The View from #410

When Home Is Cohousing

Jean K. Mason

iUniverse, Inc.
New York   Bloomington

The View from #410
When Home Is Cohousing

iUniverse books may be ordered through booksellers or by contacting:

iUniverse
1663 Liberty Drive
Bloomington, IN 47403
www.iuniverse.com
1-800-Authors (1-800-288-4677)

Because of the dynamic nature of the Internet, any Web addresses or links contained in this book may have changed since publication and may no longer be valid.

ISBN: 978-1-4401-7982-2 (sc)
ISBN: 978-1-4401-7983-9 (ebk)

Printed in the United States of America

iUniverse rev. date: 7/28/2010

For all those who have ever
undertaken the risks and discovered the rewards of
a new venture

Contents

Also by Jean K. Mason

Intimate Tyranny: Untangling Father's Legacy
(available from Centora Press.com)

FOREWORD

A true story, set in an innovative cohousing community in Cambridge, Massachusetts, *The View from #410* is among the first books written by insiders about the development of such a project. The author is a woman intimately involved in the creation and the ongoing life of a thriving cohousing community. Written with wisdom and style, *The View from #410* is a warm, personal story, and culturally significant; a book about home, community, and the evolving American Dream.

"Cohousing" is the name for a special kind of intentional community, an idea that was imported to America in the 1980s from Denmark, where the concept originated in Copenhagen among friends grappling with the stresses that urban isolation created for their young families. After a slow beginning, cohousing is now embraced throughout Scandinavia. In America, where an ethos of rugged individualism and the ideal of the single family home are still iconic elements of the American Dream for many, this old/new approach to life has produced a wider range of reactions.

The View from 410 is an insider's story, one woman's view of life in one of the early American cohousing communities. After living for fifty years in one house, and raising their three children in a fine residential neighborhood, Jean Mason and her husband Ed made an adventurous transition in their seventies—to life in a cohousing community of forty-one households. Although Ed was initially reluctant to throw in his lot with a cohousing community—not to mention the many meetings involved!—both Jean and Ed abhorred the idea of life in a retirement or assisted living community. And, as a professional psychologist with a focus on how people live, Jean Mason was eager to participate in the founding, design, development and management of an urban cohousing project. Once there, Jean found their new home an ongoing source of revelation about the quest for home and the good life. Fortunately for readers, she began to take notes.

As her story moves from the heady planning and design stages to the early years of an embryonic community, Jean offers a candid, affectionate, and thoughtful chronicle of what it is like for a diverse group of modern Americans to forge a new way of life together. How do the new neighbors learn to use consensus to make lasting and sound decisions? What is it like to prepare dinners for fifty people, some of whom have food allergies, all of whom have preferences? How does a group of people create a place that is safe, diverse, and beautiful, and affordable?

Jean Mason's stories about these matters, and insights about the cohousing experiment, are a wonderful contribution to the American literature of place.

—Emily Hiestand, April 2009

From the "American Dream" to Cohousing

An old world is collapsing and a new world is arising;
we have better eyes for the collapse than for the rise,
for the old one is the world we know.
—John Updike, 1992

The house where I was born in the 1920s, in the German immigrant community of South St. Louis, no longer exists. The city was aging; development was calling. In a significant step, my struggling but ambitious, upwardly mobile parents made a life decision every bit as agonizingly complex and challenging as the one my husband and I had to make seventy-five years later: they elected to leave hearth and kin to join the waves of young families populating the new western suburbs.

I'm sure my parents had all the mixed emotions of pioneers anywhere, anytime, tottering between feelings of loss and gain. They were proud of their ability to purchase property—an act that immediately promoted them in their eyes and the world from fringe status to respectability.

The new house sat in a ten-block development, still dusty with construction. It was a modest, square, eight-room, center-entrance Dutch Colonial, with one bathroom, a garage, and a yard. To be strictly accurate, there were in fact *two* bathrooms. The second, never mentioned, was one of many symbols of the racial divide I grew up with; in a city never united after the Civil War, there was complete agreement about its dependence on the huge minority service population. This meant that while a family of five used a single bathroom, the "colored" maid was given exclusive use of another, off her bedroom and off-limits to us.

In our house, first Annabelle, and later Hallie and Mary, helped my mother and shouldered the physical labor of the household. Each, in turn, became my mother's partner of a sort and often, during those long, lonely days, even her hapless confidante.

After we moved, the long-awaited promise of kindergarten for me was delayed by several months because my new school had yet to be completed. But I found much to keep me busy. My siblings and I gained a neighborhood, an expanse of unfenced backyards, access to many households, and a wide choice of playmates.

Over time, I discovered what a shamelessly inquisitive child I was. Emotionally keyed into my parents' turbulent dynamics and now in touch with a whole new set of neighbors, I had plenty of source material to help me hone my skills as a keen observer of family life. I would often put myself to sleep at night by mentally retracing the Halloween route, making my way around several blocks, house by house, thinking about each family in turn: what was unique about this one, what made that one tick. Why, there was a house I had never been in; how could I maneuver an invitation. I became an ardent student of the secrets that I sensed existed behind closed doors (ours, foremost), of the discrepancy between public and private behavior, a topic that I later read about in works by sociologist Irving Goffman.

Listening to the adults, I also learned the axiom that to own one's own home was one of the compelling motivations of the 1920s and '30s. It is almost impossible to overstate the significance, the emotional meaning of that hunger for ownership among the millions who were buying their first stake in America back then. As urban scholars, like Gwendolyn Wright, wrote about much later, it amounted not just to a trend but to a national pastime, an obsession, and was equated with patriotism, business success, social status, and individual self-esteem. It symbolized the very essence of being an American and helped explain some of the strongly held attitudes about ferocious independence, privacy, and property that now seem embedded in so many older people rooted in those times.

Along with this phenomenon came another axiom: No matter what horrors might occur there, within the confines of the home, people were not accountable for their own behavior or attitudes. How often did we children hear from impassioned adults, "Under my own roof, I'll discipline my children any way I choose..." We now know that that belief often shielded a lot of abuse.

And so it was that from a collection of immigrants who still shuddered at horrific memories of dislocation and crowded tenements, we became a nation of private real estate holders, rearing families in, and thus institutionalizing, isolation and secrecy—the ultimate prizes of home ownership. It was that secrecy which I plumbed in solitary darkness.

At first look, the American Dream appeared to be thriving in my town. But a closer inspection exposed chinks. My town was, in fact, not one community with a diverse population but several stratified communities. Bordering my grid of single-family homes was another grid, consisting of blocks of apartment buildings, where some of my schoolmates lived. Whenever one of these schoolmates invited me for a visit, I very early sensed a stigma attached to apartment dwellers. Only gradually did I deduce the disparaging meaning of *renters* for my parents. A foreclosed mortgage? An ineptitude for business? The reason was irrelevant. A renter took on a second-class cast around my dinner table. More chilling even, though stated only in broad hint and jocular innuendo, were the implications that Jews were not by nature property owners. According to my relatives, they "preferred apartment dwelling among their own kind."

There were other grids too, other layers of neighborhood. One, just a couple of blocks away but vastly more distant in spirit, was separated from us by only a tree-lined boulevard and formidable gates with signs saying Residents Only. The gates opened onto wide, winding roads scattered with homes of palatial proportions peeping from behind mature trees. These were the domiciles of the very wealthy who lived on estates, not on blocks or streets edged with newly planted saplings.

Another neighborhood stratum, equally impregnable, held even greater interest for me. Our town had a wall-less ghetto. Black children—or "colored," rather, was the only term in those days—did not venture from their eight-block area, nor did we enter theirs on foot. I suppose my school system funded their one-room brick schoolhouse that I was dying to see, but there were no interracial friendships or even opportunities to cross paths. Teach-ins? Workshops? Unheard of! I learned in subtle ways about exclusionary and discriminatory practices, the building of patterns of social and residential segregation that have been described so poignantly in such works as Lorraine Hansberry's play, *Raisin in the Sun*. In fact, I used to think that Harper Lee had written *To Kill a Mockingbird* about my town.

The messages of my childhood were jarring. Besides secrecy and deception, engraved in my mind was the motto "Mind your own business." I learned that there was little help for families in trouble, that short of a dutiful response to the events of birth and death, neighbors rarely expected or offered support or counsel. I observed competitiveness, divisiveness, and very little compassion. Discussion of personal finances outside the home was forbidden; so were the topics of marital discord and nettlesome children. Sex was a vast and thorny abyss; adult illness was whispered about but only among adults. On the other hand, infantile paralysis or the *scourge of polio*, as it was more familiarly referred to, was on everyone's minds and tongues; children were not spared a depiction of its savagery. All of the above, however, was fair game for gossiping adults. A cagey child with acute hearing could learn much.

A respectable family was required to be an island of self-sufficiency, absorbed with getting ahead, paying the mortgage, educating the children, and maintaining an image of righteous, productive living—a tall order for the inhabitants of the detached single-family house. The result: the moral rectitude of these strivings threw up a screen that allowed us kids to escape into a freedom that today's protected children can't even imagine. Thus, *to play outside*, a euphemism for unsupervised experimenting from our early childhoods on, brought its own insights and experiences, and eventually liberation from our parents' truths.

Now because this book is to be a review of the feelings and experiences that result from where we live and what we call home, and how these feelings influenced my own decision to live in a cohousing project, I shall jump over my college years except to say that my father believed that money spent on women was wasted. So although he finally was persuaded to fund my tuition at the local university, until I was married, I lived at home and was a streetcar commuter. In other words, whereas so many have opinions about living with others based on college and dorm life, mine are restricted to observations from two weeks at a Girl Scout summer camp and a few Ozark hosteling trips.

In the midst of WWII, after Ed and I married, we lived in a number of places, both alone and together. During a military assignment in Texas, we rented a large furnished house, and I, restless and unemployed and ignorant of the term "communal," started just such a household. For some months, until husbands received the inevitable military transfers, six or seven of us played house. One couple opted out after several weeks, reportedly seeking more privacy.

When Ed was assigned to a barren prison outpost on the Jersey coast, I was drawn to the Boston area to await the end of hostilities and his return. We then did what millions of our generation were doing—had babies and bought a house. That house was large, old, in Cambridge, and in retrospect, remarkably inexpensive. It became our home for fifty years. The post-WWII's Levittowns, held in disdain by the newly minted Harvard-trained architects, were in retrospect seen to have created cohesive and supportive communities for young families.

As a homeowner, I was beginning to discover more fissures in the American Dream. My career-building husband, a good and caring father, was rarely home; I was a displaced stranger, struggling for identity, required to assume a multitude of unfamiliar roles at a young age. Some of my most vivid memories are of pushing a stroller around our neighborhood of similar houses and feeling desperately alone, inadequate, and isolated, all the while assuming that my peers were on top of their lives. What were we doing, I wondered, sealed up in these enormous wooden boxes, outfitting ourselves with identical appliances, reinventing child rearing? We, the Super Moms, were pretty good actresses, something I discovered only decades later when we, as close friends, confessed to one another the desperation we'd experienced in our early years.

My day-and-night fantasies were poorly disguised attempts to rearrange my environment in order to extract a measure of support from my overcommitted, fragmented life. For example, on those walks with the children, I would mentally redesign the imposing homes of the neighborhood to encompass aspects that would meet the needs of a small community. I imagined a communal laundry in one, tool sheds in another, hobby rooms here and there. I "closed" our side street to traffic and created a safe, sociable play area. (Imagine my delight to discover only recently that a century ago, a similarly frustrated Harvard professor's wife, who had lived within blocks of me, had had the good sense to record her complaints—and her solutions. Melusina Fay Peirce proposed in a small volume, *Cooperative Housekeeping,* that housewives band together in spaces designed for the purpose, in order to reduce their lonely, burdensome chores.)

One night, at a time when our teenagers were driving Ed and me crazy, and I was longing for some helpful community norms, I woke him at 3:00 AM with the news that Harvard University's Stillman Infirmary along the Charles River was for sale. (Ailing students and faculty were to receive an up-to-date facility in Holyoke Center, in the midst of Harvard Square.) Ed obligingly accompanied me in the dead of night to prowl the grounds and peek through dark windows. Wishing I were an experienced draftsman with access to drawings, I played with the imagined interior space in order to develop it for perhaps half a dozen families like ours, with private and common areas. I even contacted that behemoth Harvard but was thwarted by bureaucrats and developers. That was the 1960s. Cohousing, still *in utero* in Europe, would not appear here for several decades. A luxury apartment building now fills that site next to Mt. Auburn Hospital.

My sister Super Moms had learned secrecy and deception well, often leading double lives. Quietly, in increasing numbers, we were visiting psychiatrists and therapists, lured by the newly popular psychoanalysis. Only rarely was the myth of our invulnerability publicly shattered. There was the occasional breakdown or a most unlikely tragic suicide. Then came the trail of broken marriages, as the women's groups of the '60s and '70s began chipping away at the isolation and myths.

In striking contrast with my closet communitarian fantasies, however, was my generation's pervasive attention to the home, particularly, to its design and decoration. The despised furniture of my youth gave way to contemporary lines, crisp functionalism. Ben Thompson (the Martha Stewart of Cambridge) set a welcome trend as founder of that little store, Design Research on Brattle Street, which sat amid Harvard Square's bustle. It was a big shove he gave to the pendulum for a whole generation rebelling against the detested stuffiness. A Saturday stop at DR, midst the Swedish modern tables, the beautifully upholstered Danish and Finnish wooden chairs, and the genial designer/manager, Claude Bunyard, became a family outing.

With his British understatement, he facilitated our liberation from the shackles of tradition. We, the doctors, lawyers, educators, rejected the family furniture! DR's semiannual sales were major social events where spouses were introduced and children romped under skeletal couches and slender table legs. Some future leaders even began to hire the refugee architects and their talented protégés fresh from their Bauhaus indoctrination by way of Harvard's School of Design. The do-it-yourselfers like us stripped away the past along with the dark varnish from our cumbersome arks.

But yet another fissure surfaced on the dreamscape: an undefinable emptiness was, for many, still there. Some learned, some did not, that a beautifully renovated house does not permanently revitalize a marriage, jump-start a stalled career, or redirect a recalcitrant child. Walls were white and spare, multiple showers replaced the claw-foot tubs, and the kitchen was a gleaming food factory, but the responsibilities of running it all continuted to fall squarely on the same shoulders. For me, a concept of a community of sharers persisted.

Until I returned to work, that is. As a psychologist, I consulted in public schools, largely with classroom and special education teachers who were integrating students into mainstream classes and with the administrators who were making this happen. I shouldn't have been surprised to discover that teachers experienced a degree of isolation in their work that resembled that of mothers with small children. It was about then that the term "burnout" began to appear in educational literature, so I developed a college course titled Stress and the Teacher; it was oversubscribed. I then realized that helping teachers to work in teams, heretofore frowned upon by administrators, markedly reduced their complaints and their gloom. Why couldn't these principles apply in a general way to the homeplace as well? The mothers, the teachers, and now the middle-aged, kept coming to mind. Why couldn't residential living combine amenities and informal social support without stigmatizing the sharers?

In a later career shift, I decided that my interests in supportive living environments might well mirror those of others like me. As it turned out, I was right. I discovered a group of midlife women who explored some of these themes along with a few other lone voices. It was at this point that I began carving out a niche I called Shared Living.

As I started on my quest for models of Shared Living, I found that the continuum of existing housing types held few hopefuls. There were the single-family homes on one end and the just-appearing CCRCs (Continuing Care Retirement Communities) on the other, with a sprinkling of genuine cooperative housing examples in between. One of the difficulties, which typically arises when you propose something new, is that people, quite understandably, want labels and concrete examples. There is a strong cognitive need to force new information into recognizable categories.

"Oh, you work with the elderly—how nice," one woman told me. "Maybe you could find a place for my sick grandmother. "No, no, this has little to do with the very old," I hastened to explain.

"Shared meals! Why that's a commune—I'd never want to do that!" was another common response, or, "I wouldn't be able to live with a stranger!" I was tempted to conclude that the legacy of the American Dream, the stereotype of the nuclear family, was so instilled as to hamper innovative thinking.

I went on to give talks and workshops and courses at churches, housing conferences, and women's groups and to consult with individuals about future living plans. And with time, the American Dream's cracks widened with the increasing failure of the promise of home ownership. On any index you chose—income, changing definitions of family, housing costs, available sites, zoning obstacles, mortgage rates, minority and racial segregation—the bottom line was constantly climbing, and fewer and fewer were able to realize a once achievable dream. So I formed an organization called SHARE to explore housing collectives.

Then an architect-friend proposed that we collaborate to offer a studio course on shared living, a topic new to the architectural design curriculum. We asked students to redesign various buildings (a two-hundred-year-old Brookline farmhouse, a seventy-five-year-old triple-decker within Harvard Square, and a third iteration of a Somerville school building, currently senior housing). For each building, their assignment was to design private living units and comfortable common spaces, combining attributes of "home" for six fictitious adults (two of them a couple). Most of the young students understood the assignment well enough, but it was the back-to-school mothers who most fully grasped and appreciated the concept. All learned from the deconstructing of age-old, often-unconscious ideas of how we live. A few students found it impossible to visualize spaces not defined by the single-family dwelling. Others were able to dig deeply within themselves to reevaluate the old stereotypes.

One day after class in Boston's Back Bay, I walked around the corner to explore a bookstore for architects. The proprietor was shelving newly arrived volumes. Low wintery sunbeams lit on a colorful cover, catching my eye as they highlighted the word "housing." Who isn't pulled in by an attractive book jacket? But who expects such a serendipitous find? The book turned out to be *COHOUSING: A Contemporary Approach to Housing Ourselves* by Kathryn McCamant and Charles Durrett (Ten Speed Press, Berkeley, CA 1988). With adrenaline rushing, I bought the store's only copy and, clutching my treasure, rushed home to read how fantasies can be transformed into reality.

The photographs and their captions alone captivated me. And the authors! A California couple, both architects, somehow engineered having a year in Denmark (practicing architects don't usually get sabbaticals) to pursue an elegantly simple research project. They rented a unit within a cluster of houses that had been designed to encourage social interactions and promote simple living and then went about their daily lives, participating, observing, documenting. Fleeting moments of envy (why couldn't I have thought of doing this?) were soon dismissed by curiosity in the face of chapter headings such as "Tornevangsgard: Small Can Be Beautiful Too," "Jernstoberiet: From Iron Foundry to Cohousing," and "Addressing Our Changing Lifestyles."

I went on to read that in the mid-'60s, unhappy with the prospect of bringing up children in the city of Copenhagen, a group of friends got together to discuss some vague ideas about some form of cooperative living.

They had read Thomas More's *Utopia* (written in 1516) and unearthed information about a Copenhagen doctors' cooperative in 1853. Although their own livelihoods were in the city, existing housing styles did not lend themselves to the supportive community they were envisioning. They finally designed and settled into a cluster of twelve houses surrounding a modest, central common house on the outskirts of the city—but not before a four-year struggle with opposing neighbors. The plight of Hareskov became public and attracted many supporters.

By 1985, McCamant and Durrett had surveyed forty-six villages, all with wonderful, unpronounceable Danish names, mostly within a reasonable commute to Copenhagen. The projects described ranged from six to eighty units each, from private to cooperative ownership. All but one village had a common house; thirty-seven of them served from two to seven group meals a week. Common facilities included laundry, children's playrooms, childcare, teen music rooms, workshops, buying clubs, and guest rooms; a few had swimming pools and sports facilities. Residents counted on solar and wind power for much of their energy needs.

McCamant and Durrett extracted common characteristics from these various villages, which have consistently come to define cohousing:

participatory process, neighborhood design intended to encourage sociability, extensive common facilities, natural energy resources and complete resident management. Similarly, cohousers have come to be thought of as persistent, empowered, and ingenious which may well be a legacy from their Danish beginnings.

Remarkable as the work was, for me, the book's greatest achievement may well have been introduction of the term "cohousing" into the Western— American and Canadian—vernacular. Sometimes, just the right word or phrase can advance a cause like nothing else. Whatever the explanation, the book caused a tiny but significant shift in the way people today are thinking about how they want to live, one that considers cohousing another option for the nuclear family.

But enough background and speculation. Let's ask the questions everyone does. What reasonably normal person would choose to give up the pleasures, independence, privacy, and relative control over one's life for the gamble of a new way of living? Yet for me, the still untried merits of cohousing seemed to offer the promise of defying isolation, stumbling into cheerful, caring companionship, sharing chores, and reducing a single footprint on our crowded earth.

Both Ed and I were well over seventy, our days of making decisions for and with a family of five were over; we had only our own lives to enhance, wreck, or experiment with. Our children, however, baby boomers all, had their own memories—mixed I would say, about those intense, exhilarating, and bruising years of "communal living"—and were less than enthusiastic to witness a *déjà vu*. Why, they wondered, sacrifice the gentle, predictable rhythms of late midlife for the volatility and uncertainty of a drastically unfamiliar existence?

To glean even a bit of the appeal that cohousing had for me, a puzzled reader could delve into my first book, *Intimate Tyranny: Untangling Father's Legacy* (Centora Press 2008). I do believe that the seeds of major life decisions are planted in childhood and, for me, my early experience with the nuclear family proved that such an arrangement was a failure. While Ed and I were proud of the life we had created for our family, it was one that we had been forced to invent due to our poor preparation. Neither of us had brought very useful parenting skills or much in the way of cherished values to pass along. Of parental support, we had very little. The attributes that allegedly make for a sense of home—safety, refuge, haven, comfort, love and nurturance, problem solving, creativity, role modeling, and humor—had not graced our households of origin, particularly mine. That said, the redemptive appeal of

9

cohousing as a late-life experiment was strong for me. It was less so for Ed, but he was well-rewarded for his willingness to try and, later, his perseverance.

Here, in this loosely chronological and peripatetic journey we took, I try to convey at times my musings and reflections, at other times some history and memories into a readable collection of personal accounts and essays—okay, a memoir. My measure of success will be whether I can convey a sense of the complexities and possibilities of community—particularly the founding of one—to the reader: the constant flux, the presence of people who have gone through a profound bonding together, which may or may not result in friendship but does breed empathy and tolerance. Though as a participant-observer, my perspective may not match that of another. The whole story has yet to be written.

Beginnings

In creating, the only hard thing's to begin ...
a grass-blade's no easier to make than an oak.
—James Russell Lowell

In the summer of 1998, Ed and I moved from our large Cambridge home of fifty years. We moved four blocks away to Richdale Avenue, #410, a condo apartment in the newly constructed cohousing project. Officially known as Cambridge Cohousing, it occupied one and one-half acres on a long, narrow parcel that stretched along a commuter rail line. It was within a ten-minute walk of the public transportation in Porter Square.

Our real move actually started in 1995, however, when Ed and I joined a small group interested in creating a diverse, participatory, urban community. After forming a legal partnership, our group's twenty-some members purchased the site in 1996, obtained a construction loan, and hired the developer, architect, and contractor. The developer was a husband-and-wife team who were a key part of the group, a driving force in the organizing phase, and also future residents in the community.

The concept of cohousing, which grew out of over four decades of efforts by Danish families to create their own supportive and congenial housing, was familiar to a few of us since its introduction to the United States in 1988. The concept would quickly give name, voice, and focus to many grappling for a more satisfying and, it was hoped, a simpler and more economical way of life than conventional housing offered.

The term "cohousing," a rough but inspired translation of the Danish *bofoellesskaber*, struck an immediate chord with many, perhaps primarily parents of young families and women living alone. It was the "co" part of the word, I'm convinced, that conveyed an instant message, one that any advertiser would have been proud to have coined. The book, *COHOUSING*, an attractive and succinct illustrated statement stressed several basic tenets: participation in a democratic planning process; joining with others to create

11

a supportive, congenial community; jointly determining the group's spatial and design needs for a balance of privacy and social interaction; and finally, an energy-efficient setting.

The book rapidly became a kind of secular bible to those with similar ideas and values. The authors of *COHOUSING*, in their onsite research in Denmark, had tapped into a need that resonated with Americans with extraordinary accuracy. They had discovered an alternative to mainstream housing and rising costs that appealed to middle-class, do-it-yourself folks. The first dozen or so projects, mostly on the West Coast, each spanned many years in the planning stages. One of the basic pillars of cohousing—participatory democracy—requires time and patience for a new group of potential cohousers to learn. In addition, moneylenders were wary of an unproven housing model. There were setbacks, failures, disillusionments. But gradually there were also demonstrable successes. By 2002, there were sixty completed projects in eighteen states, in addition to seven in Canada. There are dozens more in various stages of planning and construction.

Cambridge Cohousing Groundbreaking

Ed Mason with camera

Through such old-fashioned methods as leaflets and word-of-mouth contacts—later e-mails and Web sites—interested individuals began to find each other, to form a group and to hold meetings in schools, churches, and homes. Surprising numbers of people turned out for these informal affairs; there was almost always sufficient interest to plan another, then still another, exploratory session. Returnees began to form a working nucleus, with the Danish model as a guiding framework to help us explore how we wanted to live. For some, sharing costs and maintenance was the primary concern; for parents, ways to share the burdens of meals and childcare were of uppermost priority. Others focused on the design as a social tool to bring a diverse group of people together, responding to the appeal of democratic approaches to planning and construction.

Harder to articulate, perhaps, but no less meaningful, were the deep concerns that many had about the specter of loneliness and isolation in urban—or suburban—anonymity; they sought a built-in social life. Still others dreamed of the joys of a semi-rural, environmentally sustainable lifestyle within an easy commute of work and city activities. And always there was the appeal of sharing. Sharing in costs, in the participation of work projects, in vegetable gardens, and in cultural and political activities.

Our construction began in February 1997 with the first condominium owners moving in a year later. All forty-one units were sold before its completion, and in the three years of nearly nonstop planning meetings, members called up inner reserves of talent, skill, patience, humor, and endurance to an extent that no one would have thought possible. By September 1998, Ed and I joined an amazingly cohesive, diverse group of sixty-seven adults and twenty-six children (bringing with it a dazzling array of visiting friends and relatives) in our state-of-the-art, environmentally sustainable housing, to begin sharing our space and our lives.

"Oh, I hope you're going to write about cohousing," our visitors kept saying. As a sometime writer, this was admittedly not a new idea to me. During the several years of planning, I now confess, I had wrestled quietly with the idea of a book. But how to write about a subject in which I was so immersed eluded me. Still, so many stories of this relentless, pioneering process begged to be told. Then again came the doubts: my friends and my neighbors, we are all joined in a common endeavor. Unique as this social experiment was, how could such a complex process be conveyed in all its reality? If I dared attempt such a task, from what perspective, in whose voice, would I proceed? As a retired clinical psychologist, I felt that a professional approach might be perceived as a barrier; there are no clients, no patients, here. The how-to manuals were already being written, and we hardly needed publicity, as there was no dearth of news coverage. Journalists from coast to coast reported on the national cohousing minimovement. Our Cambridge project alone was often a focus of print, radio, and TV features and spots; we used up more than our assigned fifteen minutes of glory. If it were a dispassionate history that was called for, there was no end to the archival material packed away in boxes. But I thought, though some day, someone may choose to write that account, it would not be I, certainly not now. So I let the matter drop.

The coaxing for the inside story continued, however, from persistent visitors and, quite frankly, from an inner voice that whispered, "Write, write." So once our flat was settled, once I'd recovered from the harrowing, disruptive surgery of hip replacement, and once the temperamental heating system was performing better, I was able to listen more carefully to the interest behind the appeals to know more about life in this place. I now heard fewer of the "It sounds like a sixties' commune!" comments and more of the thoughtful inquiries, stripped of a confrontational tone, regarding why an older couple—specifically, Ed and I—would choose to throw in their lot with others for such an uncertain outcome. An inordinate amount of the interest came from my age cohort, often the very ones who had blithely dismissed the concept as "socialism" or an "idealistic nightmare" not long ago.

True, an urban cohousing project is in itself worth inquiring about in detail. But something else seemed to be nagging at Ed's and my questioners—real concerns began to eclipse mere curiosity. Worries about their own aging appeared to surface. On the cusp of retirement and housing decisions themselves, might they be asking themselves if they could adapt to community living? Was our unique experiment one they now thought they could tolerate? Was cohousing in action—despite the intergenerational messiness—forcing them to reassess some assumptions that they had been assiduously avoiding about their own futures? These were the nature of the questions that I began to hear:

"How could you give up your big, beautiful house after fifty years and all those memories?"

"Didn't you have to get rid of lots of treasured things?"

"But you're all so different there—how on earth can you get along with all *these* people?"

"You mean you really cook together!"

"Your neighborhood looks, well, ah … a little dangerous. Do you worry about safety?"

"I love my grandchildren, but I wouldn't want to have those kids around all the time" and "What is it that the children add?"

And finally:

"You must write about cohousing. There are so many of us who will soon have to make decisions about the latter part of our lives."

I hastened to tell these folks, and there were many of them—the empty-nesters, those who dreaded the idea of age segregation, the about-to-retire-singles, the back-to-the-city crowd—that cohousing was for kids, families, all kinds of people. That it was not exclusively an old-age or retirement option. That it was a huge stew of differences, and not primarily defined by the needs of the elderly. But for some inexplicable reason, in all my years of promoting the cohousing concept, I'd been unsuccessful in getting this idea across; the presence of children always surprises people. My failure or their denial? I gave up explaining and left it at what I knew they were probably thinking: "Just another of Jean's quirky pursuits."

That was, until they came to visit. Then their defenses melted. Jaws dropped, silence descended followed by reverent exclamations: "Why, I had no idea *this* was what you were talking about!" I could see it on their faces as I guided them through the sunny common dining room and well-equipped kitchen, the large but cozy living room, and the library. I could see it as we peeked into a noisy playroom, as they met a friend of a friend in the elevator.

Once, during such a tour, a woman blurted out, "I didn't think it would be nice like this. I expected it to look like a college dorm!" And from another: "So many children—where do they come from?"

Throughout the tour, there was always growing amazement at the size and the amenities, more disbelief and awe at the decor, at the quality of the personal interactions, the geniality, and the detailed knowledge of the residents about one another.

"You mean you know everyone here?" asked one visitor.

"Why, you're your own concierge and security guard!" remarked another.

And finally, upon seeing the spacious, airy, sun-filled flat where Ed and I lived, our aerie in the sky, they would register downright envy: "Now *this* I would love!" At this point, they would ask for the real stuff, the *truth*, how it all *really* worked. Then, ultimately, we'd hear the clincher: "Do you suppose there's a place here for me?"

Here, finally, was the perspective that had eluded me all along. Blinded as I was by my voluminous notes and rough drafts, I hadn't fully comprehended that most people cared less about the analytical, carefully researched account of cohousing than they did about the look from the inside. A grandson's favorite phrase—the "up-close and personal"—came to mind, and along with it, in a flash, a title: *The View from #410.*

And so, hardly scholarly, rarely methodical, this book is a memoir, a journal of my experiences of living here from my particular vantage point. As one-half of the oldest couple here, as a cofounder, and as a biased and committed participant with an initially reluctant husband, I have written this story about my own transition, in narrative and essay, from nuclear household to polyglot community.

Can I be truthful? Only up to a point. The preservation of the ever-developing bond of trust that is essential in this community is more important to me than any tell-all exposé. I remember reading a book once in which the author said, "Everything here is true, but it may not be factual." In other words, my observations are as accurate as I can make them without revealing identities to outsiders. They are what I see, altered only where necessary to maintain privacy and confidentiality.

They are also unsystematic, fragmentary, impressionistic, unofficial. They are without benefit of collaboration or even confirmation of chronology or fact. I did not delve into the many notebooks, the hundreds of memos and documents, the countless e-mail messages I had access to. And so bolstered by only enough background to lend credibility, this is my story about living at Cambridge Cohousing.

Now twelve years postoccupancy there are no scandals, though there is gossip, there are interpersonal tensions, and there are clashes of values. There are moving moments, and there is incredible generosity of spirit. Most of all, there are stories, stories, stories, a vast wealth of them; and because of that, I love living here in a way I never thought possible.

In total, in recounting my view from #410, I hope to show a balance between the strains and the rewards of people creating a new way of living together without betraying the fragile bonds that allow it to happen.

Trains of Thought

*"His own life was no longer a single
story but part of a mural, which was a
folding together of accomplices ...
a wondrous web—all of these fragments of
human order, something ungoverned by
the family he was born into or the
headlines of the day."*
—Michael Ondaatje, *In the Skin of the Lion*

I grew up in the Midwest, in train country. The tracks were a playground, for jumping over, for balancing on, for diving from into the weeds at the first vibrations, before the sound of an oncoming train. The railroad bed occasionally yielded data to ponder over. Newspapers, coins, toilet detritus were all clues about the oh-so-fascinating lives of the train's passengers. (The word "tourist" was not then in my vocabulary.) To the west, the tracks, arrow straight, blurred off toward the dust bowl—in those days you could taste the grit that had been carried hundreds of miles by searing summer winds. But it was the East—a capital letter place—that held the greater pull for me. Just across that muddy Mississippi lay the beginning of the whole world. I had no particular destination in mind, no gigantic railroad terminal where familiar faces would loom to welcome me. Just the lure of the tracks: Away. Elsewhere. Anywhere. But especially to the East.

By the 1930s, my father had a car, and on Sunday afternoons my parents and my brother, sister, and I would gather up the old folks—my paternal grandmother and great aunt, who conversed in broken German-English patois, and my mother's mother and doleful sister—for the the obligatory Sunday drive. The car was roomy, the children skinny; the era of auto-safety consciousness had not yet dawned to determine the seating arrangement. Our route was always the same. First to North St. Louis, then South St. Louis, to pick up our passengers, then to the west past an occasional farm and toward our goal, the family graves in two cemeteries, Valhalla and Lake James.

For us kids, the cemetery offered a site for a welcome romp, unless we were caught in the grievous error of stepping on a grave. My parents, aiding the elders through the uncut grass, proceeded slowly to "our" graves, inspecting the plots, commenting on the headstones.

"Didn't the first Uncle Harry die in 1891, not what it says here, '92?" asked my grandmother of no one in particular. Valhalla's maintenance, I recall overhearing, was felt to be marginal. After a brief stop, my father, ever the get-on-with-it organizer, summoned us to the car.

On those rare occasions when my immediate family went any distance, it was by train. And when I was old enough to travel alone, maybe ten, I was allowed to visit a great aunt in Illinois, and at thirteen, another aunt in Texas, a journey of twenty-four hours. For a lonely, hapless child, this was heaven. Essentially undisturbed for hours at a time, I was free to let fantasies build in sync with the hypnotic clackety-clack of the railroad. With nose pressed against a window darkened by gritty black ash from the coal-fired steam engine, I could give endless reign to the fascination that life along the railroad held for me. That absorption kept me in its grip like a vise.

The only dilemma on these rides was where to sit—the "inland" side with its potential for more abundant human life or the river side for sightings of rushing water and the occasional stern-wheeler through scrubby trees. But Tom and Huck notwithstanding, river life was sparse, the river itself dizzyingly swift and muddy.

Life along the tracks! The train never went slowly enough for me to take in fully the shanties spilling over with ragged, scrawny kids engaged in fleeting play, worn and weary mothers, tough but defeated-looking men chewing on straws, tobacco, anything. And then there were the mansions perched on hills, encasing their residents in remote luxury. I never really understood the pull these moving targets had for me, the draw I felt toward intimate encounters with strangers—only that I longed to bring them into focus. To freeze-frame them, if only for a moment, was my overriding goal. A collage of pale Ozark faces and straw-colored hair remains vivid to me to this day. Through blinding sun, headaches, and rain-smudged glass, I struggled to search for answers to those big questions about life that plague kids. Poverty and plenty, struggle and ease, fairness and injustice, fear and safety. Two worlds, my worlds; would they ever coalesce?

Over the years, symbols for cohousing have occurred to me. The cocoon is opaque and lifeless as seen from the outside, but, if you dare to pierce the squirmy sack, you find a swarming, even frightening, tangle of larval life. Or take the ship—not, let's hope, a ship of fools—but a cruise ship, brightly lit at night, gaily plying the waters, visible and yet its innermost workings unknowable.

But of all the possible metaphors, that of the train is the most appealing to me. From childhood on it has been a significant presence in my life; it was my means of dreaming about a different kind of life. Here I have my own train that passes our home only feet from my pillow. And as an adult, I am no longer the observer, watching life from the window of the moving train or the staccato flashes of the passengers in the dining car from the railroad crossing; I have become a player in the scene along the tracks. Looking out from #410 onto the six-car diesel commuter four floors below, I now know that I am rooted, anchored, in this place.

Finding land on which to build multifamily housing in a densely populated, old American city is a next-to-impossible task. Nonetheless, our fledgling cohousing group, led by our intrepid developer and flag waver, Katherine, was uncompromising. "No farther than ten minutes by foot from public transportation!" we insisted in a single voice. Some of us already knew of Katherine's talent—she had an eye like a water diviner's willow rod for finding heretofore unavailable, unused land. But "unused" in urban parlance is a misnomer; it's more likely to mean used up or used many times over.

Katherine once said to a small group, "I've got to do this before I die!" What most may not have known was that her great-great-great-uncle, John Humphrey Noyes, founded the utopian Oneida Community in New York State in 1848. In her turn, she regularly haunted the public land registry, the land courts, and maybe even obituary pages in her quest for the odd land parcel. I, too, was on this track but lacked her expertise. For years, I had been obsessed with transforming every run-down building and rubble-strewn vacant lot into unconventional floor plans. From inside my car, I would morph them into shared houses—small individual units with ample common space, as options for women who wanted independence but not loneliness. You see, a creative property searcher is first and foremost an iconoclast; razing, levelling, and renewing are her tools. And she never rules out anything. No neighborhood is too unsavory, no building too deteriorated. Zoning ordinances, variances, appeals, tax liens are all vehicles for the persistent developer; after all, good architects can design or transform an unseemly mass into open space, making cars disappear underground. And to the visionary, class boundaries and existing structures are rendered invisible. But let's get back to the story.

At our earliest sessions in 1995, several dozen of us watched as Katherine brought to us her carefully mined treasures, displaying them with tools of her trade. Maps, charts, and color-coded drawings of buildings and neighborhoods, blown up to better facilitate our group discussions, were unrolled, taped to walls. If we responded with interest, a site visit was planned. "Good, let's make a picnic," she'd say. (I came to learn that a major building block of cohousing was food, another tool that Katherine understood how to use).

A few days after some hurried arrangements, with Katherine patiently coordinating schedules, members gathered after work on a summer evening, children in tow, to trudge around a factory or a landfill, surveying the latest "find." Our requirements were stiff, and in the end, only four sites made the cut. All abutted railroad tracks!

That our searches all ended at the tracks was not really an accident. Unconventional housing must seek out unfashionable sites, real estate discarded by the mainstream developer. It must jump some barriers and take some unaccustomed leaps to the edge. I have come to think of "edge" as the planners' euphemism for scarcity, a code word for upgrading ugly to pleasing. For urban historians, one image triggered by the concept of edge is the railway system, which helped define our nineteenth-century cities and neighborhoods.

There was one handsome brick Nineteenth-century bastion in the city of Somerville, next door to Cambridge, a building for the sole purpose of powering Boston's electric surface trolley network. This veritable fortress, which I'd been eyeing for years, was begging for imaginative reuse. Railroad tracks alongside had been converted to a bike path, bringing the industrial edge into the heart of the city. A perfect cohousing site, I thought, but for these purists, nothing outside of Cambridge could possibly qualify.

The City of Cambridge is both lure and snare—it seduces and enchants and often refuses to release its victims. Many fall captive to its educational riches as well as to the romance of skulling on the Charles River, with Boston's cultural offerings within easy reach. Its neighborhoods and "squares" are crossroads of ethnicities, with their shops and restaurants. From its famous Harvard Square (its once funky appeal is rapidly giving way to national brands) to the more modest but colorful Putnam and Inman Squares, I counted at least seven distinctive squares. Though a square is not square at all but an intersection that was made necessary by the original colonial transportation and communication network, aka cowpaths. New arrivals from Midwestern cities made up of orderly grids are charmed and bewildered by them, while residents publicly dismiss their chaos as failures of geometry and at the same time take pride in their personal mastery of the disorder.

Mighty Harvard University, in all its red-brick-and-ivy majesty, is fair game for irascible neighbors who periodically feel required to stem its rate of usurpation of their favorite places. For political watchers, the town-and-gown scene, played out in city hall on Monday nights at city council meetings, is rich and endless. My all-time favorite outrageous drama, now legend, was the proposal by an oft-elected mayor with a large Italian following that the city pave over historic, magnificent Harvard Yard to create a public parking lot. "The Peoples' Republic of Cambridge," is affectionately referred to, by both its proponents and opponents for its social and political querkiness, and for its liberal stands. Cambridge City Council was the first in the land to ban smoking in public buildings and to vote to establish a peace commission. It also should be remembered that Cambridge citizens did *not* vote to eliminate its controversial rent-control policy—Massachusetts voters did!

Harvard Square is a lively cross-section of the educated and the wannabe worlds; it daily hosts not only the university community but retirees, runaways, entrepreneurs, tourists, and homeless alike. A few blocks away across Brattle Street is a quiet bulwark near the Longfellow House, the Society of Friends, whose building for worship has a large social and meeting center. The Quakers responded to a cohousing proposal for support from their member, Katherine, by offering their encouragement and a space to meet. For a struggling group, no gift is more valuable.

In an era and an area of soaring wealth, another goal of our cohousing group was to put the project within the financial reach of those who were not full beneficiaries of the boom years. As such, "affordability" became a second mantra, ranking right up there with "location." No one knew exactly what affordability meant, especially in a still-rising real estate market. Nor did we yet know who could afford what. Neither cost estimates nor recommended income levels discouraged anyone from attending our meetings, although a few early attenders claimed "insufficient funds" as the reason for dropping out. However, we actively courted the financially distressed, especially those of color, couples with children or who were child-friendly or child-hopeful, and those with gender and religious differences. The greater the deviance from the white middle-class norm, it seemed, the stronger the invitation to join.

If you sense a tinge of sarcasm in my tone, I confess to swinging between waves of skepticism and excitement about our aggressive outreach. And in the end, we did have to admit to failure in our collective efforts to attract minority prospects.But that was not the cause of my concerns. My concern, to put it bluntly, was that I believed we had all the diversity we could handle within our forty-one households and that we were only inviting trouble to actively recruit more. This was but one issue that made me wonder sometimes whether Ed and I should withdraw. That and the fact that cohousing encompassed a group culture that somehow made it feel shameful to scrutinize something so morally righteous as diversity. At the end of the day, though, I knew that I wanted to be a part of figuring out just how we could fold all these disparate opinions, incomes, and living standards into our multimillion dollar experiment.

Money is always a delicate subject—a truism in any group. Most of us, however, had no precedent for bandying about the large sums that were being estimated for a project of this size. From early on, each cohousing resident wore several hats beyond the conventional one of buyer. We were each in turn customer, realtor, buyer and seller, banker, bookkeeper, payor and payee, lender and receiver. Many of us, accustomed to playing the money game close to the chest, suddenly woke up in a public arena.

Then with little warning, the moment came—just when we were exhaustively discussing the merits of three versus five common meals weekly and debating our ideal window type. The owner of the site preferred by all announced a deadline: he requested a down payment of a hundred thousand dollars by week's end. Sitting in a large circle with perhaps forty-five people who had been unknown to us a mere few months earlier, we were now destined to become linked for life in a committment, involving money, and lots of it.

A defining moment, for sure. How did we even begin this discussion? There was no Bill Gates to raise a hand and magnanimously offer to bankroll us. Someone bravely broke the silence by speculating that since the incomes of those present varied from "subsistence to comfortable, maybe even affluent, there may be resources within the group willing and able to finance the property." No one spoke out, but within a matter of minutes, another voice proposed a loan fund, and, with no further ado, consensus was reached. Then in a kind of charade of privacy, someone passed around pieces of paper, on which each of us jotted down a sum we felt able to loan the infant LLP (Limited Liability Partnership). Finally, we formed a voluntary task force. And it was thus that the financial entity known as Cambridge Cohousing was born.

We now know that the still neophyte cohousing concept has not been the usual choice of the wealthy; nationally, it appeals largely to a moderate-income, middle-class, white subset of the population. However, our mission states that we strive to create an ethnically and racially diverse community; therefore, like a "color blind" college admissions program, we should be prepared to offer financial aid. That said, how will the LLP survive the inevitable pitfalls in order to repay, with interest, the eight coresidents who, after weighing the risk, put on their lenders' hats for the total cost of the real estate—to say nothing of funding an affordability program? Though the subject has arisen off and on through the years, we have never found a way for the latter.

Those beginnings were euphoric times, even though new complexities surfaced on a weekly basis and I found myself with quietly disturbing thoughts. In hindsight, I think perhaps I should have given them greater voice. But among the swirl of property pursuits, they seemed out of place, even cynical: any one of us would have said that this was a time for bonding around the design of our future community, not for brooding over the prospect of our group's finances or composition. Yet my thoughts continually returned to one of the pillars in our vision statement (see appendix)—that of equitable participation. There were several prospective members whose personalities suggested to me an inability to adopt and pursue group goals. And I continued to stumble over that word "diversity." A laudable goal, indeed. To me, it dramatized the collecting of physical differences—color, language, dollar signs, religious status, physical and mental disabilities, gender. But for the most ardent members, every worthy cause and liberal value should be incorporated into *one* housing project.

In vulnerable moments, I questioned the reality of such virtue. Such an ambitious stand, it seemed to me, besides heightening the risk of success, also failed to take full cognizance of the incredible diversity that already existed in the group mix: diversity of spirit, talent, and personality, of the richness and nuance of different classes, of the psychological motivation and emotional make-up that are the strengths and the gut-wrenching challenges of this way of life. There was already more variety in our midst than many of us had ever experienced. A general call for inclusion, rather than turning us into a Noah's ark, would have been my preference. Another worry that crowded my thoughts, but ... whoa, hold on a minute. I see that scene again—of me and the train. That little girl, the observer, watching from alongside the tracks as life speeds by, always the outsider looking in. I wanted to hang onto the player role, but before I return to it, my other concern is still worth mentioning. I was concerned about how successful our conglomerate commitment to participate in group work would be. Was my sense of commitment comparable, for example, to the next person's? And was one's commitment during this initial planning phase predictive of the next phases as we grew as a group? If so, it was a little unnerving to observe early on that some were simply more involved than others. They took on all the jobs: the cleanup, the bookkeeping, the grundge work, the leading, whatever was called for. And then to see that the remaining few—not many, but almost invariably the same few—were invisible.

AMTRAK Boston-Fitchburg Commuter Rail along rear of Cambridge Cohousing

Take one example: that of attendance at scheduled events, one of the few tangible criteria we can actually observe. Oh, there are lots of reasons for being remiss now and then—single-mom stress, work pressure, theater subscriptions, travel, poor health. But participation being one of the most sacred values of our cohousing path, mightn't we suspect that regular absence, emotional withdrawal, or personal demands at the beginning stage might be predictive of a lack of involvement in, say, a future work project, a critical vote, a cook team, a grounds crew? Mightn't a growing sense of unfairness, with seeds planted in these first meetings, grow into one of those invasive botanical nightmares, a kudzu that consumes time and thought, obscuring our vision? Self-selection, however, was and remains our motto: there were to be no judges, no screening, no attendance records. Trust was our operative stance—the belief that fairness and an individual sense of responsibility would prevail. I would have liked, however, to have talked about that more.

Everyone who sat in that Society of Friends' meeting house Sunday after Sunday had wish lists for our new housing. Open space for children, vegetable gardens, cars banished to underground parking, spacious light-filled units with pollutant-free fireplaces, state-of-the-art energy-saving equipment and nontoxic materials, climate control at our fingertips, and all in a safe and environmentally sustainable "green" setting. The list continued: a rooftop gazebo—next to a hot tub and clotheslines—from which to sip our wine while watching the sun set, gleaming hardwood floors, a greenhouse, and more and more and more. The inexhaustible resources of Boston's "Big Dig" might have been our model in those early planning days.

Into small multifamily units were to go every amenity known to the decorator's trade. In workshops, the housing dreams of each were polled, ranked, and starred on newsprint. We even asked the kids what they wanted. But did we stop long enough to ask ourselves how our goals of affordability and diversity squared with our extravagant fantasies? Did we more than graze over how a community deals with, for example, substance abuse in its midst? Yes, of course, but I felt that our "fast-track" pressure tilted us toward trying to fulfill concrete and material hopes over less tangible, much more difficult concerns. And early as it was when Ed and I joined, matters of membership, (e.g., screening, criteria) were not discussed.

This was all prelude to building and living alongside an Amtrak commuter line. For me, the impassioned debate about whether to purchase the Richdale Avenue site was associated with trains—balm, stigma, nostalgia, class symbol? Threat to life, limb, and hearing? Or resale risk? Could the presence of a railroad be separated from the adjacent run-down neighborhood it bisected? With its noise, dirt, and trash, even its romance, could our group possibly reach consensus on such a controversial location? Well, we did. And while some of our early decisions returned as ghosts to haunt us, the railroad was not among them.

To boot, Ed's and my grandson Alex, then three, was already deep into a love affair with trains. The promise that each day he could get exactly thirty-four glimpses of the real versions of his adored toy engines Charlie and Thomas from our window lured him and his mother to give up our family home. For me, the railroad proved to be a magnet to childhood that linked my new life with a past I had imagined I had long abandoned.

If It's Tuesday, It's the DOC Meeting

All the hours of meetings, the melding
of our individual ideas into a group
vision, the making of that vision
practical and real have paid off, and
cohousing works!
—A cohousing resident of Muir
Commons, Davis, California

Looking back at those beginnings, I now see that I had little idea what "oversight" entailed. Had I known as I headed to Cambridge's Central Square (the step-cousin of Harvard Square) that the approaching scene would be reenacted each Tuesday afternoon, beginning at five and ending at seven (or often much, much later), and would continue for a period of three and a half years, I might well have refused the invitation to join the Development Oversight Committee. If I had, I would have been spared years of frustration, confusion, tongue-biting restraint, displays of temper, undisciplined arguments, feelings of helplessness and inadequacy, and the often unbearable pressures of small-group dynamics. Add emotional exhaustion, and you have a prescription for insanity.

I could only admire anyone who might have been inadvertently drawn into this sweeping experience with us. An overly dramatic statement but, of course, my way of saying those meetings could be tough-going. Not just for members; tough also for spouse, partner, child—anyone passively caught up in the second-hand smoke.

This Tuesday, as I trudged up the three flights of stairs in a partially rehabbed building of jaded vintage to Katherine and Brent's office overlooking "Mass Ave" (Massachusetts Avenue), I realized I was preparing myself for another tension-filled several hours.

But first things first: Having stumbled over the name "Development Oversight Committee," we easily settled on its abbreviations. The DOC (pronounced as letters, not as in "Okay, Doc, what's the diagnosis?") was a greedy boss, leaving neither room nor time for much else. It replaced movies, novels, and a social life. But saying no to the invitation would have meant missing unbroken participation in a landmark venture as well as immersion in a group effort that transcended the talents and scope of any individual. Accepting the invitation seemed to bring the true meaning of participatory democracy into focus; it was a concept that was somehow embedded in creating this community. Although every now and then, I did ask myself whether this sense of belonging—what I thought I wanted—was for me. I still do. The intensity was, on occasion, personally shattering; it took over one's life. At times, the DOC floundered, seemingly rudderless, only to snap back, on track again through someone or other's courageous efforts. In the process, we endlessly defined and redefined the prize—the living together—which I could only hope would prove to be more serene than the planning.

Site preparation

To fuel that hope, I drew from another parallel venture, one imbued with extraordinary idealism. In the mid-1980s, I was introduced to three young men who had just started a unique corporation for which they were looking for funding. "But," they hastened to warn me, "you shouldn't expect to make money and you might even lose your investment." Equal Exchange began as a worker-owned cooperative. From the beginning it was a radical departure from business-as-usual; the challenge to large corporations held special interest for me. The three incorporators had met each other in the natural-food-distribution business; their political activism on behalf of the growing economic plight of Central American coffee farmers led them to attempt change. They had learned about fair-trade programs in Europe that they hoped to put into effect by importing coffee to the United States and returning a certain percentage of the return to farmer coffee-growing cooperatives. I was impressed not only with their motivation but with the inventiveness necessary to forge a new path.

They launched this new program but not without first carefully thinking about the business ethics they wanted to pursue. Their humanitarian goals were foremost—rather than simply the profit motive—and much time was spent—and still is—considering the ethical aspects of relations with farmers, customers and employees. One example tells a lot: the founding mission states that the ratio between lowest and highest paid employees is one to three! The ratio was raised from one to four recently, about when Wall Street executives were receiving millions! New employees are rapidly involved in decision making and participate in creating company policy.

Just as in cohousing, everyone's on a committee or task force; unlike cohousing, meetings are usually held during working hours, rather than on nights and weekends. Growth has changed much, including a thriving coffee-roasting-importing enterprise for EE in its own building, but major decisions continue to be made not only top-down but bottom-up, with the lively input of all. Salaries are relatively low, but morale and benefits are good; lateral job transfer is encouraged; job rotations permit many to learn the ropes; coop worker-owners (requiring a year's employment for membership) elect the board members. Policy is created through evaluations, surveys, interviews, workshops, discussions, and of course, freely expressed-opinions. Not always 100 percent efficient in the usual sense, but invariably respectful and humane. Now more than twenty years later, EE is a formidable, influential actor in the specialty coffee, tea, and chocolate markets, and an ethical business model. And, idealism aside, EE has only once failed to pay a 5 percent or higher dividend to its stockholders.

The bottom line for me, however, is that as a trustee in one and an active resident in the other, I think of fair trade and cohousing as my two "movements," my apprenticeships in participatory democracy. Both are rewarding beyond measure, but can, at times, be incredibly trying. Both leave me convinced that efficiency alone as a governing criterion is a worthless priority for humanitarian, social, and business endeavors. To reconcile conflicting beliefs into a reasonable working organization appears to be the only bumbling method for building a sturdy foundation, humbling though that may be.

But somehow, despite the demands of our other lives, weekly we returned to the DOC, voluntary captives of a kind, bonded together by a blend of rejected and brilliant ideas, jokes, and the recurring dream of creating a cooperative community.

This Tuesday, from her computer behind a temporary partition, Katherine called out, "I'll be there in a minute. I'm finishing the agenda." Each week's agenda was numbered, we were now at #39.

Countless times, all of us had climbed those same three flights and others as well, following Katherine and Brent around Cambridge as they, in the mobile style of architects and developers, put their classy stamp on run-down, available, affordable space. A year ago, it had been another: Katherine had a talent for breathing life into deteriorating lofts as well as forlorn, abandoned land. A splash of color here, an antique table there, a Chinese screen and *abracadabra*—a new office!

The two reminded us now and then that this cohousing project was, for them, a labor of love and not meant to be a profitable venture, that high-office rentals were not affordable. Katherine and Brent were also founders, members, and, more recently, employees of the newly formed Cambridge Cohousing LLP. We would live together as fellow residents; they would need to ante up their down payment like the rest of us. At the same time, we were their bosses; we could even fire them. A high level of trust was the basis for this unconventional arrangement—a risky one, according to the lawyer Ed and I turned to, to advise us through the venture. Our attorney insisted that his job was to inform us of our level of personal risk, not to make judgments about our housing choices. Though, in an aside, he said he liked the idea.

Now, Vinita was settling in, emptying her briefcase. What one noticed first about her were her smile and her voice. The former was welcoming and contagious; the latter crisp, announcing her English childhood and her legal training. She left her government job on the other side of Central Square a little early to come to these meetings. Proud of her common-sense view of the law, Vinita had already saved us a fortune in legal fees.

Ned soon bounded in, carrying his bike, face ruddy, balding except for white fringes, now wet from the melting snow. Fresh from his ride from the Prudential Center across the Charles River in Boston, he was just in time to hear Vinita and me bemoan the near certainty of yet another parking ticket. Ned good-naturedly lorded his "free transportation" over us.

Merna, long hair flying, was hauling a bike up three floors "for safe-keeping." A social worker with much experience in housing management, she was just back from her ancestral Lithuania, where she returned twice yearly to teach health and social policy.

Dick, the most recent member, graciously agreed to replace Clara on the DOC when she dropped out, although I know he was concerned about fitting it in with the evening courses he took through Harvard's Extension Program in pursuit of a master's degree in literature. He worked up to the last minute before DOC meetings for an academic publishing house.

Like me, Clara was self-employed, and I'd guessed that we'd been selected to serve on the committee for our flexible schedules, as well as our skills and training in architecture, psychology, and housing. In addition, we had a deep commitment to the cohousing concept and, possibly, access to funds. Clara, however, for personal reasons, had just withdrawn from both the cohousing meetings and the DOC.

This was the only cohousing committee that was not open to all members, the only one presuming regular attendance. Over the next couple of years, several other members would join the DOC, for a short period, or for longer, but this original group of seven would remain for its entirety. When we began to meet in the unfinished, heatless library of our own property, free of concerns about parking meters, others would come to listen, cajole, complain, take umbrage, but not to vote or be accountable. For now, our official complement was full.

One additional presence—more than a shadow, less than a ghost—was also a member, but a nonparticipating one. Initially silent, moving only pen on notebook, this presence was not granted entry lightly. An early member and a sociologist, a woman who moved to Cambridge solely to join the project, commuted to her teaching job in Connecticut. Velma proposed to follow the DOC for a book she was researching on cohousing. Her plan was to conduct interviews with residents before and after moving into their cohousing units.

When she had initially approached our committee, we had met the idea of her dual member-researcher role with consternation. A spy in our midst, we thought. Our gaffes, our conflicts, our off-color jokes exposed! Velma might just as well have asked to sit in on the weekly meeting of the Joint Chiefs of Staff at the Pentagon. A research project! Egad, we thought, matters of confidentiality and content should be decided by the entire membership.

It was thus that Velma was hastily dispatched to plead her case to the full membership at what had now become regular monthly general meetings. As was our procedure, that body talked, debated, and then most likely formed a task force.

Eventually, the task force recommended approval of Velma's protocol and asked to review the book's final draft. It observed that we now had some guidelines for others who may be interested in cohousing research. Velma was now free to become the DOC's silent member. And with that, the stage was set for the meeting to begin. (A couple of years later, when I began to think about a book, this incident came clearly to mind and was a factor in shaping the concept of a personal account).

#410

Sketch of Common House Entry by Bruce Hampton

A voice came from our long table, directed toward Katherine who was dashing from behind the partition, with Agenda #39 in hand and colorful scarf arranged just right to set off her handsome dark jacket.

"Where is Floyd? Is he going to be here today?"

"No," reports Katherine. "His brother took a turn for the worse. He took the shuttle to Washington."

A few muted moans could be heard, heads bent in respect for a tragic illness and for Floyd's family loyalty, with just a tinge of resentment for the project's disruption—unfortunately for all, a continuing saga. For me, Floyd the committed architect and Floyd the devoted brother was becoming a metaphor of hope and promise on the one hand and of despair and the specter of death on the other.

"Brent will be late," Katherine quietly added.

We all understood that, although we had engaged the couple as our development consultants, in fact, cohousing had been a long-nurtured dream of Katherine's, and Brent saw himself in a supportive role; he was also the financier of this project.

Weekly Agenda #39 was distributed. Old Business was first: Item #1: Ongoing Negotiations with Century required explanation. Century was a New England firm that manufactured the modular housing units that our developers recommended for our dwelling structures. With their new technology, the owners promised faster, more economical, and more energy-efficient buildings than was possible using traditional construction. Katherine's attempt to persuade us that this method would be superior to the traditional stick-built construction was repetitious for several but an update for Merna and Dick.

"The units are well-made, and they can be substantially completed at the factory—even complete with appliances and carpeting—then trucked to Cambridge in batches, and hoisted in place by a crane. Any necessary finishing is done onsite. By manufacturing the units in the winter slow season, they can give us a discount. That should help our goal of affordability."

Then her voice dropped a tone or two, and I wondered what was up. "There are some problems," she said.

Turned out, Lewis at Century was strangely sluggish about negotiating with us, and Don, who had signed on as general contractor, was digging in his heels about working with them. His company was responsible for the basement, ground floor, roof, and grounds, and for tying the whole thing together.

"They'll simply have to work together," Katherine said.

It always makes me nervous when two parties to an agreement, both of whom stood to benefit, were unready or unwilling to show enthusiasm. I recall remarking that this didn't bode well, but no one wanted to pursue it.

Katherine looked up as though gauging her audience's tolerance for problems. "Another delay is that the cohousing Design Committee is creeping toward consensus at tortoiselike speed. Different members come to each semiweekly meeting—anyone is welcome—so a lot must be repeated, any new ideas require modifications of earlier design elements. For example, will there be fireplaces or not? That's still a big *if* so it has to go to the general meeting." We all knew that meant maybe fifty people discussing air pollution, incidence of asthma in children, cost factors, firebox efficiency . . .

"The meeting isn't scheduled for two weeks, and the information is needed ASAP."

Ned, always optimistic and known for quick decisions that tend to carry an air of finality, this time surprised us. "I'm for giving them another week or two. I never have understood why we're on this fast track Katherine and Brent talk about."

Vinita, our legal watchdog, weighed in, clarifying parts of the contract.

Jean wondered aloud. "These procrastinations could be read as a danger signal for smooth working relations. Does Century really want this contract? Do we? What about pursuing other avenues before we're locked in?"

A few murmurs but no "right on" comments.

Merna, with an unfailing ear to community concerns, said, "People have talked to me. They're worried that they can't afford to stay in if costs go up."

It was now six fifteen, and we were no farther ahead with our three-way contract than when we'd commenced. A long list of new items awaited us. Next up: Common House Laundry.

Katherine explained. "Betty wants a washing machine in the third-floor unit she has her eye on, apparently a long-held wish of hers. Since we eliminated a laundry for each floor in the Common House to cut costs, she's unwilling to go to the basement. Do we make this change or do we risk Betty and Mike pulling out?" (In this project I realized we dealt a lot with wishes, dreams, and hopes.)

As happened every now and then, this particular matter touched a nerve that ignited heated argument, to which our normal, respectful exchange gave way. This was our third round about washing machines, an emotionally laden topic for homeowners, architects, and plumbers alike. We took sides, quick to recognize a budget-breaker in the making. Floyd, Don, Katherine, and Brent had all drummed into us the danger of the dreaded Change Order—the single biggest cause of cost overruns, they explained periodically.

Several talked, or rather shouted, at once, and the loudest, strongest voices ruled. Fragments of homespun cohousing philosophy replaced whatever semblance of order remained. The tangle of voices sounded something like this.

"This makes no sense—we already consensed on changing the plans to remove the plumbing line from the three floors in the Common House." ("Consensed" was only one of several butcheries of the language to lay at the feet of cohousing devotees.)

"Remember, we hoped the basement laundry would become a social center of sorts. As people go between garage and elevator, they can stop and talk."

"The plumbing estimate—please don't interrupt me!—is already in."

"How can we call ourselves environmentally sensitive if we give in to washing machines everywhere?"

"The townhouses will have washer/dryer setups. Have we forgotten about fairness? What happened to our egalitarian principles? We'll be accused of pandering to those who can pay."

"I thought we hashed this out long ago—we deliberately agreed to reduce our unit sizes in order to increase our shared space. One of the things that makes ours different from other condos is a design that attempts to reduce the feeling of isolation."

"Oh, c'mon, it's only a laundry!"

A burst of laughter broke the tension, as someone added, "Okay, but who will pay the extra bucks for a new plumbing line? And won't it take space away from the units below? Boy, who wants to enter that lion's den!"

Another voice timidly suggested that this sounded like a matter for the general meeting. "We're not even close to consensus."

With a collective sigh of gratitude, we rubbed our bruises; on this point we could agree.

(The general meeting the next Sunday afternoon had a field day with the laundry conflict. Katherine assigned herself as advocate for Betty and Mike's home laundry; my memory is that they did not attend. Because they had been unofficially promised this amenity and because no one wanted to test the strength of their request, it was granted with a cost-splitting proviso.)

We had little energy for the remaining agenda items: our dwindling balance, overdue bills—which to pay, which to postpone. How to collect the 30 percent down payment from the last few holdouts? With that money in hand we could pay the civil engineer's fee. (We did not assume the roles of taskmasters well; our philosophy—with a lot of time hammering out ingenious approaches to members' consciences and pocketbooks—assumed that all would act responsibly in financial matters.) The construction loan, still not finalized—well, that was Brent's bailiwick, so we left that to him. In our growing fatigue, our ability to resolve these final items came to symbolize the almost impossible task we had undertaken.

Driving back to my house for a late dinner with Ed and Anne, Dick and I confessed our discouragement.

He claimed not to be suited for the task. "I don't know what I can contribute. And besides, I guess I'm not a yeller."

I felt much the same. "We need a peacekeeper, a facilitator to guide us through the morass. I can't stand it when everyone speaks at once."

A postscript. Betty got her washing machine, Jean and Ed their west-facing windows, Theda her pocket french doors, and Velma her fireplace. The dining room had enough lights to host a night game at Fenway Park. We postponed a prohibitively costly dishwasher installation in the common kitchen with a simple, ingenious BYO practice: Going to dinner meant bringing our own place settings to the common dining room, and then taking them back to our own perfectly good dishwashers. Residents then boasted of a handsome assortment of basketry with wine glasses snuggling in amongst fanciful plastic dishware.

Delivery of modular units, 1997

The Lottery

All of life is a battle for the ears of others.
—Unknown

Thoughts raced through my mind during the five-block walk, some months later, to Katherine and Brent's newest office. The real work of the DOC today, I remind myself, is to go beyond that of our usual Tuesday agenda. The eagerly awaited time had arrived to plan for the unit selections. It would be the moment when we would know where we will live for perhaps the rest of our lives. When each of us had officially signed on—by contributing one hundred dollars to the LLP—we became cardless members with a lottery number burned into our brains; participants in a transaction based on trust. Number 18, I still recall, was ours. (*Will this turn out to be a crazy or wise move?* I wondered). Number 18's only function was to indicate the order in which Ed and I would choose our unit.

In their quest for the perfect office location, Katherine and Brent had abandoned Central Square for Harvard Square. First floor this time, awfully tight temporary quarters in an old house awaiting renovation. Katherine greeted us with toilet bowl cleaner in one hand, mop in the other. "This place will do for a while. Office space in Harvard Square is at such a premium that we're lucky to find it. Meanwhile, we'll be searching for something better, more permanent."

"Coming up in the world, are you?" Ned said cheerily, more statement than question, as he squeezed between the door and an outsized desk.

We were about to inaugurate the new office with the fiftieth agenda. We were all prompt; the excitement was palpable. Today represented a milestone we'd been heading toward for what seemed like forever but for what was more like a year and a half. Floyd, doffing his dapper little cap, joined us.

"Okay, folks." He grinned as he unrolled the architectural drawings. "We're at the point now where individual units can be designated and matched up with their future owners."

Did Floyd say "owners?" I got goose bumps as I came to grips with this new idea; it took me by surprise. The full meaning of owning private space in a collective project simply hadn't fully registered with me. It would be the place where I would sleep, eat, write, see friends! Why such a strange reaction? I think I had unwittingly harbored a kind of department-store view of our complex. I knew the street, the address, the geometrical shapes of the blue architectural drawings, and the schematics representing the common space on the first floor, but I had no idea where to find the underwear, the pots and pans or the shower curtains. Cohousing up to now offered me no single bounded area I could point to and say, "This is my *home!*"

Ed and I often talked about our hopes—top floor, a little removed from the crowd, southern exposure, a gigantic sky vista, good sound insulation, sky lights . . . only now did I see how etched these elements were in my vision. What if the lottery came out wrong? With all the other concerns, day-to-day decisions, and deadlines, I had not once faced the possibility of such a fateful outcome.

The agenda began with an announcement in bold:

THE FIRST BOXES LEAVE VT TOMORROW

The "boxes," our homes-to-be, had been in manufacture in New Hampshire for months now. After many delays and false starts, the way through state and city regulations appeared to be clear. Permits were issued, staging areas were arranged; would weather be forgiving? Cohousing members would be notified via the phone network; those who could, would stand on chilly corners to watch the flatbed trucks maneuver through the maze of North Cambridge streets.

Odd little facts: by law, the boxes could not travel during rush hours or rainy weather. Also boxes could be arrested—and one was. My daughter called from Route 2 that morning, very excited. "I just spotted some boxes heading toward Cambridge! They're huge! Maybe one is yours!"

Back to the real business, the DOC authorized Katherine to pay some bills and to give Don, the contractor, hell for taking so long to finish the foundation. Cash should have been flowing in soon; residents had two weeks to pay one-third of the total estimated costs of their unit and a portion of the entire project. The remainder was due at closing, a still unknown date and amount.

Katherine reviewed the status of construction: the foundation was dry, ready to receive the boxes. She and I recalled a number—something like 122 boxes (was that possible?)—would be brought to Richdale Avenue on flatbed trucks. We had neglected to budget for the required daily police detail, but traffic would be stopped one hundred twenty-two times, as each box was slowly lifted by crane and then, one by one, set in place. That meant a lot of disgruntled neighbors and drivers.

"From macro to micro." What better way to understand my ownership panic? My absorption, like that of the other members of the DOC, was with the overall project—site search, land acquisition, hearings at city hall, the budget, the contracts. Only at rare moments could I focus on plans for our home. I did carry a little list that I added to periodically—those things I wanted: good tight windows, the latest word in insulation, electric outlets at desk level, a high-rise sink faucet, a suitable area for chamber music—but it was really hard to concentrate today as I shifted back and forth, between the general and the particular.

For years, I had lugged my cello to Max and Sheila's house for evenings of string quartets. Until 10:00 PM sharp, we'd transform ourselves into musicians, dropping the cares of our day roles as we soared to other realms. Then at the witching hour, while packing up the instruments, we'd briefly rate ourselves: "Better than last time," the second violinist said, optimistically. "Well, what can you expect from amateurs?"might be the violist's retort. "That was fun!" or our highest mutual congratulations, "We're really good tonight!" as we make our way from Brahms and Beethoven to beer, to cheese, and then to fruit and cake. Sheila was every bit as ingenious as Mozart in the variations of food she put before us.

We touched upon politics, local personalities, even cohousing progress. No social session was complete, however, without an update about Max's invention. Max, a professor in Harvard's Chemistry Department and gracious, modest, and as ardent a teacher and researcher, I'm sure, as he was a violinist, would never himself bring up the subject of the Low-E glass he was working on. Just as he would never cancel an evening of music for other than a hurried trip to the large manufacturing company in Ohio, which was gearing up to produce "miles and miles" of the unbroken sheets. Low-E insulating glass was not yet a household term, so in these discussions, we felt conspiratorially included in a coup that would dramatically increase residential comfort levels and represent a major environmental advance.

During one such post-quartet supper, Sheila—not Max, who just looked embarrassed—proudly showed us drafts of ads and an article about Max, who was pictured standing in front of a sheet of his glass. The second violinist, in the process of building a house with lots of windows, became intrigued by the glass's promised energy savings and became the first in New England to install them. Ed and I followed close behind, replacing some sliders in our cold living room, rendering it comfortably useful in winter for the first time ever. Now these windows, known as Max's glass to us cohousers, were high priority on my wish list for our new building.

Unit selection by future residents (Plan by Oaktree Development)

"So how shall we go about seeing that people get what they want and that no one pulls out at this stage?" I heard someone say.

Katherine cautioned us—always with one eye on the budget—as I tried to refocus my full attention on the DOC meeting.

Recalling my recent house fantasy, I said, "People have dreams and expectations about their homes—many hope this is their last move—so they're heavily invested in having it be just right."

"That's true," said Merna. "But people like me are constrained by limited funds, so I don't feel like I have many options."

"Let's remember our own history for a minute," opined Vinita. (Opined. There's another word for the cohousing glossary, "opined" like "consensing," that we seem to have adopted.) "Very early, it became clear that there had to be a fair and orderly method for allocating the units—a method that wouldn't lead to chaos. Good idea or not, that's the reason for these lottery numbers."

"For the meeting on Sunday, we have charged ourselves with making the lottery work," added Dick, looking up from his minute-taking. "Everyone already seems to know it's coming. The tension is mounting." (I really did forget about her; there is Velma, in the corner, true to plan, quietly taking her own notes).

We paused, all reminding ourselves, I suppose, of our main challenge and responsibility. Then, as though on signal, everyone spoke at once, shouting out ideas for this procedural dilemma in rapid disorder.

A bidding process! No, definitely not. That seemed antithetic to our commitment to affordability.

First come, first served? Hardly. That would give unfair advantage to early comers; we should all be able to see what's available before making a choice.

On the drawings, Floyd pointed out examples of the several-unit prototypes: studio-, one-, two-, three-, and four-bedroom apartments and then the three- and four-bedroom, three-story townhouses. "I have made every effort to distribute the goodies as evenly as possible throughout the project. All units open by door and/or windows onto one of the four open spaces. All have at least two exposures. All have a southern orientation. The Common House, equidistant from both ends, with its mailroom and garage, is the focal point, easily accessible if not visible from every unit. Thirty units back up along the railroad tracks; the remaining eleven are sited near the street. So pick your poison—train or car, pollution or noise."

Brent got up and squinted at the drawings before saying, "Not that it was moribund before, but these drawings really bring the project to life. I can begin to imagine living here."

Several of us chuckled. This was, from Brent, a remarkable statement; it was no secret that he would prefer to remain in their present Cambridge condo, in a building that he and Katherine developed with a wondrous view of all of Boston.

"Seeing these in groups gives me an idea," offered Ned, who had been oddly silent until now. "It seems to me that all we have to do is have a plan for those times when two or more choose the same unit. This probably won't happen too often, but we should be prepared just in case. We should determine what motivates people's choices—whether it's price, size, or location. Can we sweeten a deal a bit? We can't change location, but we can help a buyer look at a second choice more positively. The size is fixed, but perhaps some interior changes can make a unit more attractive or functional for them. And then there's price; maybe some fiddling is possible. I'm leaving now—I'm off to the theater. Those are my ideas."

As so often happened, Ned seized the role of Summarizer—in rapid, declarative sentences, sometimes outrageous, sometimes profound.

"And don't forget," he hollered from the doorway, grinning impishly, "the selection requires consensus, just like everything else here!"

At that Sunday's well-attended meeting, those with potluck dishes headed for the kitchen, and the three childcare workers gathered the children and headed for the basement playroom. No one, unless out of the country, would have dreamed of missing this one. I understood that Joy and Sam had cut their trip to Washington short in order to choose their "flat" (Katherine introduced this term early on and most of us never stopped using it. I liked it. It suited Ed's and my space—oops, that is, the space we *hoped* to draw).

This may be a long meeting, so we were fortunate to have a great space, thanks to the Society of Friends. We sat in folding chairs around the edge of the room, forming a huge circle. No one could hide. But first, the customary calming moment of silence, a Quaker ritual that we had adopted.

Then, the silence over, the facilitators were ready. On well-displayed newsprint pads (we had made a large investment in easels) were the numbers one through thirty-one, writ large. With each number representing a unit ownership, this meant we had only thirty-one current memberships; however, the full roster would be forty-one. Next was a list of the would-be residents, along with the dates that each joined the Cambridge Cohousing LLP; in case of a tie, these dates would be a determining factor. Then, on the far right, a blank column, where, by the end of the day, the assigned unit number for each new owner would appear. On a large table in the center of the room were the enlarged plans, spread out for ease of viewing, showing the entire narrow, elongated site. Heavily outlined in red was each unit with its numbered location; for example, "East End #120," "Common House #410." On another easel appeared all of the possible housing types—for example, we saw that there were three one-bedroom units available—along with the vital statistics of each: location in cohousing plan, view, floor level, dimensions, exposures, balcony or roof deck, and estimated final price. Ellen introduced the other members of the facilitator team, Mike and Kirsten, and explained, "The plan is to proceed with the selections until 6:00. That gives us two-and-a-half hours. If we do not finish by then, we will stop for a quick meal and resume after supper at 6:45—the children get hungry and the childcare people have to leave. And, oh yes, we have been asked by The Friends not to use the refrigerator; they are having an event in the front room. And, very important, do not park in the handicap space unless you have a visible permit. You will be towed." Her final instruction: "We have to finish this *tonight*."

Mike then took over, explaining that he and Kirsten would be responsible for running the meeting and would field any process questions. "Katherine, representing the DOC, will be recording the choices that people make, and responding, along with Floyd, to any specific questions about the units. Does everyone understand the plan?"

A hand shot up. It was Ruth, at the far end of the room. "I think that of the units I can afford, there are only five with two bedrooms. From the talk going around, I can imagine that there are more than five of us who might want one of those. What happens then?"

"Hey, you struck on one of our knottiest questions! A tough one. I'll just pass it right along to Katherine."

A ripple of laughter followed as Katherine, knowing she'd been hit with a hard one, hesitated. "That—this—well, this is something as developers, we try to figure out ahead of time. Remember those surveys we asked you to fill out, months ago, questions about size preferences, needs, and price range? Ordinarily, developers do some market research, look at the demographics, and make educated guesses. When units go up for sale, then we see how accurate we've been. For cohousing, we know many of the buyers early on, but you can never be sure. People change their minds; their lives change.

Really, this is the basic reason for the lottery. We hope we have assessed the needs and hopes accurately but, in the end, it's somewhat arbitrary."

Katherine, perhaps conveniently not hearing some grumbles, went on. "You should know that size and number of bedrooms are not the only determinant of price. That's why we urge you to study the drawings carefully before making your choice."

With no other questions, Mike announced it was time to move to the next item, at which point, Kirsten posted a large "Number 1" on the easel. Heads swiveled, and a quietly tense silence descended, followed by murmurs, when no one responded. The whispers grew in volume, reaching an outburst of hearty laughter when Mike, puzzled, went to the master list (a record of all the names in the lottery) held by Ellen.

Ellen replied, "The name here is Caswell. They dropped out some months ago, concerned about the ultimate cost and not happy with the idea of pulling their home out of a hat."

"Right," Vinita added. "They were here for our big drawing, but we haven't seen much of them lately. They have asked for a refund of their original one hundred dollars. Remember that some time ago we agreed that wouldn't be possible." Her last words were drowned in the rising waves of mirth, the irony of the absent Number 1 having broken the tension.

Number 2 is put up on the easel. Merna pops out of her seat and goes up to the table to speak with Katherine. I couldn't make out their words but, after a few brief exchanges, Merna turned to the group and promptly bursts into tears. "I can't tell you what this means to me," she sputtered between sobs. "My girls and I now can have a home of our own. Ever since I lived in Holland in something akin to cohousing, I have dreamt of this, a dream I never thought could happen in this country. And then cohousing came along. I work three jobs to pay for this, but that's fine. I just hope I can manage the condo fees as well as the mortgage."

At the tail end of a round of applause, Merna rushed downstairs to tell her girls (Pam, seven, and Lise, nine) that they would live in a two-bedroom apartment in the Common House overlooking the proposed Shade Garden, now a jungle of weed trees.

The mood of the group was now decidedly high-spirited as well as respectful of Merna's happiness at the fact that her efforts from the onset would be rewarded. Perhaps we really could create an income-diverse community, I thought; this was one of those inspiring moments that made all the effort worthwhile.

One by one, Ellen posted the next few numbers, and Katherine noted the choices; there were no surprises. With Number 8, Roger and Clea, with a nursing infant and hopes for a second, spoke up, caused raised eyebrows.

Others seemed to share my assumption that they were a couple with financial concerns as well as a carefully worked-out life plan. I, for one, was sure they'd pick a small unit in the Common House while Roger finished his book. Hadn't they been asking a lot of questions about flats in the Common House?

I drifted off, thinking how amazing it was to be choosing your home midst people you know, many fairly well, a few even intimately, after two years of intense planning. Then both cheers and groans jarred me to full attention. Roger, following a conversation with Katherine, smiled broadly, his eyes rolling to the ceiling. He and Clea chose one of the large townhouses, the last before the driveway in the West End. Well, that was a surprise! Never trust one's assumptions, I remind myself—a good thing to learn when living closely with others.

Obscured by the applause, a fleeting memory of groans returned to me. Then I noticed the downcast expressions on Marsha's and Shan Shen's faces; several people hovered around them, speaking softly and reassuringly. Though their hopes for that unit had obviously been dashed, they were too polite to publicly remonstrate, so the community's support went out to them.

"There are others that size." An encouraging voice rose from the group.

"But we have such a high number," added Marsha, glumly, slumping in her chair. "Victor's only our first child, and a lively one at that. I don't see how we can fit into anything smaller. And I love that view, looking over the playground across the tracks."

Kirsten gently reminded us that it was 5:40 and we were not yet through a third of the units.

Admittedly a relatively easy way to feed a gang of people, potluck meals used to appall me. The haphazardness, the quantities! Now I joined in, with relish, bringing my chicken dish, my dip, or my pasta and was always in awe of the balanced spread before us. My neighbors-to-be were inventive and generous, creating wonderful smells. They seemed just as obsessed with food as I am. It was one of our bonds, a basic one; by feeding one another, we were making the transition from I-them to we-us.

Then with serving dishes empty, trash stowed away, flatware returned to labeled drawers, and the kitchen restored to institutional cleanliness, we reconvened in our circle of chairs. Children were everywhere, but they seemed to have some sense of the specialness of the moment.

Number 6 appeared on the easel. Betsy set her knitting aside and rose slowly. She had joined several of us in our campaign for accessibility of the flats (see the chapter, "You Can't Get There From Here"), and she was now choosing a unit served by our triumph: the stair chairs. She walked heavily; her knees must have hurt. Boy, did I understand that.

"With my rotten hip, we'll have to drop out if we can't have a Common House apartment near the elevator," I whispered to Ed. Fortunately, no one had yet chosen the third-floor flat that Betsy had had her eyes on. Her face was wreathed in smiles as we made eye contact and she serenely resumed her knitting.

Now only Joy and Sam preceded us.. Tall, shaggy Sam, who ran the external communications at a nearby startup.com, loomed over tiny, squat Joy who is a teacher at a suburban independent school. Both dreamt about retirement. When? "Depends on how much it will cost to live here," they always say on cue.

My moment of panic was unwarranted; there was no contest. Unit #410 was ours! Either the fourth floor was too far from the center of things or the final price was expected to be too high—not everyone had a large house to sell. I knew it was exactly right for us. Two of the four bedrooms, while small, would become office for me and studio for Ed. Clouds would course across the sky, treating us to ever-changing pantomimes; sunsets would beam in from two of the three exposures. Our next task was to reduce eleven rooms, plus cellar and attic, down to five. We'd think about that later. Now, the lottery swept us along.

The Spitzers, a blended family with four children, needed space, a lot of it. Like us, they got their first choice: a large townhouse opening directly onto the open "glade" area. The two youngest, rather shy girls, showed no visible reaction; they had been bored and begging to leave. The older two, teenage boys with interests other than living with many parents and a lot of small children, were decidedly cool to cohousing, this nutty idea of their parents.

Doris's quandary captured everyone's attention. Fresh from divorce and a career change, she explained that she must scrape bottom in order to live here. "I see there's a studio in the Common House, where I'd like to live, but, yikes, I simply cannot live in one room, especially with Luna." (Lovable Luna was a member in good standing, one of three grandfathered dogs for whom the "no pets" by law was waived).

A serious conference among Katherine, Brent, and Floyd took place, one that we all could hear. There was a possibility of taking space from an adjoining apartment to carve out a small bedroom. But there was another problem. No one had shown interest in that four-bedroom unit; we should save it for a family who might need it.

Doris looked worried, thought a moment, and then said, "This is a big gamble for me, but I'm deciding to take the studio on the condition that, if a family doesn't come along, cohousing will let me have that one hundred and twenty additional square feet for a bedroom. I think I can swing that for now; if something larger opens up later, I'd like to have the option of moving." How was that for commitment and trust! Would I have been able to do that? The applause was strong for Doris; no one wanted to lose her for a few square feet.

It was Theda's turn, but she made no move to leave her seat. Her face was white, in stark contrast to her thick, long, dark hair, now pulled back in a ponytail; her eyes were on the floor. Was she trembling? Norm, her longtime friend, was encouraging her to stand, to walk to the table.

By now, her hesitation has silenced the room. The carefully orchestrated momentum of the lottery was interrupted; there's a feel of growing drama in the air. We all knew Theda as a thoughtful, meticulously careful, unhurried person who continually reviewed all of her options and then asked for more. Theda was notorious for postponing her observations right up to the end of a meeting. "I have just one comment and two short questions," she was likely to say, just when people were folding up their papers to leave. Affectionate laughter accompanied the sighs of those who had already dressed to depart. Carefully worded and deliberate, however, Theda's questions were elaborate, pithy, and valuable. It was her timing that brought the laughs.

Finally, she mumbled, "I have two equally wonderful spaces in mind, and I can't decide between them. No one has picked either."

Mike stepped in and suggested a ten-minute break to give Theda some breathing room. People relaxed, moved around, talked to friends. One family brought out pajamas and was preparing their small children for bed.

After a few minutes, Mike raised his hand for attention. Theda had moved to a corner of the room with Norm, who was holding her hand; they were speaking quietly. Mike asked how the community might help her with the decision. Did she need any more information? Theda drew herself up, thanked Mike, and began to talk about her dilemma.

"As you know, I'm an artist ... but first, I want to say I'm very sorry about the delay. But I'm almost fifty and have never owned anything before. I find it unbelievably stressful. I haven't slept for nights. I intend to live here with all of you forever..."

"You were saying something about being an artist, Theda. Is that where the problem lies?" asked Ken B. from across the room.

"Yes. I want a studio where I live. The space in the Common House is wonderful, so is the light, but then that's true of the East End, too. I've made sketches showing the light in each for all hours of the day. I also want the kitchen to be ... I really can't go on. I'd like to ask you to give me more time. I think if I go for a walk by myself, I can figure this out. I know this is hard for all of you, but I hope you'll allow me an extension of an hour. I so want to make the right choice."

Mike surveyed the room. A few, citing other commitments, seemed unwilling to grant the request, but noting the sympathy level of the rest, withheld their objections. And with that, what had been a long and often tedious process, with moments of humor and excitement, suddenly changed gears. The mood altered. The warm, friendly, postdinner, settling-in-to-see-this-through spirit halted. A remarkable bonding activity showed signs of splintering.

The room looked like a dormitory. Facilitators had disappeared for a powwow. The circle rent, some kids whining, others scooting around the floor on coats. A board game appeared at the far end. Some families had taken their children home to bed, one parent to return, an option not open to single parents, someone ruefully pointed out.

Little groups were forming, and it became obvious from body language alone—faces intent, postures strained—that our patchwork was at risk of coming unstitched. Feelings of frustration and disappointment may have found a target in Theda's paralysis.

It was particularly strange to me that very few of those whose housing was decided, for whom the lottery was history, were making overtures to leave. Maybe we were a cohesive group, I mused. Or, less hopefully, I muttered to Anne, did our cohesiveness just require a scapegoat?

The facilitators returned; it was now 9:30. At best, we wouldn't roll again until 10:00.

"It is tempting," Ellen said, "in view of what has happened and that we allowed Theda extra time, to rethink our selection process at this juncture. But we have rejected this idea because a number, precisely ten, still haven't chosen their units. It seems unfair to tamper with the ground rules now."

"But what's fair about allowing Theda leeway that no one else has?" someone pointed out.

"No one else has asked," Ellen said, then without a pause, she went on. "Betty, always with a pocketful of activities, has offered to organize a game. Do I sense any interest in this?" She scanned the room. "Not much, so let's just take a breather, visit with our neighbors."

Theda appeared at the door, drawn and limp. The roomful of waiting people snapped to attention. With tears streaming, she walked slowly toward the center, and lowering her voice, said, "I didn't have the epiphany I hoped for, but I know I have reached the limits of your good will. I choose the East End three-bedroom flat."

This was the stuff of legend. And, as such, it would soon sit alongside our other stories, those already past and those that have yet to happen: our homes delivered in boxes; our dedication ceremony, complete with a parade through the property, carrying candles, beating drums, and burying a time capsule;

Ed's eightieth birthday celebration and Kara's birth party; our continuous wrangling over the uses of the roof. Also not to be overlooked: some family, I forget who now, dropped out; and Marsha and Shan Shen got their large townhouse and filled it with three more children before leaving for a larger home in the suburbs. All of these stories and more would become part of who we are. They would become the stories that a family collects about itself.

Public Space, Personal Boundaries

*Our goal is to create a mixed-income
Community, where children, adults, and
elders of varying race, ethnicity,
religion, sexual orientation, and ability, can thrive.*
—Cambridge Cohousing Vision Statement

The construction period seemed interminable, especially to those homeless souls, including children, who with each delay were forced to search for still-another temporary living arrangement. The completion date was postponed again and again, leaving more cohousers to live out of suitcases, schlepping their goods from one friend's house or furnished rental to another. Nine months of this speaks to the devotion of those ultimately committed to inhabit our urban village. That is not to say that morale didn't suffer; it did. Tempers were short, blaming became a daily pastime, trips to storage warehouses were more frequent. The only winners were the pizza emporiums and Chinese take-outs.

But at long last, the local newspaper got its photo ops and reports to the effect of "Only in Cambridge! A Housing First!" The first few families moved into the East End in February 1998, a scant three years from conception—actually a speed record for cohousing projects nationwide.

The prevailing cohousing mode was to "process" and plan, often for years, before purchasing land. Cohousers were notably careful to cover all the bases, scouring the preselected area for available property, meticulously scrutinizing mortgage rates and all other financial obligations, and monitoring consultants with a watchful eye.

In contrast, Cambridge Cohousing had plunged headlong into a land search, fully aware of its scarcity. Most commonly a group of potential residents organizes itself as an owner-driven model. When pretty sure what they want and can afford, they begin to search for and hire developer, architect, builder, and other consultants. But a few projects, in a developer-driven model, were envisioned by developers who then recruited from those interested in the cohousing concept. Cambridge Cohousing was a blend of the two. A group of Quakers, including Katherine and Brent, mobilized the original core group and steered the development process, but the membership was increasingly proactive in running the project.

When the units were finally ready for occupation and passed city approval, no one was thinking about anything beyond the move-in date. Nothing—not nonfunctioning plumbing ("My kitchen faucet activates the third-floor shower"), seas of mud and rubble, an inadequate heating system ("indescribably constructed," commented a consultant), a refrigerator blocking a cabinet door—could staunch the excitement nor the steady flow of the curious.

Friends, relatives, reporters, doubters and promotors, city planners and TV producers, all responded to the contagious high spirits engendered by this forty-one-unit urban phenomenon along the railroad tracks. We, in turn, opened home, hearth, and hearts to all comers in one long, jubilant celebration. Cambridge Cohousing was hot news on the real estate and living pages. I, targeted by and for my white hair and early role in the project, became a blase' interviewee. Ed and I, as the oldest couple, were sought out for wise guru-like remarks about intergenerational living. Hinted at, if not asked directly, was always the question: "What on earth about this crazy scheme can be attractive to people like *you*?" 'You,' I took to mean retired but active professionals, who held interests in the arts, who travelled, and who were financially able to live in a much better neighborhood than others like *them*.

By the time we moved into our separate cohousing units, Ed and I, Anne and Dick had a leg up on the others, as a fortuitous rehearsal period of close to a year had enabled us to ease into the main act. In the spring of '97, when Anne and Dick too were caught in construction delays after being told to sell their house. They had done their part, but by their closing date their Common House unit, a floor below ours, was far from ready.

"Certainly by midsummer," came the word.

Although we did not know them well, we liked what we saw, and Ed and I had a large house. And so, with their belongings in storage, they accepted our invitation and joined us as houseguests for those few weeks. We enjoyed being together, and rapidly eased into a routine, sharing meals and chores, movies and families. Besides, after our late-night Design Committee meetings, they, like we, had only to go upstairs to bed.

Ed and I found that more considerate "guests" could not exist. And while we laughed with others about the the-man-who-came-to-dinner scenario, well-intentioned friends advised us to be wary. Nevertheless, with the next construction delay, Ed and I proposed to continue the arrangement, with a change of our joint status to "housemates." They balked, we urged; they feared intruding on our privacy.

"Think of it as a rehearsal for living with a hundred people," Ed countered.

Truth be known, we actually dreaded their departure; they were helping us pass through this frustrating period more than they knew. With Ed's continuing uncertainty about our cohousing decision, their presence helped reduce some tension between the two of us. Humor, in particular, was a big help. It became our metier; some of our jokes were even, well, pretty good, if immediately forgettable.

In the first few weeks a plan evolved, a household business arrangement of sharing expenses along with the promise of a monthly "house meeting." This was to be a session to air gripes, though, frankly, while we loosely honored our plan, the biggest joke when we settled down over wine in the living room, was the absence of complaints. Then someone, probably Ed, mentioned a movie, and we were off.

Anne and Dick to us seemed remarkably sanguine over being separated from their belongings and living under another's roof. "We'd always talked about simplifying our lives," they'd insist, gamely. They'd usher in each new season with a trip to scattered storage sites, bringing home appropriate clothing, holiday regalia, tax records. Ed and I felt the strain was theirs, and the benefit ours: snow magically disappeared from cars and walks, the morning paper was on the table (Dick continued to deliver it to #410; he heard me say once that what I'd miss most was the morning newspaper at my front door), all before they soundlessly left for work. Ed could count on luscious desserts and ironed handkerchiefs (neither in my repertoire). Fresh flowers filled the house, every dinner was a mini-party. We celebrated special occasions, gave each other space during stressful events, turned deaf ears to spousal tiffs, and fretted and rejoiced together over the lives of our six collective offspring.

Asked by friends, poised to commiserate, how the arrangement could possibly work, I was unable to support their predictions (perhaps tainted with hope) of disaster.

"It just does," I lamely replied. "Really, there's no friction."

It were as though two unrelated couples weren't *supposed* to cohabit comfortably for very long, that if they did, it was almost unAmerican. Though to be fair, with very few exceptions, most of our curious friends as well as most of the cohousing residents came from traditional households.

It became all too clear to me then that while cohousing's mantra of "interdependence" may have rung with magnetic appeal, it also was looked upon with some disbelief. Ed and Jean and Dick and Anne, abstractions aside, were now getting the chance to refine what that mantra could mean.

Possibly the most predictive single factor of our success was that Anne and I worked happily together in the kitchen, each preferring different ends of the meal—a soup kitchen for me, a bakery for her. Housekeeping was another non-issue: another myth exploded. Our standards of order and cleanliness were in reasonable synchrony, as she was a vacuumer, I a straightener.

It was in our kitchen that it first dawned on me how skilled Anne was in camouflaging a real handicap in her social exchanges. She at a counter across the room, I at the stove, our backs to each other, I said something but heard no response. I repeated myself—still nothing. Only after I got her attention did I learn that she was very deaf, having worn two hearing aids since childhood. She somehow had combined a keen observation of facial expression, body language, and lipreading with current technology to be a superb listener.

And Dick, I learned, worked with books, lived with books, had thrown away enough books to fill a bookstore, and yet never found enough time to read. It was not unusual to find him downstairs, in the early, early morning hours, preparing for his evening classes. Yet he never claimed fatigue or impatience, as I would, and was always ready to take on the next task.

I think we all worked hard to establish a *quid pro quo*, a recognition of one another's needs and individualities and, without ever talking about it, boundaries. Through birthday celebrations, an auto accident, basement floods, a job change, we unconsciously—and this is the miracle—sensed one another's limits as, simultaneously, we set our own. And in this way, day by day, we reinforced a future of unbreakable bonds for just under a year.

Having passed the clinical trial, maybe we were ready for the full-blown cohousing experiment.

"I don't want to hear about the budget," said my friend Tim. "I want to know how you get along together, how you establish boundaries. I'm pretty sure I couldn't stand living like that—in fact, it would drive me crazy. I need my *privacy.*"

His question jolted me. In talking about himself, he could have well been describing me. I was a very private person, an observer at heart. (My painfully acquired social bent, I understand, may be deceptive). So how could I love being in this place? Could I, a woman in her midseventies, really defy the habits of a lifetime and refashion myself as a communard? Or had I just forgotten, buried, or deluded that part of myself?

Tim's reverberating question then challenged my own decision. Would I find the interruptions unmanageable? Would I feel constrained by the many people and tasks I would have to adjust to, take time for?

I knew that I could reverse the isolation I sometimes felt at Raymond Street by taking a short walk to Mass Ave to window shop, select a birthday card, bump into an acquaintance. In a few years, however, the short walk—going to the common living room by elevator, exchanging words with a friend to alter a desolate mood—may well become a long or impossible walk. And what about pursuing my own interests without the interference or judgement of others? Would that be possible?

Years later, writing *The View from #410* over a several-year period was, I suppose, the test. No one ever indicated any knowledge of my endeavor. With a modicum of care, I could write away in seclusion without being questioned about my progress, probed about locating a publisher, or even cheered on.

On the other hand, other authors here have expressed annoyance when peppered with such intrusions, so I suspect that it may be a matter of knowing how to set personal limits—and that takes practice. I am also aided by living on the top floor, relatively far from the center of things, where I have more control over my space than some.

Still, much as I have tried, I cannot imagine living here as a young family, although I admire those who make it work. I suspect our children would have loved it!

Back when Anne and Dick and Ed and I were comfortably managing our microhousehold, we were also engaged with the membership in often stressful planning sessions, confronting multipronged issues. The most difficult one was to determine how much our individual units were going to cost so that, as purchasers we could review our finances and investigate the mortgage scene. Just *how* to arrive at these values with fairness to all was our next big hurdle. The dilemma for homebuyers everywhere is to choose housing that is both desirable *and* affordable. Since we had already paid one-third of the estimated final cost when we chose our unit in the lottery, we now needed to accurately know what the amount of the final balance would be. That figure would eventually lead to the percentage of ownership for the entire project that each of us would own—an amount that would determine our condo fees, assessments, utilities bills, for as long as we lived in cohousing. Eventually, the range turned out to be from 0.88 to 3.75 percent.

But how to reach a level of accuracy that would be fair to all owners. The Pricing Task Force was established; Nathan volunteered to be the convenor. From the beginning it was clear to all that a price based on square footage alone might not be fair; Unit A may have a variety of amenities absent in

Unit B, although be the same dimensions. What appeared to be a desirable feature to Unit H might not apply to Unit E. The task force undertook the gargantuan job of developing a process that could be applied to all units and would have the approval of the membership.

The Cambridge Cohousing Newsletter of late 1996 in a heading said that "The Unit Pricing Saga Continues." The article reported that "there was no clear plan for resolving the issue other than to meet again (and again and again) . . ." The large amount of group resources which have been devoted to this issue reflects both the complexity of doing this as a group as well as the acknowledgement that a fair resolution of the pricing issue is essential to the progress of our community." Imagine, if you can, house shopping with a realtor and being told that the price of a condominium hadn't yet been decided. Without deep pockets, you'd simply leave! I was amazed that we were able to veer this far from our culture's rigid home-purchasing practices. The experience not only caused us to reveal much of our financial affairs to one another, but also gave us a new depth of familiarity with working together—and fortunately so, because at no point are people more vulnerable than when both their housing preferences and pocketbooks are at stake. On the contrary, as the stakes rose, our progress seemed less bumpy. It must have been that we were *agreeing to agree.*

The dedicated task force struggled throughout the Christmas holidays. I recall learning, when we returned from ours, that it had pounded out a detailed set of criteria, something called the amenity point list, that took into consideration features that added value based on the community's preferences expressed over the past weeks. Here, in descending order, is the list: private basements, garden/deck/balcony, elevator access, abundant light, no stairs, three exposures, convenience to garage, convenience to common house, wheelchair access, garden view, direct access to storage, high ceilings, and multiple levels. In addition, a base dollar value per square foot of $142.50 was established; an amenity point was worth $750 each. It should be said that everyone was not completely satisfied with this solution; some wrote to the task force with specific complaints. I do not know how these were worked out; I do know that no one withdrew.

Fence painting by volunteer work crew

In our early meetings, we were not prepared as a group to resolve serious conflicts; we had not learned a process yet that could help us reach big decisions. Personalities tended to dominate. When Ed and I had first met with the maybe eight to ten original members/founders, it had already been decided among them that all decisions affecting the group would be made by consensus. (Later, our bylaws stated that the only exception could be a financial issue of the entire association; then, majority rule would apply if efforts toward consensus had failed). Originally laughed at by cynics, the idea is now a maxim of the national cohousing scene. But how a roomful of people with diverse ideas, opinions, and beliefs could possibly come to agreement was a process that very, very few of us could truly understand or even envision. I speak only for Ed and myself but I also suspect not a soul could have predicted the intense, emotional debates that have erupted over the years, based on differing ideas around a combination of money and values, such as a frontyard ice rink, clotheslines on the lawn, holiday meals and a few other topics.

In our beginning meetings, we resorted from habit to Robert's Rules of Order, but it very soon became clear that "rules" wouldn't cut the mustard. The very act of voting is polarizing—some win, some lose—and therefore not conducive to living together in harmony. Slowly, slowly, as we, as a goup in our general meetings, traversed the rocky road to consensus, the process was beginning to make sense.

Some visual, concrete aids were useful. By means of bright color-coded cards, using a technique borrowed from one of the earliest cohousing projects that Ed and I once visited near Seattle, we were getting to consensus a little faster. A small cardboard carton, filled with about fifty sets of four-by-four-inch colored squares, permanently rests in the mailroom between meetings. Each set of five cards, held together by a ring, contains brief instructions for their use. Packets are passed out at every general meeting. A member with a "question," a "comment," or a "clarification" holds up a specific color card to aid the facilitator in expediting an informed and orderly discussion. The same cards are used in arriving at consensus. A red card will stop the discussion or block consensus in a vote. The facilitator will help the group respectfully explore the objector's reasons. But until that individual is convinced, or at least can live with the decision, a show of cards will not be asked for.

The idea of *color cards* as the basis for signifying major life decisions seemed ridiculous when I was introduced to it. Although awkward to use at first—some hated giving up the right to speak spontaneously and off-topic—after time, the act of calmly raising an orange card signalling "Serious Reservation" and knowing you would be heard became reassuring. In addition, we all learned how to flush out those dangerous red cards, which signified vetoes, and to keep the discussion open until differences could be fully explored and resolved.

It didn't take me long, however, to realize that when we learned how to use the system well, the benefits of the technique were real. The rotating facilitators (volunteers from the group) became more and more adept at keeping us on track, and creating a nonhostile atmosphere that would encourage the voicing of opinions. To boot, dominant personalities dominated less, timid ones spoke more often as the abilities and skills of all gained credibility through this structured environment. The goal, an atmosphere in which everyone feels safe to voice an opinion is not easy to achieve.

Now and again, we did slip from grace. Then the meetings would be raw and emotional, and conflicts would reveal deeply felt needs, values, and the very core of personalities. A lot of credit was due to the steadfastness of the group during these times. The mediating talents of various members emerged during such trying periods. At those moments, my faith in the capacity of this group was unbounded. Of course, the end of a successful meeting was always a triumph, but even if we could not resolve all of the conflicts, at least we could demystify, de-emotionalize, and reframe them through our persistence. And the growing repertoire of negotiating skills we adopted brought us growing confidence in our ability to manage the inevitable issues ahead

In the end, for an increasingly cohesive group, these cards proved to be ever-ready tools—like a flashlight always within reach, lest the electricity fail. They helped us jumpstart a new phase of our joint life, that which started upon our leaving the security of the Society of Friends for our new neighborhood. The next challenge was to explore how to establish personal boundaries and group limits on the large—and the small—intrusions that were becoming daily occurrences.

Our immersion in design, construction, legal, and financial matters was so consuming that we tended to forget that we were not alone on our street. Now that our housing was close to completion, so-called boundary issues began to arise. Discussions focused on the kinds of interactions we wanted to have with our immediate neighbors. How ready were we to share our fledgling community? How comfortable would each of us be with the trail of guests, clients, and associates of our fellow residents? And don't forget the just plain curious who were beginning to swarm over the property. The gate or the picket fence were not perceived by all as the demarcation between public and private the way they were for the single-family home. As a result, there existed a large gray area of semipublic, or if you prefer, semiprivate space.

To solve the problem, it seemed we must either raise our trust threshold beyond the traditional level or determine alternatives for distinguishing between friend and stranger. That bothered some, threatened others. And for still others, it seemed an opportunity to enlarge our world. Regardless, I began to suspect that, along with a solid bank account, a clear sense of one's personal boundaries was the best equipment to bring to a new community.

Most of us hailed from single-family privacy, where a homeowner's friends may well be strangers to his neighbors. Now we were asking ourselves to treat our neighbors' guests as ours. That seemed to mean creating an oasis of safety and security for ourselves and our collective legitimate visitors.

Today, most visitors, I believe, feel welcomed, but a tinge of wariness still underlies the informality. Many of us have been known to remind our neighbors of nonconfrontational language and behavior ("Remember to smile!"), to investigate unfamiliar people in the common areas by politely asking, "May I help you find someone?" or "Are you lost?" We introduce our families and friends to residents who share the elevator, unlike in the prevailing condo culture of avoiding eye contact. This open, friendly style reflects, in part, the spontaneous pride of the new homeowner and, in part, a covert, implicit security measure designed to enlarge our circle of familiar faces.

In our first summer, boundaries became a major theme of discussion. The early hopes of a free flow among cohousing residents and our adopted mixed-income neighborhood were waning, and tensions mounted as the idealism of our original vision collided with the realities of our new way of life. Was it that some inhabitants of this fragmented neighborhood were not overjoyed by the prospect of a social phenomenon in their midst?

Only one example of our naivete: unlocked bicycles, customarily left in front of units, attracted a brief rash of thefts. Did the owners report them to the police? Some did; others were reluctant to cast suspicion, fearful of antagonizing neighbors with whom we were on uneasy terms.

In a potentially more serious incident, Cai Yi surprised an early morning intruder rummaging through our basement storage room. Like a pit bull—bravely, if unwisely—she went after him, literally chasing him away. In the ensuing powwow on the patio, we learned that notifying the police was repugnant to her; in her country of origin, the police were considered part of the authoritarian system, never to be appealed to. We tried to persuade her that in America we preferred to view the police as protective. She relented; a meticulous scientist, she reported the incident in full detail to a nonthreatening police officer.

In this single encounter, we leapt from the politics of the '70s to the realities of the '90s. Together, we acknowledged one of those areas often rife with misunderstanding: creating a sense of fellowship does not require tolerating crime. We had to define where to draw the line between building a relatively open community and retaining some appropriate urban wariness. Reporting attempted theft we could concur on; more subtle transgressions gave us pause. For example, what should Merna, who is typically friendly and welcoming to all, do if an unfamiliar family lays claim to the common living room while waiting for a visiting child? Or what if the owner of #309 were to find the library door closed with a taped notice announcing a "private counseling session" in an unfamiliar signature? Should he knock, enter, and explain that the room is for the use of residents only? Or, what do I do when the UPS delivery man rings the #410 buzzer for entry, having learned that Ed and I are often at home in the daytime? I may have signed up for creating a hospitable environment, but not so that UPS can gain easy entry to forty other units besides mine. Or say a very determined architecture student from Amsterdam turns up at the front door, pleading for a tour of our cohousing miracle between flights? Would I send her back to Logan Airport unsatisfied, just because our tour guide is not available?

In our general meetings, we tended to lump these incidents into the category of security risks. True, in one sense, but they also had deeper, more emotional overtones. "Comfort level" was a term I heard often: I understood it as the amalgam of a sense of physical safety, a reasonable certainty that one's personal and psychological space and values would be honored, and all within the rubric of the myriad meanings of home.

I also came to recognize instantly what a threat to my own comfort level felt like: a sudden wordless gripping of the gut, a nameless pinpoint of physical unease that slowly radiated to my mind, and *ah-ha!* It is then I knew that some line or other had been crossed.

Now, as wariness has slipped into casualness, we slack off, assume that the tall bearded man with a backpack and a purposeful stride is a legitimate visitor, only to take up our vigil again when our turn comes for the nightly security check.

In our polite and rational discussions, we speak of our public rooms as extensions of our own living rooms: hospitable sanctuaries for ourselves and friends. Making that idea work is the subject of many conversations, both brief and extended. In e-mails and at the gossip level, however, varying views about what hospitality entails, about one's comfort level with strangers, about the uses of our homes, all get analyzed. It's a much more slippery subject than the word "security" suggests. A concierge is the answer—but we're affordable, remember.

I can look back now at that honeymoon period when I had welcoming words for every passerby. When we were all settling in, when the air was electric with the excitement of finally inhabiting a dream. There were introductions, furniture swaps, spontaneous outings, joint forays to Home Depot, food exchanges, impromptu walks and dinners, moving assistance, wonderful jokes that evaporated with the laughter.

When I remember that, I realize we are a work in progress, sculpting a cohesive community with a distinctive *identity.*

Over that first winter, we reached a kind of stability in our standing with the neighborhood. Mostly we went our own way, and they theirs, though boundary disputes occasionally still erupted. The signature style in our cohousing world was to talk a problem to death. Nevertheless, sometimes an individual, faced with sheer frustration, instead of drawing on the customary rationale, would react spontaneously. Like Lois, who by spring, after many nights of loud rap music issuing from a neighbor's car had enraged all within hearing, struck upon a unique antidote. That particular night, the ear-splitting music was accompanied by an offensive argument among several young African-American men perched atop the car. She had reached her limit. No more letters to the managing board or complaints at the general meeting for her; she chose musical action! Passionate about all things Irish, Lois selected her loudest Celtic CD and set it at full volume on her balcony. Ear-piercing rap gave way to strident Irish dance tunes. The shouts from the street were loud, but midst laughter and some colorful language, the decibel levels of both soon went down.

Stashing the Stuff

When you lose your story, you
have lost something that nobody
should lose.
—Garrison Keillor

"I *must* have a temperature-controlled, locked area in the basement to store my wines" was Gerald's answer.

The question, often asked by facilitators in those early Design Committee meetings, was what was important to us as we thought of living in a smaller space than to what many of us were accustomed.

"Right now, my cellar is full of boxes and filing cabinets crammed with my research notes and all my husband's writings that I want to edit for a posthumous collection," lamented Velma. "When I retire from teaching sociology, and I no longer have a big house to take care of, not to mention this commute from Connecticut, I can get to that project. For now, I need storage space."

Ken and Lynn, after many years alone and then some together, announced they had acquired belongings from their global past—big things, like furniture from Asia. Ken added, "We're getting married soon and hope to have children. And Lynn's mother will bring her things when she comes to live with us in our small townhouse. Without a basement! Where on earth do we stash the stuff?"

Sam, a self-confessed collector, was particularly attached to the geology period in his life and to his extensive rock collection. "Maybe I can display it all in the common living room," he posed winningly.

"Jean is after me to simplify my ... our ... lives, and I am ... really I *am* ... trying, but my various careers have left huge storage needs in their wake. By law, I must preserve psychiatric patient records for a certain number of years. From forty years of teaching, twenty of those producing documentary films, then videos, I'm faced with a warehouse-sized amount of stuff. Some of that will be sold, some stored in a Harvard library archive, but then there is my whole new venture of computerized photographic art that I need close at hand. And framed photos are bulky." Ed sounded desperate.

I sighed audibly, thinking of Ed's accumulations. Would the contents of our third floor simply be transferred to a condo? Later, back at home, I would hear that he really can't go ahead with the move. And I didn't even mention the crates of records in our garage, from my family's one-hundred-year-old business!

"I cannot ever face my widowed father if I don't make a place for my mother's clothing, jewelry, and furniture," moaned Anne. And in a postscript, Dick reminded her and all of us not to forget about his books; even after generous contributions to the cohousing library, their apartment would be filled with them.

For Paul, it was quite clear. "I *must* have room for my woodworking shop or I can't leave my home in Brookline!" Paul and Ann-Marie had only recently joined the Sunday meetings. I was just getting used to Paul's dry wit, with his crooked smile and twinkling eyes; was he delivering an ultimatum or tossing fuel into the embers? Later we would learn this was his dead-serious mode. Some offered reassurances that accommodations could be made for his shop; after all, a retired child psychiatrist, he would perform woodworking miracles—for the two of them, and for all of us.

A single, middle-aged woman, who I never saw before or since that meeting, remarked timidly that she was still the caretaker for the possessions of her three grown, scattered children. Had I noticed a catch in her voice, a sense of entrapment? Had this, for her, been one of those revelatory moments when she would realize that she had some very hard decisions to make about the stewardship of her children's belongings before considering a move *anywhere* an option?

Others spoke about the pianos, the cookbooks (no one can part with her annotated, much-prized collection), the toys, today's plastics and yesteryear's antiques, the infant equipment and the outgrown clothes that just might be needed, the family silver. To calculate the enormity of the storage challenge, reflect a moment on your own can't-part-with items and multiply those by forty-one households.

Lise, a rising seventh grader with a twinkle in her eye, broke the mounting tension with, "I think I'll be able to find a spot for my grandmother's button collection."

A small sample of "stuff"

One of many yard sales

Even before selecting an architect, when cohousing was still a grandiose concept, we aired our most pressing expectations and concerns. (Naming hopes and fears remains a useful group exercise to alleviate strong feelings

63

or serious disagreements.) Within a few moments of the start of any general meeting, we could all see the range of thoughts scribbled on newsprint and note the clusters of similar ideas as somehow comforting. Not being the only one to want something is less lonely. It means less likelihood of rejection or dismissal and more chance of arriving at consensus. In other words, one is heard.

And we're not talking about exotic hopes or fears, like the controversial hot tub on the roof, but down-to-earth necessities. Right near the top of the list: "Storage! Plenty of storage! Please!" Walk-in closets, cabinets under and over counters, locked bins for personal items, secured bicycle storage (at one count, the community harbored a hundred and seventy-nine bikes, less a few stolen ones), as well as accessible but protected areas for strollers, gardening tools, exercise equipment, movie projectors, unused microwaves, and crock pots—and don't forget the books and back issues of *The New Yorker* and *National Geographic*, along with collections of baseball cards and Barbie dolls. We would bring the treasures and detritus of our lives, from sprawling family houses and tiny apartments. And, magically, there would be space for everything. After all, Katherine promised, didn't she?

In a phenomenal denial of reality over fantasy, every single person over twelve *overestimated* the space that would become theirs. From grand pianos to decades-old textbooks, from gadget-filled kitchens to basements full of family lore, our overloaded brains anticipated niches for them all. Yet ironically, at one time or another, a *raison d'etre,* expressed by each of us for joining this experiment, was the opportunity to simplify our lives. Each of us struggled to balance these strongly opposing basic wishes as we handled each trinket, each photo, each high school English paper. We asked ourselves: Can I afford to lose this part of myself?

The depth of feeling stirred by an attempt to pare down, to simplify one's life, forces me to wonder why a perfectly rational move is so universally painful. Oh yes, everyone understands why it is difficult for the elderly pressured into giving up the family home for retirement living. It signals the onset of the final phase of life and, for many, is perceived as one mountainous loss—in social status, independence, and control over and familiarity with one's environment.

But this was not a retirement community; it was a vibrant experiment, an adventure we'd elected to take on. And "elderly" applied only to a few of us. A third of our members were families with young children; a third were couples; a third were singles spanning a broad age range. Regardless of age, we were all bubbling with life as we neared the fulfillment of this complex vision.

Still, we all clutched desperately to those furnishings of our past that tended to privatize rather than communalize us. We, who liked to think that identity was not defined by our belongings, were in for a surprise.

The realization of my past disdain for those paralyzed by change, captives of their possessions, came as a jolt. As Ed and I rifled through our own histories, labelling things with #410, Trash, Sell, For Kids or "Goodwill," I gained appreciation for others hung up at this stage. On the other hand, quite frankly, it could be pretty tiresome hearing about forty other similar journeys, which all had the same ending: "Let's have a yard sale!" Why? Because the daguerreotypes of *our* forebears were worth saving; theirs were dull. Had I really heard myself think that? Here we were, coming together to support, understand, and listen to our neighbors, only to have my uncensored reaction erase in a millisecond the empathy I was so carefully cultivating. Maybe I didn't belong in this experiment.

Ed and I handled our anxiety in our typical fashion: we bargained. A brief digression here will explain what was really a complicated and extended process. Early on, just after the lottery, a period fraught with tension, we reviewed the preliminary sketch that Floyd had prepared for our flat. The overall unit size seemed all right: over sixteen hundred and sixty square feet of comfortably affordable space. But where would we *put* things—not furniture, but, well, just *things*?

In our meetings with Floyd, Ed and I pleaded for more space. We offered to buy a few square feet from the abutting unit, still ownerless. We paid extra for a seventeen-inch bay; every inch mattered. We squeezed thirteen inches from a bathroom to enlarge a closet. Somehow, still within the footprint of our two, side-by-side, sixty- by fourteen-foot manufactured boxes, by losing a lavatory, we carved out a small all-purpose room that was the envy of all. We eliminated bureaus, replacing them with wire storage components. We discarded our king-size bed and, on the eve of moving, the family grand piano. We asked a furniture designer to sketch a plan for multipurpose built-ins that would provide both seating and storage for books, china, bedding, the works. Later, looking over the unused plans, I wondered how we had maneuvered him into such awkwardness—all for the sake of stuff.

In emptying our large house, every item seemed to take on fresh emotional significance. Those family keepsakes, untouched for decades, hidden under the eaves, suddenly become precious. "Aren't your 'Saves' bigger space-eaters than mine?" Ed and I accused each other.

One laughably ridiculous example comes to mind: a pair of bristle hairbrushes that had been given to my father (who'd been dead for over half a century) by his fourth wife (whom I'd never met), spilled out of a box of keepsakes. I argued that our son, Jeff, the first of my father's grandchildren (though never seen or acknowledged by his grandfather) would surely want these. Ed and I collapsed into helpless laughter at the absurdity, thus ending that sorting session. I am ashamed to admit, however, that I still have one of the hairbrushes. Though I'd like to say it's for the beautiful tropical wood, more likely, it's for the sentiment—a symbol amid the absence of other mementos from my father, with whom my relationship had been hopelessly severed.

While Ed was gamely tossing all but a token selection of the small metal foundry of awards he'd won for his films, I was wistfully absorbed by a mother-of-pearl gold-pointed pen, a legacy from an unknown German ancestor. Might Herr Von der Au also have harbored ideas of writing? Had its gold nib been dipped into an inkwell for over a century? Once, as a child, I had tried it, but gold or not, it scratched on the paper. These mementos were small, requiring little space; they told a lot of little stories that added up to who I was, were threads to a past I'd often wished to forget yet somehow defied obliteration. However, saving them conflicted with my primary rule: if I don't use it or love it, I toss it. And unlike some who moaned over this process of dispossession, I came to enjoy the opportunity for a life review. I thanked our wayward contractor for the extra time.

Obsession with the destiny of our concrete objects accomplished another purpose, as well: the threat of change was so powerful that focusing on mere things helped to put a lid on the mounting anxiety. When the tension reached an uncomfortable level, and no easy decision was in view, I would find rare spare moments to rush out in a reassuring search for shelving, bins, and stackables. Since I'd last noticed, a whole new industry had sprung up to placate the terrors of change—the space-savers, the hold-everythings that house the hoardings of a consumer society.

The angst over divesting our stuff was not without bonus, however. A repertoire of jokes about everyone's hoarding, buying, and ownership habits helped forge a group cohesiveness and a new part of our cohousing culture: Kevin's tapes, Rose's fabrics, Vinita's seed catalogs, Greg's reading lists, Dori's 1970s feminist tomes, Roger's—"No, *my* boat," Clea interrupts. "I was the sailor first. I earned the down payment!" Ruth's designer cleaning tools, Dennis's high-tech gadgets, Tamara's Russian toys, Velma's ancient first editions, moldy and disintegrating. The jokster sensed the emotional potential of this humor—a time-tested tool for making friends.

By move-in time, the construction budget was hemorrhaging. New common-house furniture—except for the carefully researched, already ordered dining room tables and chairs for sixty—was one of many items scratched from the wish list. The growing controversy over new versus used or comfy, however, was thankfully over.

The design task force had worked for months to create an informal, pleasing, and durable atmosphere for community use: high on comfort and low on the decorator look. In fact, the task force had rejected the interior design firm that Katherine had employed to assist us and took on the task ourselves. In keeping with our democratic process, everyone had opinions, and they wanted to apply them to the decorating. This was never more true than with the dining room furnishings, and more particularly the chairs. From local furniture stores, the task force assembled seven—count them, seven—different styles of dining chairs to be tested during an intermission of the general meeting. They asked members to perform a "sitting test," using colored dots to rank the chairs using criteria such as comfort, height, sturdiness, design, cost, even environmental sensitivity of materials. After elaborate calculations, a modified Windsor chair of cherry, made in Massachusetts, was selected over more expensive, contemporary models. Now showing signs of wear, the chairs have hosted thousands of dinners.

So, with no money for furnishing the common areas, donations of our castoffs to cohousing served multipurposes: a well-used, oversized couch looked fine in the common living room, helped the budget shortfall, enabled those moving in to unload their items, eliminate wrenching separations and still keep tabs on them. The Design Task Force gave way to IDA (Interior Decoration and Art), which bravely assumed the task of screening, and sometimes painfully rejecting, the donations that made the transition from private household to public common space.

In spite of a very small budget, IDA continues to be conscientiously managed by Anne, who always has a vision, though not always achievable, of how the common spaces should look. "This place," she says firmly, "is an extension of my home, and I want to feel good about bringing friends here."

Early in 1998, the parade of vans and rental trucks began. The eleven units of the East End had been the first to receive Occupancy Permits by the city. Heavy rains brought tears of frustration as mud was tracked onto gleaming floors, walls sprung leaks, showers ceased to work. From my unfinished flat, I watched the chaos. Every traffic jam and honking horn from the street heralded another cohouser unloading his belongings, dancing around the construction workers, loudly exchanging their now tiresome hippies/commies in-jokes. I imagined that, eager to begin their long homeward commute to the serenity of rural New Hampshire, these laborers had little sympathy for this screwball outfit that suffered endless contortions to live together in what their belief system told them was communism.

By summer, the units in the Common House were occupied, and then finally, half a year later—and a year behind the first projections—the West End townhouses and flats. Living here, witnessing the changes, I swung between feeling exhilarated one minute and irked by unfinished construction the next.

Most of our interactions in those days was pleasant and casual despite an occasional blistering e-mail. We were learnng that this new technology could be an outlet for new homeowner frustration. But also, like new homeowners everywhere, we were absorbed in feathering our own nests, our first priority was to stash the stuff. For some, the process would go on for years. Not many days went by that I didn't see Sam, from my lookout at #410, pushing a grocery cart spilling over with cartons and files. From his third floor flat he had to go down two flights of stairs, load the cart, go outdoors on the Spine to walk to the Common House, get on the elevator, and fnally, into the over filled open storage room in the Common House basement to add his belongings next to those of others. Could we have improved and lightened this process? Probably.

So for anyone facing a required shedding of belongings, maybe our collective experience can provide a few tips:

- Sort and throw away *before* a move. Handle items as few times as possible. People postpone this essential phase, erroneously persuading themselves that they'll have more time after the move. Not true. In other words, have your own yard sale.

- Expect that you'll make a few mistakes. The profound feelings of regret, loss, and grief that you may experience from getting rid of something you later wished you hadn't will, in fact, pass, so don't be too hard on yourself. Just think: the resulting story may have more social value than the sacrificed object.

- Insist on and accept nothing less than secured *individual* storage bins/rooms, however small, rather than sharing an open area. You want to remain on friendly terms with your neighbors. Our open storage area at Cambridge Cohousing would arguably receive the highest ranking as a source of friction.

- Do not be shocked by or disdainful of the objects other people are emotionally attached to. Because we are not usually privy to the contents of houses, they can come as a surprise: a large box of wigs, identified when the precariously perched carton falls into the aisle and disperses its contents, the mattress "my father died on," countless foam-filled boxes of computers past, five used adult bikes from a single unit, untied cartons of unsorted recipes dating back to 1963.

- Remember that auction houses, consignment stores, and antique galleries are, most likely, where the stuff caught your eye in the first place. Going back there to attempt to resell it, then, is setting yourself up for failure. Best to look to your town's recycling services and charitable organizations, or, as a last resort, to explore what used to be your local dump, but is now a sanitary landfill.

Space, Personalized

The House As Mirror of Self
— by Clare Cooper Marcus

"You must miss your old house so much. Do you think about it often?" asked my friend Sonia, a frequent guest from my precohousing days on her maiden visit to #410. One of my very best friends, she was now seeing what she had only heard about for many months from me. Her blessing mattered to me.

We were both being very careful neither to ask too much nor to say too little, but her tone—how should I have read it? Whenever she would express a kind of cautious curiosity, devoid of comment, I took it to mean that she considered my loss in excess of my gain.

"No," I answered. "It's strange even to me. Wouldn't you imagine that I might have a few wistful, teary moments? You know how I loved that house, quite consciously loved it, every day, and it's not mine anymore. But it rarely crosses my mind, unless I drive by. Then I look for the latest changes—and the new owners are doing a good job. I don't resent them; I'm glad they're taking care of it. Is this aberrant behavior on my part? By chance, they even chose our old carpenter—that fence is an improvement. But I wish we could have salvaged the myrtle from the garden before they dug it up. Cohousing could use it."

There, that had to be the explanation! Whether it was about myrtle, happy memories of family get-togethers, or Ed and I cooking dinner together, I had managed to transfer, part and parcel, my lasting memories from Raymond Street to this mystical place called cohousing. I had simply trundled all of those associations the few blocks to Richdale Avenue.

"All this ruminating helps," I muttered to Sonia. "But it still is puzzling to understand how I can put my beloved home of fifty years at such emotional distance."

Here was my second epiphany: houses became a subtheme of my grown-up life after my turbulent years of childhood, at which time the house was a mishmash of a home and a vault, embodying the terrifying and dangerous secrets of my dysfunctional family. It was little wonder, then, that all of those adult interests emerged—in design, decoration, and setting, in the psychological meaning of home; not to mention interests in providing places for the homeless, for families and singles, for the lonely and the poor, for people of color.

And with that, I convinced myself that it wasn't denial, favoring the idea that I had just dragged all the memories with me, along with the boxes and baggage, and would open each one in its turn.

"Funny, but it's been easier to shed furniture and works of art than all these cartons of housing files, stacked in my office," I went on to say.

Raymond Street had all the attributes that scholars ascribe to home: safety, shelter, setting, size, style, security, snugness. All of the elements were there. In the eyes of many, I had perfection, an old Victorian, renovated over the decades, made comfortable and workable. And yet, with nary a backward glance, I was able to just leave it for a vision of home that was neither finished nor guaranteed.

At no time has #410 *not* felt right to me. Our condominium, impersonally described in the deed as so many feet of walls, floors, and ceilings, has never disappointed, has always led me to further discoveries, has always pleased me every time I open the door. I have never taken its offerings for granted. It's wonderful, it's ours, and I hope to live here until I die. In short, it is the encapsulation of home.

Dictionaries fail miserably in defining what the word "home" means. None of these examples—"a residence," "an environment which offers security and happiness," "a refuge"—fully conveys the ineffable quality writers struggle to capture. Architects, designers, sociologists, novelists, memoirists, philosophers have all taken their turn at analyzing the meaning of home. Literature has given us rich accounts of inhabited spaces. Home is one of those overarching ideas, like love, motherhood, patriotism, that teases writers to search deep within ourselves, to grapple with our own interpretations.

"I could stay here forever and never be bored," I solemnly told Sonia, whose eye was caught by the bathroom tile.

"Now what kind of an off-the-wall, dramatic remark is that?" she tossed back to me.

"Well, it was an instant love affair from the moment the first of the two boxes was set in place. The way that swaying hulk of raw lumber against the blue sky created geometrical space of the surrounding air. I just couldn't wait to live in it. The way the windows framed the exposures that I never tire of watching—the anonymous apartments across the street, the street itself with its trucks, its walkers, its "fuck you" toughies aimlessly shuffling out of my sight, the sweep of the gleaming railroad tracks in the moonlight, the urban oasis across the tracks, the southern, western, and northern skies, all constantly changing, the crow sanctuary. I can walk through my rooms at night guided only by the yellowish pink glow of the urban sky. I have just enough barrier from weather to feel close to the stars but protected from the cold. In a magical moment, I discovered that I own not just a piece of real estate but a chunk of the universe."

Sonia and I looked at each other, both our eyes wide, stunned at the long speech that had just spilled from me. But then my thoughts immediately went back to the old house.

The gestalt of our former house—though I really should call it our former home, since I'm well aware that a house earns its way to *becoming* a home—is what I was bonded to. That home really did give off an impression of serenity and harmony that, admittedly, I strove for. My eternal battle against clutter, without destroying the comfort, ease, efficiency, and flow of the place may have been responsible, but in the end, it was not just an amalgam of rooms. It had integrity and inner consistency, and it said something about its inhabitants: Ed, me, our children.

Then #410 took me back further—to the early years of coupledom. I figured out once that Ed and I had moved ten times in the four years before children. In each forgettable house, I was a visitor, a squatter.

Now, I realize that my sense of home combines both my pre- and post-children housing experiences. It may be newborn, but it has been evolving for decades, enabling # 410 to be hatched almost full-grown as a refuge for this couple, for Ed and me as we enter the final stage of the housing arc.

A first-time visitor, stepping into our flat from the spacious fourth floor lobby, might well make some inferences about us. Ed's cane stands just inside the entry—really the beginning of a narrow hallway. Just to the left, is a dark space (Is it forbidding? I hope not), that is my cellar-pantry-attic storage room, a treasured amenity for any apartment dweller. I am proud of it, and rarely close the door; it is crammed full but organized. (I'd heard myself say once that I couldn't have moved without one of these to come to; in fact, the very decision to move may have hinged on the architect's ability to give form to such a space). The entry hall is devoid of furnishings; our daughter's weavings dress the wall. Already the visitor would have gleaned we are halt, spare, and not at all modest about displaying what we like and use.

Inside the hallway, the visitor gets a first glance at what appears to be a railroad flat—a bit of New York cachet doesn't hurt. Then a low-ceilinged "tunnel" after passing two offices, a guestroom and bath, quickly opens into pristine, unadorned, sun-lit space. (At first, as I am so in love with sheer openness, I couldn't bear to spoil it with furniture. Then reluctantly, I added one piece at a time, and only after each passed the test for function, beauty, and enough reticence not to overpower the space). I often appreciate how Katherine and Floyd envisioned our unit—I never could have done it myself.

The tour continues through the kitchen area, the absolute center; a bench is a visual echo of the blue couch in our Raymond Street kitchen, which becomes a greeting and gathering area when I am cooking meals. The long white wall on the right filled with Ed's photographs, is both art gallery and family display. It overlooks dining area and also separates the public and private sections of the flat that is simply a sixty-by-twenty-foot box, bisected the long way. Beyond the dining table a glass slider opens onto a small but functional balcony which figures into the title of this book. A few steps farther—remember, distances are very short—you come to a small, cozy sitting area. To the right is the doorless opening to our bedroom; a Japanese screen serves as token barrier. The bedroom, its bath and large closet wrap conveniently around the far end of the apartment and have their own set of views.

Now comes the controversial part: our Russian neighbor took a strong view of our flat. She is not bashful, either, and once reprimanded me. "Jean, I'm shocked! You *must* put a door between your sitting area and your bedroom right away."

There are others, I suspect, who silently harbor this view, but who are too polite to tell us; Katherine, and Floyd, too, once tried to discourage us from organizing it the way we did. "Think of resale," they said.

Too public! "But there's only the two of us here," I replied meekly, feeling I must have unwittingly trespassed in some vague realm.

What was this issue? Were we shamelessly at risk of exposing the marital bonds? Had our unconventional room arrangement crossed some line that shattered the intimacy of the bedroom, a place of refuge and solitude? And so all this time, I was waiting to hear Sonia's opinion. She is known for her honesty—some of our friends even call her blunt.

As I finished giving her the tour, I could see that it was time for the promised cup of tea and a talk. I reassured her that, whatever she thought, it was all right, because I was really interested in what she had to say about this new venture of mine.

"I'm glad we took our time," she said. "If you had rushed me through this apartment, I would have had to tell you that I was really turned off. Oh yes, the floors are nice, you'll see a lot of birds from here as well as the rear ends of gardeners across the tracks. Those windows you enthused over made me dizzy, they're so low. And I really jumped when the train went by. How can anyone live next to a train? No wonder the land was a bargain; they should have given it to you—"

"Whoa, Sonia, maybe you'd better stop there. I'm not sure I can take any more of—"

"But you're not letting me finish," she interrupted. "What I'm trying to tell you is that what I saw at first was highly colored by what I've been hearing from you, and others, about the problems, the incredible efforts of so many in order to pull this off. I can tell you my expectations weren't very high when I came today. To be honest, it appeared a little bleak on the first round, with so much that's unfinished … and railroad flats don't do anything for me. But then I started mentally decorating the place with your furniture, hanging Ed's pictures. Well, the result will be fantastic. Now I can see what you've been talking about. It's all come together, like an epiphany. What imaginations you people have."

I smiled, but she went on.

"Frankly, I'm jealous as hell. I've been a little angry that cohousing has absorbed you so much; you haven't had time for your friends. But now I see why and I really love the apartment. Ah … hum … do you suppose I could get on the waiting list?"

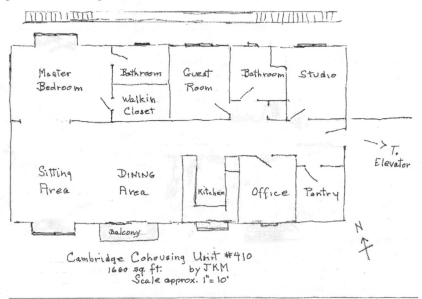

Sketch of #410 floor plan by Jean Mason

Cambridge Community Gardens from #410

The Big Sky from #410

From the Balcony

You shall no longer take things at
second or third hand, not look
through the eyes of the dead, not
feed on the spectres in books;
You shall not look through my eyes
either, nor take things from me:
You shall look to all sides, and
filter them from yourself.
—Whitman, *Song of Myself*

A family, I was guessing, the turbaned husband with stolid, measured step leading a little raggle-taggle parade: the wife, whose colorful, draped sari partially enveloped an infant, was followed by a reluctant child, a boy dragging behind, hands jammed in jeans pockets. The adults stared impassively ahead, while the boy's head swiveled around for one last look at the goings-on across the street. They all exuded silence and impenetrability.

As I stepped out onto my fourth floor four-by-twelve-foot platform— labeled "Balcony" on the architect's drawings—I wondered how the boy read our multi-windowed, yellow, airy buildings on his walk to the subway from his cramped apartment a block away.

Behind a raw wood picket fence, "our" children were cavorting on a new play structure positioned on a plot of wood chips—an area that we had demoted in our idealism from the Great Lawn to the Pretty Good Lawn. A couple of mothers were chatting, one periodically throwing a frisbee to a panting dog. On the concrete patio (which also served as a roof for the underground garage), a man lounged in the sun; another pulled alongside, bringing his motorized wheelchair to a sudden stop. A middle-aged woman, with graying hair straggling outside a red bandana, transferred perky marigolds from pots to newly spaded soil. It was Anne, who dedicated every spare minute to bringing a garden to life from these clay flats. When she lived at our house, she missed the gardening, but I wondered whether she had yet fully realized the challenge this rotten clay soil presented. If humanly possible, she'd be among the few who would convert our "estate" from industrial to residential. Her eye, like mine, was always drawn to children, and I noticed that she was watching the same child I was. We'd compare notes later.

If the boy had dared look up, he might have noticed book-lined walls behind curtainless windows, open, unlike those in his high-rise, the concrete housing project. Heavy curtains and shades sealed his family's doings from the world. He must have puzzled over these people who exposed themselves to prying eyes. The indoors was visible from the street! And children and adults alike played with unguarded abandon on the spacious lawn.

Overlooking Common House Patio

Overlooking Spine toward West End

Our architectural yellow oddity, altering the face of the surrounding somber, gray, working-class neighborhood forever, was, quite literally, dropped from the skies and plunked down on a long, narrow parcel of rubble bordering the commuter rail line. Off limits to my own children, who'd grown up decades ago only a few blocks away, the land was, sequentially, brick factory, slaughter house, and city incinerator.

As I settled into one of our two new white metal chairs, I again asked myself whether it could be true that Ed and I, parents of scattered, grown children, were really here, joining with others in this country's first large urban cohousing project.

More walkers passed. Some stared shamelessly; others glanced furtively, then ignored me. What was behind their grave, somber gazes? Envy? Culture shock? Hope for friendship? Curiosity, resentment? A wish to join us? For many of our nonnative passersby, the street, in their countries, is the center of life. But here, in this bewildering land, the street was for stealing glimpses of the public life of their strange hosts. An invitation to voyeurism.

Laden with the ubiquitous assortment of plastic bags, the walkers were part of an endless and varied procession along the pedestrian route to and from nearby Porter Square—the shopping and transportation hub, a station for both the metropolitan subway and the commuter rail.

One morning, during breakfast on my balcony, I took a ten-minute sample and came up with the startling calculation that, adjusted for the quieter hours, hundreds of people walked past our Richdale Avenue condo daily. "A little United Nations" as one friend dubbed the flow.

How hard it was for our friends, even our family, to understand this move from our large, lovely house in an area of other large, lovely houses. Not forced by adverse circumstances—unless aging fell into that category—Ed and I deliberately, thoughtfully, chose our move. And, in sharp contrast to the low-rent requirements of many who passed my balcony, we had many choices. Going against the expected tide every step of the way, we were now aligned with this self-selected group that spurned suburban order and long commutes. In the eyes of some, we had given up the assurance of privacy, serenity, and convenience for the gambled promise of a vigorous, supportive community.

The sound of voices exploded across the street—a wail here, a lusty shout there. The day-camp bus dropped off tireless, high-spirited kids who headed for the dusty homebase, marked by telltale patches of once-obliterated grass. The ascending decibel level was a blend of ball players' shrieks, exchanges among mothers at third-floor windows and their defiant kids on the ground, and rap music at top volume. Endless backing and filling of cars vying for the single driving lane between parked cars provided constant excitement. These sudden exclamatory outbursts, resulting in such cacophonies of sound, prompted me to remind myself that I did *choose* this. This was the neighborhood in an urban village. This was a life that I had bargained for, was getting in spades, and never disappointed me.

What did we cohousers beam back to our neighbors? On our side of the street, a work group was hammering on what must seem to observers incomprehensible boxlike structures that resembled a row of crude oversized toy tanks more than the architect-designed tree planters that would line our walkway, demarcating entrances to half a dozen townhouses. Gentle murmurs rose from a two-person team painting the picket fence; across the lawn voices carried parts of a strained discussion about where to plant some donated shrubs. A toddler, having doffed clothing, tottered merrily across the lawn. From a second-floor open window flowed a powerful soprano voice that, for a time, prevailed over all.

Long before we all moved in, we looked at our Vision Statement (see the appendix) and, in accordance to our goal of assimilation, appointed a task force to consider how we might best fit in with and add to the existing neighborhood. Concerned about our reception, we, invited everyone on the block to a groundbreaking ceremony, held an ice cream social for neighborhood families, sponsored a meet-the-candidates night before the city elections, and staged a couple of yard sales (the best attended activity by far).

We found that the neighbors' explicit worries about our construction phase were simple: an infestation of rats and a shortage of parking places. The former didn't occur. As for the latter, parking was tight and tempers were short until our underground garage was completed. Now enough room for all on the street, however, the peace has been restored.

Still, aside from the few personal contacts that some have made, our overtures fell fairly flat. It seems we are viewed as a daunting neighbor—not because we bring our rather tame versions of diversity to an already diverse neighborhood but because our imported culture stirs up deeply rooted class barriers. To all outward appearances, the neighborhood's United Nations characterization is an accurate one. In time, perhaps, these rich textures will be fully woven into a tapestry. Assimilation takes time, however, and often depends on spontaneous acts of chance.

You Can't Get There from Here

All community spaces will be handicap
accessible and private homes will be designed
to accommodate a variety of physical and
social needs ...
—Cambridge Cohousing Vision Statement

I woke up smiling: it was Wednesday! Today I was to pick up our grandson, Alex, at school and bring him to #410 for lunch and the afternoon. Now seven, he had spent one day a week with us since he was born. Every Saturday, Ed and I had him to ourselves in our big house. In safe steps, he explored Raymond Street, inch by inch, incrementally making it his own. He climbed our stairs; my closet became his "elevator." Perched on the edge of the empty hot tub, he spent chunks of time "fishing for cuttlefish and shark," carefully giving play to the string on the end of the yardstick.

As a toddler, he circumnavigated the entire first floor, then reversed direction at the front hall in order to avoid an Italian wood carving of a mustached man that held unknown terror for him. Before going home with his parents, in some gleeful ritual of mastery that only he understood, midst squeals and chortles, Alex tossed the orange straw clothesbasket over the second-floor railing for a soft landing in the front hall.

He was enlarging his world by memorizing the geography of the house at the same time we were immersed in planning the cohousing project a few blocks away. Watching him raised new questions for me about our plans: How could we leave this much-loved house? How could we sell our children's childhood home? Was it fair to deprive this little boy and the other grandchildren of the family homestead?

The young ones would adjust, I realized; and hiding behind the cloak of family was the real question: Could we, in our seventies, pluck ourselves from our familiar, traditional lifestyle to one fraught with unknowns? Ed couldn't imagine it; I couldn't reject it.

When we finally moved, Alex was six. By then we had known for three years, and were learning to live with the horror and heartbreak of his chilling diagnosis of muscular dystrophy. That adorable toddler waddle I had always loved so much—a last mark of babyhood and a first of the emerging child—just didn't disappear in Alex. From developmental endearment to clinical symptom, for us, the waddle now held a name as well as a morbid future. Studies and tests over a several-month period prolonged the suspense and briefly, but only too briefly, extended hope for his parents, family, and friends.

We were a medical family, but neither Ed nor our daughter, a pediatrician, had ever seen a case of MD. A retiring pediatric friend had seen only two in his long practice. Jerry Lewis's annual telethon was about as close as we had come to this cruel inherited condition. We cried, we tried to comfort our devastated children, we read, we bargained, we questioned. Nowhere in the collective family memory was there a remote hint of this crippling, degenerative disease. Research! That magic word was all that held out a shred of hope.

The irony of placing all hope on a slightly slower path of physical destruction did not escape us; you grab for anything. Then, with a heavy finality, the DNA results indicated a mutation was responsible. And it spelled out Duchenne. Among the several dozen forms of Muscular Dystrophy, an immense difference was found in a name: if only the dreaded Duchenne had turned out to be Becker. Though in his regular visits to Children's Hospital, Alex was doing so well as to give his doctors pause. could there be a mistake? Further tests showed without question there wasn't; malfunctioning muscle tissue, like a tornado, would eventually destroy all in its path.

That day, Alex joined multitudes of others with genetic disorders for whom the only solace is still the speed of modern research. The Muscular Dystrophy gene was identified as early as 1986 by Boston researcher Dr. Louis Kunkel at Children's Hospital but between discovery and cure, a lot of birthday candles are wished upon. A nanosecond here, a generation there—we helplessly await the ebb and flow of the research establishment. While I have a layperson's confidence that, in time, this condition—like polio, syphylis, tuberculosis—will be conquered, maybe obliterated, at the same time, I am learning not to allow hopes to rise with each reported mini-breakthrough. But, research is spelled F-U-T-U-R-E; while living is spellled N-O-W. So what can we do day to day?

Alex's impaired mobility could not be separated from our housing plans. Meanwhile, "handicap," "disability," and "accessibility" were pushed front and center in my vocabulary. If any further reminder of these terms was necessary, it came from my decades-long losing battle with arthritis. Throughout the arduous emptying of our old house, that fourth floor *level* flat, only feet from the elevator, was a heartening image. I planned to celebrate move-in with a hip replacement followed by a stress-free convalescence.

So it was that both Alex and I became part of a "customizing" procedure. His parents were beginning to think about his future needs and would soon renovate their old house to accommodate a ramp, widened doorways, a special bathroom, and a household elevator. We, also, at #410 have enlarged our bathroom and hallways, simplified the layout, installed extra grab bars, all with the inevitable wheelchair in mind. He was fortunate in that he would be able to move about comfortably and relatively independently in at least two households.

And shortly after moving, Ed, who had always been active and vigorous, fell, and suffered some impairment to his mobility, convincing me more than ever that our decision had been good. Our experience is the example I offer to those in their later years who say, "I'm not ready to move out of my large house." For us, the unpredictable period between healthy and partially impaired was only a few months.

Until then, however, the weekly visiting rhythm remained unchanged. Alex continued to dutifully greet us with, "Play trains, Papa," as he headed for the dining room where the growing collection of wooden Brio train components was stored. And yet another complex track system, wending its way around table legs, evolved throughout the day to engulf the room.

Alex's passion is trains. Ours are twofold: cohousing and the wonders of our grandson. But like an unwatched TV, always on in the background, sadness and worry are ever-present, a lump in the stomach, a nagging thought. Realization comes in small doses, the "he will nevers" accumulate, little daily reminders of what he will not be able to know—climbing a mountain, riding a bike, participating in a team sport, the unrestricted freedom to come and go at will, even to decide to run away from home.

Now, after hip replacement, followed by three hip dislocations, I must regretfully face my "will never agains." I may never again canoe, play tennis, hike a forest trail, wrap my legs around my cello and play string quartets. I have already given my bike away. What is a loss for me is, for young Alex, a void.

Our family crisis preceded by Ed's fall had the effect of perforating his fierce independence and denial about aging. As a result, we shifted our focus to what we could do for our family—not just for Alex's, but for those of our other work-driven, distant children.

One answer was easy: we could spare them future burdens by simplifying our lives, letting any lingering reservations about the path we were on fall away. Thus, wholeheartedly, we plunged into the cohousing planning process, shedding our ambivalence. Much as he hated the often tedious meetings, Ed was becoming a serious, committed participant, while I was becoming an advocate for the disabled.

Aghast at my lack of prescience, I look back on my years of lecturing about and promoting housing options for women in midlife, and I never truly saw *myself* as becoming disabled. Someone else—my mother, Lynn's mother maybe, almost anyone could be, but not I! In fact, for years, women whom I counseled or taught would ask me whether I intended to live in such innovative housing myself. "Oh no, my husband won't be budged," I'd say, blithely. "We plan to live in our house forever; it suits us just fine."

When I began my alternative housing business, I was sixty, of the generation and temperament to defy retirement, senior housing, and other such stereotypes of aging. Cooperative living, on the other hand, offered options to living alone for women of all ages. (Men didn't seem interested.)

When I organized workshops and spoke at symposia, however, I always promoted universal accessibility as essential for modern living—all the statistics and demographics cried out for it. The healthiest of us can slip on the ice!

When Kevin, in a wheelchair, his wife Rose, and his daughter Erika, began coming to our cohousing meetings, it raised our awareness to the point that we reviewed our commitment to accessibility, and our passive compliance turned into active advocacy. Our planning shifted, veering from the coldness of statistical probability toward the real and human needs of present and future Kevins and Alexes.

And even then, Ned and Marion were way ahead of us. Their son Curt, disabled since birth, now a strapping, amiable twenty-two-year-old who was outgrowing his family, would need supervision throughout his lifetime. Marion had already paved Curt's successful path through his high school's special programs and was now focusing on the years ahead. Empty-nest time for most parents, an offspring's adulthood places a unique responsibility on those with dependent children. Creative families, however, face this as simply another challenge, and Curt was blessed with unusually creative parents.

With energy and good will, Ned and Marion were part of the core group of founders. They knew, however, that Curt would also need his own companions; undaunted, they established a large apartment—a separate condominuim association within Cambridge Cohousing to be owned by the parents of four dependent adults—along with a small unit for a live-in helper or supervisor. This mini-community is now managed by a private agency, which is responsible for its residents there, as well as their integration into the larger cohousing community.

Gradually, Patrick, Evan, and Dave joined Curt in the experiment of living in a diverse community. They all now leave for their various jobs in the morning, returning at different times, at which point they are free to sign up for meals in the dining room and, with some supervision, to shop and cook for themselves. Each sometimes takes a turn on a meal team. (Residents volunteer to sign onto three meal teams every six week period; there is a lead chef who plans the menu and oversees the dinner preparation with three helpers as well as a cleanup team).

Curt can be seen striding through the complex in perpetual good humor, ready to tell one of his limited repertoire of jokes. To every "Hi, Curt, how are you?" he responds cheerily, "I'm here!" Evan, from the sidelines, silently watches the kids playing on the lawn. Two of "the guys," as they are collectively referred to, have also volunteered to bring in the emptied barrels from the street on trash removal day.

As far as I know, this precedent-setting private group home model, integrated within a larger, housing project, is unique to Cambridge Cohousing. It requires private funding, a willing community, and careful up-front design planning, but the cost is more than worth the results; I like to think that, collectively, we've had a part in reducing the rigidity of the long-held stereotype that some people of limited cognitive abilities cannot live among their peers.

To go back a little to the early construction phase, budget concerns could not be ignored, as costly construction Change Orders mounted. The budget-watchers among us were sending alarming messages: we were in danger of losing our young families and fixed-income members if costs continued to escalate. But in spite of financial constraints, there came to be a growing concern about the physical inaccessibility of some units. First, there were the three-story townhouses, with their steep, turning stairways. Their front doors, however, were at ground level. Logically, could we presume that their occupants will be healthy and vigorous young families ... and ever more shall be so? Second were the eight flats in two three-story buildings. So, for a group which prided itself on access to all common areas, we needed to ask: was accessibility—beyond that required by law—meant to vie with affordability? Must we make choices here?

Still vivid to me, probably twelve years ago, is a warm, sunny, Sunday afternoon at a general meeting under the leafy shade of Clara's Cambridge deck. Perhaps forty of us clustered around architectural drawings pinned to trees at eye level. Triggered by my question about the inaccessibility of the flats, someone said, "Older people can choose to live in the Common House near the elevator."

"But anyone," I said, together with Betsy and a couple of others, "regardless of age, can break a leg, have a debilitating illness, be pregnant."

That did it! Two impassioned and especially vigorous women rose as one with nearly identical responses. Something to the effect of "I had two babies in a Manhattan five-floor walk-up. If I could do it, you can too!" End of statement, but not of debate.

At the risk of appearing weak, some recalled post-op complications, chronic back trouble, not-so-healthy pregnancies. Still others remembered a disabled friend or relative who would never be able to visit them. Ed brought up Alex, how totally unexpected the MD was and how grateful (even though required by law for new buildings above the third floor) we were for the Common House elevator.

The debate wore on, the filtered sunlight on the deck gave way to dusk. Picking up the pace of the discussion, a Greek-like chorus marked the dichotomy. "Accessible, accessible" alternated with "Money, money." After several hours of exhausting pros and cons, the meeting ended with a plan: the next day, the architect and contractor would be asked to revise plans and estimate costs for improved access in the two sets of flats.

We departed, feeling by then like a cohesive group, congratulating ourselves that we were giving priority to quality-of-life issues. We'd worry about the money later. A Change Order requesting that the stairs be widened by two feet to allow for the installation of stair chairs, thus extending the length of the building, would play still greater havoc with the budget. But somehow, consensus reigning, somehow we would find the money. The extraordinary power of talk, talk, talking, so frustrating in itself, had once again prevailed.

That hard-won consensus survived for ten years while the stair chairs served those in need. Betsy had already jumped at the opportunity to move to the second floor of the Common House. At that point, however, Sam, suffering from cancer, required a wheel chair. A captive to their third floor flat until, fortuitously, a ground floor apartment in the Common House became available.

Whose House Is This, Anyway?

In our interactions we seek a balance between
privacy in our own homes and our wish to be with others.
—Cambridge Cohousing Vision Statement

The Saturdays of Alex's babyhood shifted to afternoons with the early-release Wednesdays of the school child. And as long as his trains came along, the move from our old house to our new flat was a seamless event. And, as mentioned, his grandparents admit to sweetening the move with the lure of a real train four stories below our flat.

The first vibration sent him dashing to a trackside window to marvel at the five commuter cars from above. Seven seconds of little-boy bliss, seventeen round trips per day! Any variation in the sound, the sudden hoot of a whistle, or an extra engine, prompted Alex into prolonged speculation. His toy engines, Charlie and Thomas, and their railroad descendants, resided comfortably in the guest room, also known as Alex's room. Papa and Oma were disoriented by the move—we still couldn't locate things (our passports, for example)—but for Alex, life proceeded without interruption.

Later, at about eight, the unbroken pattern of train play had lost its rigidity, and fanciful variations crept in. The Brio components were transformed into a fortress, and the cars were clustered in hidden locations, presumably for protection against invading Martians. Once, during such creative play in "his" room, he informed me as he closed the bedroom door, "I want my privacy"—just as Ed and I occasionally had shut the larger world out of #410. I was secretly glad he felt at home enough to request his own space. He may well have viewed #410 as cramped, despite its light, airy living area. Regardless, it brought up, once again, an important cohousing precept—the unconventional allocation of space. That is, giving up square feet of personal space in exchange for roomy common areas for the use of all. If, to our unit's sixteen hundred square feet, we added our percentage share of the common areas (included in our monthly fees), we would have a condominium of close to nineteen hundred square feet. More than we need! And think of all the duplication throughout the project. In exchange for less room, we have access to two guest rooms and bath, which, for a pittance, cohousers' guests are welcome to use.

Eventually, an entire Wednesday afternoon could pass without a train reference or a scurry to the window. Alex's interests and range expanded to include the elevator, the buzzers, the dogs, and Erika's pet cockatoos on the second floor. But he continued to ignore—really, to avoid—the resident children. He was just more comfortable with adults. I believe he perceived the children in the cohousing community—the coho kids, we call them—as a formidable, inseparable mass, a phalanx. If not menacing, at least intimidating, and certainly puzzling.

The new Ping-Pong table in the basement recreation room was a ready magnet and claimed his attention early. However, he rapidly discovered that neither he nor his grandparents were very adept at keeping the ball in play and even less apt at recovering it. Luckily, through a generous, anonymous donor, a pool table appeared soon after, and tackling the game of pool became the afternoon's high point.

To this day, however, his reluctance to meld into a pack of kids remains. Apparently, he hasn't yet received the warm, welcoming message of cohousing.

Recreation Room in Common House basement

On this Wednesday, the rec room, usually uninhabited, was occupied by a man in a suit and tie (already an outsider sign). He lay stretched out on a beat-up couch, nose in a book. Slouched on the floor nearby, with his back to us, a boy, maybe ten, worked over a pad of newsprint. Surprised by what I judged to be a tutoring session (could that be Jason, a coho kid, under the baseball cap?), I heard myself say, "Oh, you're working. Will we disturb you if we play pool?"

"Not at all, go ahead," the unknown man replied in an offhand manner and returned to his reading. What I really meant to say but was too cowardly to explore was: Who are you? What business do you have making yourself so comfortable in *my* place? And why am I lowering my voice to oblige you, a total stranger? The experience reminded me of the feeling I get when I cannot distinguish whether a person in a store is a salesperson or a customer; I was thrown off. The game of pool became sluggish after that; I was preoccupied.

The incident revived for me, however, many further cohousing discussions about what approach we should take regarding the use of our common space, which could range anywhere from community-spirited generosity to a let's-keep-it-for-ourselves stance. We flirted with a whole gamut of scenarios from musical and dramatic events to crafts, children's parties, a film series, discussion groups. Looking back, it was Katherine who, early on, promoted the idea of a large Recreation Room in the basement as a necessary step toward "integrating the neighborhood." Her vision was clearer than that of most; she spoke of political events, lectures, square dances, singing groups—anything that would promote the assimilation that most gave lip service to. Working with the architect, she presented us with drawings that reflected her ideals, stemming in part—I guessed—from her Quaker roots.

Cohousing was akin to sanctuary. That's how I understood Katherine's almost spiritual image of our Rec Room. A haven, a refuge even, for simpatico groups, ones similar to ours that had no access to meeting places. Cohousing as an urban oasis was a view shared by many of us, and the early drawings she showed us embodied these beliefs. In particular, I remember the depiction of a ramp from the street level to a beautifully landscaped, welcoming community entrance leading to the spacious basement Rec Room. In a gift to our neighborhood, we would play host to square dances, yoga classes, local activists.

At the next Sunday meeting, only half-listening to the gentle murmurs of good fellowship so in tune with the Quaker setting, (without the generous contribution of a regular meeting space from the Society of Friends, cohousing might well have floundered), I was jarred from my reveries by a new, strident tone. Just as six-foot-six Ken entered with the sleeping Ronnie slung over his shoulder, the debate took a sharp turn. Someone had just introduced one of those cusp issues, the kind that could pierce the balloon of idealism.

"We can't just open it to the public—this is our *home!*" several voices rose in unison.

"Well, one of us will just always have to be present at any gathering as a sponsor," said Ruth, who hoped to use the room occasionally for her nonprofit group's board meetings.

"But, gee, I don't quite understand," said Merna. "Who's going to clean up? And you know, someone always has to use the bathroom—do we escort them to the first floor?"

Never stymied, always armed with pencil and indispensable trace (the architects' roll of semitransparent paper), Katherine quickly sketched a lavatory onto the basement drawings.

"How would we keep people from roaming around the common house?" sputtered an aroused future property owner who had imagined the Recreation Room to be an adjunct of his living quarters. "I absolutely refuse to do guard duty!"

And then, the perennial conversation stopper: "How will this affect our insurance coverage?"

A few continued to rally to Katherine's undaunted enthusiasm, but the bell was tolling for the ramp, a designer's bridge between social worlds.

Tweaking the drawings did not quell the questions: the controversy would not go away.

"Let Design deal with it," Ned, always eager to get on to the next agenda item, said to a grateful audience. This posed a real challenge for the overworked Design Committee—one of several committees that had evolved such as Membership, Finance, Meals and, of course, the original one, the DOC—of which I found myself the coordinator—or the convenor or the facilitator. (Our egalitarian practice eschewed any hierarchical word such as "chairperson.") But to be honest, I must have volunteered because that's the way we operated. One thing was clear, however: my role was to give everyone who wished it an opportunity to add their voices to any decision, however trivial, so they would be fully heard when the time came to arrive at consensus. For many months, Design had met weekly in my living room; if you wanted to attend or bring an issue, you turned up on our front porch on a Tuesday night.

The ramp issue, as it came to be known, grew to tremendous proportions. As an architectural embodiment of a vision, the ramp had implications for the entire project. It was big in terms of money (maybe a thirty-thousand-dollar item without the landscaping), of philosophy, of personalities.

At first glance, the ramp issue represented concerns about time pressure, cost, and potential use. The initial debate started over the Spine, that path that went through the entire project. The Spine, it was argued, would also serve as a bridge over the ramp—a construction challenge and perhaps a safety hazard. A closer look at this debate over design, however, suggested more profound cares.

Whenever a design element became the fulcrum for strong vocal expression, as it did here, it was a sign to me that we were unwittingly touching upon emotions buried at unknown dimensions. This time, the debate over the ramp design unearthed many unvoiced anxieties and assumptions that had become obscured in our feverish action to create our cohousing dream. Time was money; we had been in a hurry. But, as always with unresolved issues, you pay at one end or the other.

Now we realized we needed to stop, to take the time to confront our fears, which were not only about costs but about the purportedly high-risk neighborhood that we were not only sinking our fortunes into but also poised to inhabit.

Somewhat to my surprise, worries about a neighborhood I had described during the site selection stage as once off-limits to my own children, were now surfacing as though brand new. I had resolved my own apprehensions—and my children were long gone from home—but I felt like saying, "Hey, didn't you guys hear me?"

But in translating "inclusiveness" from an abstract idea to an acceptable architectural form—all within the context of a new lifestyle that none of us had yet lived—how were we to know how to get all of this right?

In our debates, "security," "safety," and "comfort level" had become buzz words we fell back on, a common language with which we could legitimize our obscure worries. Some had an it-can't-happen-to-us response to a recent murder outside the corner store; others pointed nervously to drug arrests in the nearby housing project.

"Crime figures are down citywide," argued Tom.

"But," countered Joy, "our area is the one with the highest risk."

More than once during this period, Ed and I left a meeting feeling discouraged; he was, frankly, ready to withdraw, disturbed by the heated discussions and the tension.

"Some nice retirement community would suit me just fine," he said once after a particularly contentious, tedious meeting. I pleaded for a little more time.

In the end, these discussions were all about control and decision-making. Unexpectedly, our group found ourselves at one of those defining moments: we were smack up against the democratic principle of participation—an article of faith in the cohousing canon. After all, just how collaborative was a decision promoted primarily by our hired experts?

"But wait a minute," both Katherine and Brent reminded us. "We're members just like you; we intend to live here forever, to make this our home, too."

Incensed at being asked to rubber-stamp a plan that could not achieve consensus, the community asserted its newly solidified position. They sent Katherine the message that she was much appreciated for her leadership and unique professional qualities but that the decision making must be collaborative, that all of us must have input into the ramp decision.

The ramp issue ranks among the three or four most tension-filled debates from our early days (two others are "the window" and the childcare payment issue), all drawing future householders to our front porch like moths to the light. As many registered strong feelings, so did I, straining my role as an objective facilitator. But all were struggling for the same end: to find that elusive balance between privacy and openness. Here, we were not absorbed with individual privacy but rather with a middle stage, with the right of a group to create a boundary around itself despite a majority of its members' sincere committment to inclusion.

Retrospectively, my own take is that words are abstractions, and not until we are forced to forge them in wood and concrete do we know how we really feel about them. In this instance, we had rejected exclusiveness in favor of diversity and inclusion by giving a back of the hand to the gated community—that most public symbol of exclusion, which I came to know as a child in St. Louis and which is being revived in pricey development after development throughout the country—yet we were now balking at opening the front door to all.

Finally realizing we were at the point where we must discern how *all* of us could share the responsibility for decisions we followed Ned's suggestion. Design set aside, for the time being, its growing collection of samples for kitchen cabinets and flooring, its fabric swatches, its paint chips. It also stopped delving into the environmental impact of unit fireplaces, halting heated arguments about cooking fuel and air quality, yet another conflict that had reached dramatic proportions: Should we favor the chefs among us with gas or the allergic with electricity? (We resolved this one on the basis of data at hand and concerns about fire. In the face of overriding evidence about gas contributing to asthma in children, I was amazed at how the chefs among us remained addicted to cooking with it. We compromised: the common kitchen stove would be fueled by gas; residents would settle for electricity.)

So now that Katherine and Floyd had brought physical form back to lofty ideals with the ramp issue, the Design Committee, a bunch of "lay interior decorators with attitude," as described by one nonmember, was now pressed into the more daunting roles of social planner and peacemaker; we faced the tough job of consolidating group opinion.

We had to ask whose home, indeed, was cohousing to be? And given the multitude of our beliefs and our limited pocketbooks, we had to recommend how far to extend the benefits of this social experiment. A necessary stage along the road to community-building, perhaps, but sometimes I just wanted to be back with those undemanding, tangible carpet samples, those lovely colored glass tiles recycled from coke bottles.

Some of us were stepping a rung or two down our utopian ladder in order to view more clearly our prospective mixed-income, mixed-everything, urban enclave. Did our individual values overreach our ability to do justice to our own community life?

I recall trying to explain, with little success, my own feeling about our emphasis on diversity: to me, diversity was a vast spectrum of preferences, belief systems, individual characteristics—not only the more visible, politically correct subsets of color, age, gender, ethnicity, and disability, which we actively recruit. Weren't we in danger of giving short shrift to the subtle differences that characterize any group of people? In other words, why take on the world? Nevertheless, we researched crime reports, we invited a police officer to meet with us, and we discreetly explored crime statistics in the area. I sensed that some of that initial trust and confidence in our ability to establish bonds with what many viewed as a wayward neighborhood element were eroding. Ideals embraced unquestioningly in our vision-writing days—before we even had a neighborhood—were now prompting second thoughts. Our middle-class slip was showing.

The debate tapped other concerns. The refrain about costs, always in the background, surged forward and center. A mixed-income project (synonymous for us with "affordable") meant just that: a financial hardship for some, a breeze for others. Some squirmed over each added dollar, while others, with deeper pockets, preferred adding value and amenities.

We weighed our soaring capital costs along with estimates of future maintenance and condo fees against the cost of building a basement community center. Someone restated the conflict and then proposed a goal that took precedence over our hotheaded political gatherings: cohousing should be affordable for all of us in the room who chose to live here.

Then, as though on cue, guaranteed to halt even the most dedicated idealist, someone piped up with, "How much will our insurance increase if we invite outsiders?" The wary legalists among us trembled at the mere hint of liability. That cinched it. The debate was over! Was Ed right, I wondered:

Did we comfortably fixed, over-seventies need all this? Was I being stubborn in defying tradition? Why not settle into a gracious old age, in a luxury condo with a concierge who protected us from the pesky public? But my question was hypothetical; I really did want to play a part in this often frustrating skirmish, this melange of problem-solving, this test of whether dreams could come true.

As so often happens, a solution tiptoed into the room, unnoticed. Our budget-watchers were getting nervous; collectively, we took yet another look at cost overruns and concluded that the ramp was not essential. While the concrete foundation was curing overnight, it seemed, the matter was abruptly resolved. On crisp new blueprints, all signs of ramp and community entrance disappeared. We had pulled in our welcome mat a bit as we simultaneously reaffirmed our commitment to affordability.

A young girl rushed into the Rec Room, abruptly ending my flashback. "My piano lesson is over. Let's go."

The lounging father and son gathered their stuff and headed to the door, but not before the girl mischievously flipped her brother's cap off. So the mystery was solved.

Pool cue in hand, Alex was looking at me quizzically. "C'mon, Oma, you never remember to take your turn."

No thanks to the now-departing strangers, our game of pool had petered out. Cohousing may have decided not to share the Rec Room with the rest of the world, but some nebulous boundary questions still remained.

When discussed at a general meeting, a surprisingly intense reaction to the public use of the Rec Room managed to raise our awareness of our flash points. Our temperatures taken, the mercury read "High Threat Level."

We all have our personal limits beyond which few are welcome. Having these lines crossed feels like discomfort, intrusion, even violation. In further refining these limits, in this instance, we found ourselves in remarkable unity.

We now are a little more careful and thoughtful about stepping over the lines. We made signs, now posted during poetry readings, art shows, and other events attended by outsiders and held in our common living room. And there are other signs on these occasions—visual barriers that separate the private spaces from those to be used during the public event: Elevator for Residents Only, Restroom, Residents Only. Now, the piano teacher is to inform her students' families where they can wait.

Now that we have come some distance in understanding our external boundaries—those between ourselves in the cohousing community and the wider world of our neighborhood—we are freer to tackle the far more complex internal ones, those between ourselves and each other. Those questions about personal boundaries, however, will never completely go away.

Living Room in Common House

An Unplanned Merger

Meaningful change doesn't come about
through lots of clout and lots of money.
It comes about through lots of
little changes everywhere.
—Jane Jacobs

In February1998, the City of Cambridge issued Cambridge Cohousing a Certificate of Occupancy for the East End units. The following is a mere sampling of what had been accomplished since mid-1995.

All modular, manufactured boxes were in place.

All forty-one units were occupied by their owners—there were no rentals, with the exception of the two units purchased by the city's housing authority.

The number of fire alarms in the first week amounted to three—all false.

The gardeners among us, determined to have a vegetable crop this first summer, were frantically adding and restoring life to what had been an urban brownfield (soil contaminated by industrial pollutants over the years).

Parking tickets during development oversight meetings were a thing of the past. Now all of us had only to compete for street space with our Richdale neighbors until our underground garage was completed.

Residents leaving for work and construction workers gathering for coffee exchanged guarded greetings and a few lame jokes. The New Hampshire workmen had been overheard to say, "Some of them are nice, but the rest are a bunch of Commies." I tried to think ahead to a workmen-free environment.

Much of the time, with questionable efficiency, the state-of-the-art ground-source heat pumps worked. Through these pumps the HVAC system (for the uninitiated, heating ventilating air-conditioning) heated and cooled the complex by way of a complicated water-delivery plan. All a layperson could say was that it had its good and its less-good days. On the good ones, despite professional maintenance, much credit must be given to the persistence and talents of the home team—the two Kens—for tackling the behemoth that continued to puzzle the servicemen recommended by the experts who had planned and installed it. They both became regular visitors at DOC meetings, which now convened on home turf. The original committee members, by then weary, touchy, irritable, captive, uninspired, were in a big push to complete this project.

The so-called home team was one of those phenomena that can occur naturally wherever there is malfunctioning technology—or an information void— in combination with some smart, highly motivated bystanders. It happened frequently in our cohousing setting. No hierarchy existed to assign jobs—"assign," like "must" and "majority," were words we were careful not to use. For example—although the esthetic touch is hardly a technology, Anne, Dalenna, and a few others, wanting their—our—home to be welcoming and beautiful, took it upon themselves to supply lovely floral arrangements in the lobby. That the flowers may have needed freshening a day or two beyond the point that a concierge would be instructed to replace them was not the point. Someone eventually would. Ken B. and Ken T., standing in the wings, saw a void and were eager to fill it.

Although they could often be seen conferring, they tended to specialize. Ken B., absorbed with our frequently malfunctioning HVAC system, was challenged to understand, fix, and nurture it, like a devoted parent dedicated to cracking the silent code of an autistic child. He was seen as a thorough, precise, and analytical techie who had a constitutional need to understand everything; he became the questioner, the disbeliever. "Why is it being done that way?" he'd ask, or, "How did this get decided? Wouldn't it be better to…?" Or, "Wait, I have a better idea—I'll check the Web."

Ken T., architect and planner then writing a doctoral dissertation, was gaining an impressive handle on our obstreperous building—its needs and follies. He was also a generous contributor to the Design Committee. His ideas were good, although less than whole-heartedly welcome when they occasionally pointed to costly course changes. He challenged decisions and assumptions the DOC had laid to rest—from the color of the building and the pace of construction, to the impermeability of our waterproof membranes and, of course, the performance of our touted heating-cooling system. His entrance timely, the DOC was only too happy to dub him czar of the Punch List.

Among DOC members there was a general mood of frustration when Katherine distributed her two hundredth agenda! Good Lord, this marked the fourth year of Tuesdays! Jean, facilitating that week's session, began gathering items for a supplementary agenda, a rotating practice begun recently to balance what some saw as one-sided. Over the past weeks, several disgruntled residents had asked to attend so we waived our policy of closed DOC meetings. Every time new people joined us, though I heard nothing personally critical, I wondered whether their justifiable impatience and frustration would target us, the DOC members. I couldn't help but wonder what I might have done differently; I suspect each member had similar private thoughts. Perhaps I should have resigned earlier; I was close to doing so, to make room for fresh views. Every one of us was discouraged.

We had reached stasis; the process was stuck and none of us knew how to move it along. Undercurrents of dissatisfaction with delays and sloppy construction were always present. Both Kens were hovering, discouraged as was everyone else but convinced they could make a difference, and eager to speed up the hellish process. Was the about-to-burst impatience of our young Turks reaching a limit? Was a palace coup in the making? For whatever reason, our meetings were longer, livelier, and more contentious when they attended.

The DOC and its newcomers covered old ground; new and unique perspectives emerged with every issue. For example, the LLP had been persuaded early on that manufactured housing was consistent with our goals: faster, cheaper, more efficient, better built. Then, about seven-eighths through the project, faced with problems, some suggested cutting our losses and returning to conventional stick-built construction. (To me, it was much too late and, in fact, that idea had a very brief life). The original DOC members were looking backward, desperately aiming to wind up our contractual agreements; the newbies, mindless of history, were on a rescue mission. Without realizing it, we were witnessing the beginning of the era of the two consultants, later in conjunction with our property manager.

We invited others to join us. For instance, athough he was a retired psychiatrist, Paul's credibility at the DOC was as an accomplished woodworker; Roger, the newly elected first president of the condo association, could, we hoped, bring focus to our disorder. Shan Shen's real estate and financial perspective were sorely needed.

The infusion of expertise and energy enhanced progress at one moment and stymied it the next. The addition of new people meant an altered learning curve. The original DOC was flat out; we simultaneously were sensitive to criticism and invited assistance. Until, that is, new ideas, exploding from several directions at once, left us limp and speechless. The contractor refused to speak with the newcomers; he set deadlines that backfired. Katherine continued to transmit cohousers' requests to Don as well as his terse replies back to us—to no one's satisfaction. There seemed to be no clear chain of command; every partially informed unit owner was invited to the DOC to air their wishes and—I never ceased to be amazed—was carefully listened to. How would we ever finish this job, I asked myself.

Don was reportedly overheard to say, "This is the worst job I've ever had. I'll never do anything like this again!" And then when the roofing was discussed, "If I go up there, I'm not walking down; I'll be jumping off! Construction by committee—what a disaster!"

The Punch List, the dreaded ritual of the building trade, was a final stage accounting of unfinished construction items that must be negotiated successfully between owner and architect/builder before the final financial settlement. It remained a major area of dispute for Cambridge Cohousing. Ordinarily an individual owner worked with a builder to complete the items on the list. But in our case, the DOC was the responsible party until the entire project was completed; unit owners did not have direct contact with the builder. As residents began to move in, they reported appalling findings: an electric outlet was wireless, a cabinet blocked the refrigerator door, a fireplace belched smoke into the room. Lists of these complaints, compiled by already frustrated residents, lengthened daily. And they all came to the DOC. Who decided which entries were legitimate? Plaster cracks, an awkwardly designed kitchen, a stained toilet, scratched mirror? The master list grew, in part driven by the illusion that perfection and full satisfaction were attainable. The contractor refused to discuss newly reported flaws. The last anyone counted, my memory was that the Punch List contained more than four hundred and fifty items—an unheard of number! While the DOC master list grew, the contractor's list, defining what constituted a legitimate problem, shortened. And the DOC couldn't decide on an official master list. That was the job the DOC gratefully handed over to Ken T.

As complaints flooded the DOC, we realized we must stem the tide and obtain agreement to fix what was not right. Desperate to create a semblance of order, we decided that we would no longer accept verbal complaints. Stacks of paper now replaced impatient homesteaders on Tuesdays; meeting time was spent in tedious debate over warped window sashes and buckling floorboards. Our two "Brits," periodically lamenting the griping, introduced another word to our growing lexicon. "Americans," they claimed, "certainly do a lot of whinging." Another word for our growing cohousing glossary: whinging seems to be a common term for complaining.

Whereas behind the closed library door, the atmosphere sometimes became acerbic and accusatory, it was in sharp contrast with what I discovered when I went to the lobby, the sidewalk, wherever a DOC member could be buttonholed. Take Ruth, for instance, in the mail room, who good-naturedly remarked, "Only half of my furniture has arrived, and my shower doesn't work. I should be furious after waiting so long, but I'm not." It was a strange thing, because Ruth was not an exception. Shirley joined us, beaming, until the word "food" was mentioned. "My kitchen! It's unusable! I expected *small* from the drawings, but this one is microscopic. And nothing works!"

So how were things really going? Almost anyone you'd meet, after a few invectives about unfinished conditions and building flaws, brightly exclaimed, "Oh, I'm so happy to be here, I can put up with anything." Or, "The long diaspora is over; the promised land is looking good."

We read Katherine's agenda item—"Time Capsule"—just as Theda arrived by appointment. They were in league, I gathered, to mark the birth of this utopian community by preserving some of its icons under our own soil: the Vision Statement, a photo history, a sampling of DOC agendas, and other such memorabilia that could be forced into a time capsule. (As in the cremation urn industry, I learned, one can select from a large assortment a strong box that promises weatherproof, tamperproof properties). Theda had chosen a spot near the front entrance and checked the plans with Floyd and the Grounds Committee.

When Don heard, however, he vetoed the location, letting the pipeline know that "a drain still has to go in there. Why don't you folks postpone your crazy schemes until I'm outta here? Everywhere I move, there's some cock-a-mamie project going on. That pear tree, now ... somebody planted that right where the path is supposed to go."

I cringed. "That pear tree" was a graft from the 150-year-old tree at our old house, which a neighbor had been nurturing for cohousing for over a year.

The comment, however, was just one example of how Don seemed to maintain a degree of detachment by refusing to adopt the cohousing nomenclature. What he referred to as simply "the path" was what we called the Spine, the connecting link through the three football fields' length of the site, a feature designed to keep us in touch with one another.

"Now you tell me, what am I supposed to do?" Katherine, in a rare lapse of professional loyalty, reported these exchanges as samples of Don's frustration. For the embattled DOC, it provided an instant of light relief; Theda insisted that the ceremonial burial of our history should have priority over the placement of a drain. And with that, we scheduled the dedication ceremony for Sunday.

The other major business of the day was to allocate the funds for the final payment of the construction loan. Unit owners found and negotiated their own condominium mortgages after lots of comparison shopping. As a result of the closing sales of forty-one condos, money was now available to pay the final installment of our nine-million-dollar construction loan. "Our creative financing," as Ned described our approach to the budget, "has worked!" It was a triumph; our detractors never expected to see this day. Someone left to get some wine for the first of many celebrations. Merna volunteered to write a message on our new whiteboard in the lobby so all could share in the good news.

Then, abruptly, as though on impulse, and speaking firmly, Ned said, "I've been sitting here thinking. The DOC has been doing our usual muddling through for exactly four years, and I think that's plenty long enough. I propose that we dissolve the DOC as of now and turn all this over to the new Managing Board. As the elected body of the CCH Condominium Association, this is their job. Right, Roger?"

Roger swallowed hard. "Right, Ned."

After years of Herculean effort, the impromptu merger marked the official start of the miracle on Richdale Avenue. We were now all bound together in the Cambridge Cohousing Condominium Association. The oversight group disbanded, and like the proverbial puff of smoke, disappeared within moments.

Ned had rendered the DOC redundant and his stunned colleagues uttered not a single objection. He had a point; whatever cutting edge we had, we had lost. Mission accomplished, development over, the mop-up begins. But I realized I had, once again, mixed feelings about Ned's style. Was it impetuous? Intuitive or seemingly irresponsible? Brilliant? Outside the envelope, certainly. Exasperatingly charming while sending explosive messages, his abrupt, succinct pronouncements, often immediately followed by hasty departures, permitted little rebuttal. This road was hardly the recommended way to consensus, but in the end, still in shock, we found ourselves agreeing.

The incident might have led a casual observer to wonder whether our commitment to decision-making by consensus was serious, or whether we were, rather, engulfed in an authoritarian, charismatically led cult. Perish the thought.

Maybe Ned consciously used this jocular free spirit to undo any suspected entrenchment, to strike at any building of a personal power base. He could be generous to a fault—with suggestions for the use of his own and others' funds. He truly believed that those who *had* should help float those who *had not*. But he could also stand being booed down, sometimes was, and furthermore, would take these observations with British good humor. Oops, to retain the English image, that should be spelled H-U-M-O-U-R.

Mechanical Room: part of HVAC system

The Power of Food

*You shall be known for your lemon
chicken, your Portuguese soup, and
your heavenly desserts.*
—Anonymous

"Close the door, sweetie, don't let the mosquitoes in." The newest toddler—
ours or those of regular visitors—in her endless search for a congenial social
center, had been taught how to maneuver the heavy glass sliders. In what
became a rite of passage requiring both memory ("remember the door") and
intricate motor coordination, each year's crop of kids was introduced to the
pleasures of "Groton."

After a few grungy summers in Cambridge with young children, Ed and
I had begun the search for a vacation retreat within an easy commute of
Boston. Our requirements were simple—trees, water, and a modest cottage.
Concord, Lincoln, Littleton, Harvard all fell within the mapped semicircle.
Our youngest was a few weeks old when, on a Sunday drive, we stumbled
upon a sign that led us, before the day was over, to a very special ten acres, a
portion of it underwater.

For us "Groton" called up old-growth pines, a mill pond claimed by
beavers with a stream running through, a broken dam, and a WWII lumber
mill. The wooden structure was transformed into our much-loved, multi-
angled, funky-shaped house full of windows with wonderful views of pond,
wildlife, and dense conservation-preserved forests—a touch of Vermont near
a time-warped colonial town, all less than an hour from Cambridge.

Family, old friends, and the annual influx of guests watched each child
become part of the two major holidays we cared about in our small but
expandable weekend/summer house. The Fourth of July and Thanksgiving
were each marked by its own unvarying menu—fresh salmon, peas, and
homemade strawberry ice cream for an authentic New England Independence
Day dinner—and, of course, turkey in November. Memorialized over the

years, these were occasions I loved for their informality, and for the continuity of friendships and family fun and history they allowed us. Everyone brought a part of the feast; everyone helped.

Still, the preholiday logistics and the postfeast cleanup fell to me alone to organize. After some years, I began to notice unbidden visions of country inns distracting me from my lists of holiday tasks. I was not only growing tired and lame, I was also betraying beloved traditions!

The dyad of burnout and guilt is a double burden at any age, and time adds aches and pains as well. So, in those early cohousing-planning marathons, I sat up and took notice when I heard my shameful, unuttered thoughts of escape echoed out loud by other women.

"I never want to handle another turkey carcass again!" said one.

Or there was the time, with nervous hilarity, that Merna sang out, "I'm giving away my roasting pan!"

Finally, I had my chance. The facilitator invited us to speak about our expectations for a life in cohousing. I bravely tried to frame mine: "I can see Ed and me, with a scattering of grandchildren, surrounded by friends, neighbors, creating a ceremony together—one which doesn't send me to bed with an aching back."

On this, our second cohousing Thanksgiving, the fantasy became reality; my ticket of admission a single dish. We closed up our vacation house on a lovely day in October before the temperatures dipped below freezing, thus averting the annual panic about the frozen pipes of Thanksgivings past.

The festive scene at Richdale capped the day's comfortable bustle in the common house. Sixty cohousers and our guests, sitting quietly midst the proverbial groaning board while Nathan coaxed us into a few moments of thankfulness.

"The children can wait," he assured the moms, putting his best third-grade teacher skills to work. And to the cooks, "The food won't suffer." Even the smallest child, heeding the cue, was lulled into silence, sensing the weight of the occasion.

All eyes focused on two plump, golden turkeys, surrounded by mounds of stuffing, mashed potatoes, and crusted breads. Beautifully presented greens enhanced the cranberry reds. My squash casserole nestled next to one of corn. Against the wall was another table, a huge half squash full of rice, end-of-season farm greens, and a blue-gray herbal centerpiece, much of which Keith had prepared himself.

Nathan asked us to introduce our guests before filling our plates. From Mexico, Taiwan, Detroit, Rhode Island, and more, they came. A first Thanksgiving for some, an eighty-ninth for one, we all celebrated together.

Nevermind that over the past week or two, a few eruptions accompanied the planning of this dinner. Nevermind memories of the previous year's barely cooked turkey. Nevermind the social crisis following the rump decision that one family could not reserve the dining room for a private party on a high holiday.

"Isn't this our *raison d'etre*," they argued?

Our dining room was antidote for holiday blues. All that behind us now, nothing could mar this scene of belonging and camaraderie, a feature any homepage editor would die for. Here in this sanctuary of security, safety, and plenty, no one was irritable or dropping from fatigue.

How did the men, especially the family men, experience this gathering? A sense of relief? Gratitude for freed-up time? I was inclined to imagine that the time-release benefits of a collective holiday meal were likely to point them in the direction of the workshop, toward visions of well-equipped, meticulously maintained rows of pliers and hammers arranged over tidy workbenches. But nothing was ever 100 percent; I nursed poignant memories of Groton's private pleasures, traditions that were beginning to fade as others began to take shape.

Food, domestic arrangements, holidays brought me to another subject that had bearing on the building of community. My family's relationship to Groton was very intense—it had come to be a three-generational rendezvous. That spot in the woods served as a crossroads, a rejuvenator, a play space, and a spot where every meal was a celebration. But how did allocating time and energy for a vacation home fit in with creating a new community? Would it deflect our enthusiasm for either? Once in cohousing, would we need an escape destination? If so, would our new friends join us there? Or would it just serve to set up "have" and "have not" barriers among the cohousing residents?

My housing workshops came to mind, in which I saw women from a wide spectrum of incomes—from bare bones to comfortable to affluent. The former, understandably, tended to measure every decision against its cost; for the latter, few choices threatened their financial equanimity. But did this kind of disparity in financial attitude bode well for living together in harmony? Or would those with the luxury of choice use it to the detriment of the group? Would the *pied á terre* crowd come to predominate, leaving the rest to take on the tasks?

I would do a little survey of my own to see what I could learn. My method was simple: by now, knowing the recreational habits of the entire community, a review of the telephone list would give information about how many had second homes. The results surprised me. Exactly one-third of the unit owners spent significant time (from the occasional weekend to six-month time blocks) at alternate homes in a spread of locations—three out of the country, four in New Hampshire, two on Cape Cod, two in Massachusetts, and one each in New York and Maine. And I shouldn't forget those who for months at a time went to Ireland and Mexico.

Even more surprising, however, was these same households had a high rate of participation in cohousing activities. In other words, owning a second home did not seem to have reduced one's interest in the cohousing community. It did, however, often keep these second-home owners from Sunday general meetings and weekend work projects. Still another surprise was that Ed and I just became less and less inclined to escape to Groton: our interest had slowly shifted to Richdale Avenue.

My mind returned to other nontraditional living arrangements. In the housing workshops I used to give, two kinds of women seemed to me to be especially attracted to the idea of shared living: those who hated to cook and those who loved to cook. The former would do anything, even volunteer to clean toilets, to keep from cooking for others; often these same women couldn't imagine sharing a kitchen with other women.

The latter, however, positively lit up over anything to do with food. They saw a common kitchen as a repository for their treasured recipes, cookbooks, and baking paraphernalia. In their minds, they moved effortlessly and rapidly from sole nurturers to collective providers. They thrilled at the mere thought of filling common rooms with heavenly aromas of simmering soups and stews, and visualized a *gemütlich* life around meals. For them, allergies, special diets, and preferences posed no roadblock—they'd deal with them. They were, in the best sense of these words, accommodators, enablers, nurturers.

The subject of food is a pervasive one that ran through our lives. It cropped up in our meetings and in talking together: How frequent should the common dinners be? Well ... not every night, mind you; what we truly crave is the freedom from routine and the luxury of choice. The choices: to dine alone, to share with others, or to sample the city's cuisines, those ethnic restaurants laced throughout Boston's densely populated, intriguing neighborhoods.

The very word *cohousing* strikes me as a brilliant synthesis of age-old ideas; in fact, a practical translation of the daydreams and fantasies of women now and through history. In each generation, a few seem to have fashioned visions of cooperative escapes from the dreaded drudgery of housework—group endeavors to get the work done and to reduce its solitariness. Others, incensed by unrewarding repetitive toil invented and designed—on paper at least—other improvements in the solitary domestic scene; for example, a centrally located neighborhood kitchen to prepare and cook all its members' meals. And a luxury apartment building in Boston with a large central kitchen in its basement to send fully prepared meals to individual units by way of dumbwaiter, butler's pantry, and warming oven.

New England women were particularly inventive. Not many blocks from cohousing, right in Harvard Square on Bow Street, one Melusina Fay Peirce put forth her ideas in 1868 in a small book called *Cooperative Housekeeping*. A suffragist, she wrote about the exploitation of women, their economic dependence on men, and their inability to develop their talents due to subjection to their housekeeping chores.

Hers was a practical solution that exhorted women to join together and get jobs done: in 1870, the Cambridge Cooperative Housekeeping Society held its first meeting. Its advocates persuaded their husbands to sponsor the venture, and the subscribing women formed committees for cooking, laundry, and "the making of garments." Melusina was in charge of the laundry, but unfortunately the collective business was short-lived; within two years, the husbands who were paying the bills withdrew their support.

Thirty-nine for dinner!

Likewise, the curious who flocked to our cohousing informational meetings were almost invariably led by women. Lena and her husband were moving to Cambridge from a Manhattan loft in search of a better life for their school-age daughter.

"I would love to join cohousing," Lena said eventually, with genuine sadness. "So would Sarita. But Michael simply cannot give up his privacy. We'll just have to drop out."

The Joys, Marions, Wha Kyungs, and Shirleys came to their first meetings armed with files and yellowed clippings about people joining for regular dinners, celebrations, babysitting, and even car co-ops. Although all had friends and devoted, if far-flung, families, each, in her own way, acknowledged the specter of social isolation and sought an alternative to "Home Alone." We talked about sharing chores, having greater economies, and shouldering less individual burden, but left unsaid that they were in the market for an insurance policy for companionship—benefits of a kind that MetLife did not underwrite.

In my experience, the woman of a couple most often takes the first steps in changing a way of life. And this phenomenon is borne out in the cohousing experience, where, with very few exceptions among the older members, men were rarely the initiators. Men typically did not come to those first meetings of their own volition—reluctant, perhaps, to be associated with this visionary group that had the lunatic potential to pull a guy out of his comfortable life.

At Greg's first meeting, he quickly hunched down in a back row seat, hoping for invisibility, until the organizers discovered the value of the no-place-to-hide circle. After that point, when his turn came, he frankly confessed his disinterest, along with his bewilderment over his partner's enthusiasm.

"I like my life. I have everything I need, and I certainly don't need all this talk," he grumbled. But in the end, he heeded the tugs of a determined woman, and though grumbling still, is a candid, valued member.

Like Greg and his wife, some couples stuck, but others slipped away never to return. Brent, whose wife was the inspirational leader of the two, once told me he lived in dread of the prospect of cooking for a group.

"I could never cook a common dinner," he said once. "All I know is how to make salad. Maybe I don't belong here."

There may well be a generational divide. But whether age or gender or something else is the root determinant—and the lines are not absolute—I don't often hear a man lobbying to repaint the lobby, to refurbish the upholstery, or to bring order to the mail or coat room. In general, they choose to manage the compost, cut the grass (although an amazing number, it turns out, are plagued by the same aches and pains as women and don't last any longer behind a lawnmower), carry heavy loads on occasion, and do detective work on building flaws. And the men do cook! Several standouts rustle a dinner together with the panache of the professional chef. And if they harbor women's concerns over loneliness, it is not apparent.

Perhaps the prospect of common meals is cohousing's strongest magnet for women. Whether three or five times a week, they spell relief from kitchen labor or, for single women, an end to the solitary dinner. And that led me to another odd gender differential: of the four or five single men with units here, only one or two occasionally show up at dinner. For most, their participation is close to zero, contrary to their involvement during the formative period. And the benchmark of shared dinners drew older couples such as Paul and Ann Marie, who said at their first meeting, "Many of our friends have chosen retirement communities—and we did look—but we really felt intimidated by the contracted one-free-meal-a-day plan. Somebody else's food seven nights a week? Dressing up for dinner? Not for us!" They turned out to be a great cook team.

I hold to a theory—my own, I hasten to add—that those whose culinary lives are fulfilling can imagine a community where food plays a central role. Those who enjoy their role as providers do not choose to relinquish it to a professional staff. And for currently single women who may have once cooked for families, cohousing is a place to revive—in welcome, small doses—nostalgic pleasures. Or, for entirely different reasons, young women who are parents can choose to reduce the lonely, daily grind of food gathering and preparation. So maybe the genius of the founders of cohousing is to have unwittingly recognized the community-building power of food, the religion of many intentional communities. Whether it be vegetarian, home grown, or organic, cohousing abhors the messianic leader; instead, it reveres the cook.

CCH drop-off location for area Community Sustainable Agriculture (CSA) delivery

A Conversation Continued

*All change begins with
a social conversation.*
—Margaret J. Wheatley

It was a rare week away from New England's winter doldrums and the stresses of work and cohousing planning. Ed and our friends walked ahead, into a small ravine and up a slope. With my hip beginning to hurt, I remained behind, happy to be alone in a vast, silent, sun-struck swath of the Sonoran Desert. Nothing in this eerie landscape looked familiar; it resembled a pop-up book about the desert that I once bought for my grandchildren.

Would the tiny elf owl peek out from its hole in the saguaro cactus? Would a perfectly camouflaged snake move, shaking its rattlers, terrifying me? Would that lone black cloud, in the next few moments, dump its moisture and bring flowers to bloom? Looking around, suddenly I spotted the dark, proud silhouette of a crow against the sky, perched on a giant saguaro, the tallest in the area. Just like a crow, I mused—he has to be top dog. I froze, as he shifted ninety degrees in my direction. My God, he knew I was here! A deliberate *caw, caw* issued forth, then silence.

I have a fairly deep voice, so it was not hard to reproduce the gravelly sounds that the cawing demanded. With my eyes on him, I chanced it. The bird straightened, arched a little, and squarely faced me. Silence again, followed by another group of caws, this time three. The duet went on.

At first, I saw this as a pretty amazing chance happening, but with growing confidence I fell in with his rhythm of vocalization and silence. Soon it was no longer clear who was mimicking whom. To make sure, I varied my sequence. More often than chance could account for, he finished my phrase. It was unmistakable. We were talking to each other, here, in this empty desert.

Maybe ornithologists have always known the social leanings of crows, but to me the experience was extraordinary. I still recall vividly those moments.

The buzzing of insects, the only sound besides our crazy cawing for close to twenty minutes. Then, suddenly, it was over. He flew away.

Bird-watching had held little appeal for me until I met Marge, a passionate birder. She and her husband Luke, and Ed and I became friends. Among us, Marge, of course, was the one to initiate all sorts of expeditions to search out birds, while Luke was only slightly more informed than Ed and I. For the four of us, birding became the vehicle for walks together—for hikes, even for weekends exploring new birding habitats, new foods. But I could hardly pass for a true "birder." Though I invested in a good pair of binoculars, I had trouble focusing them in synchrony with my glasses. When I looked up, I stumbled; my back hurt; the sun was always in the wrong place; and my experience as a cellist proved inadequate to the task of distinguishing between song sparrow and warbler. Oh, all those warblers! I gave up. Nevertheless, the four of us happily explored woods, fields, rivers, and seashore. Wonderful new terms like "pelagic" had me scrambling for the *Peterson Field Guide*.

In time, however, our outings tapered off, as Marge began taking exotic trips with serious birders led by even more serious world-famous guides, returning with new checks on her Life List. Amateur though I was, I found that I was hooked, for a time, bird guides were my bedtime reading. I also found I had learned more than I'd thought on those hikes. Every now and then, I was rewarded with a successful identification. Once, on a shore in Holland, I knew immediately that I was seeing a skua! The thrill of bird recognition was addictive and the drug was cheap. I realized I was content to satisfy my habit on the ecological microcosm of our woodlot and pond in Groton and my own backyard.

After returning from that magnificent Sonoran Desert, the next time I packed—a few months later—was to move to Richdale Avenue, a place where crows, brash and unafraid, abounded. Longtime inhabitants of our cohousing site, the crows clearly had no intention of giving up a foothold to the newest stewards of the one and a half acres. Unfazed—this was their Gaza Strip—they tormented and buzzed and teased. At lunchtime, a centrifugal gale of noisy activity took place as the crows, watching from the rooftop, descended upon the workmen's lunch remains. These clever thieves waddled awkwardly into paper bags and trash bins, clawing their way through the construction debris.

I began to think about the crows a lot. Even as they appeared to be ignoring us, I felt they were revealing something about themselves: that they, like we, need social connections. They don't fly *from* us. On the contrary, in an enormous ruckus of mysterious origin, they pointedly call attention to themselves. My curiosity about these amazing birds led me to find out more about the Corvidae family. I learned that our common crow was overshadowed by his better-researched cousin, the raven; that the North American branch also included jays and magpies; that Corvids were considered among the smartest of birds; and that crows were reputedly able to associate sounds and symbols with food. In an experimental setting, a crow could count up to three or four, could solve puzzles, and could mimic animal sounds and the human voice.

By day, the marauders circled our area, carrying noisy dialogues among themselves. Most of my neighbors hated the crows; only recently did I discover a soulmate, Ken T., who loves the crows as I do. Where are the young, we wondered together. Who'd ever seen a fledgling crow? Where did they go at night? A timely local newspaper article reported that thousands met at dusk to roost at a shopping center rookery located thirty-five miles to the west, "as the crow flies."

Residents took sides on the subject of the crow. In addition to his offensive, early-morning awakenings, some bird lovers were convinced that—perhaps in the absence of his favorite food, corn—this egg robber was responsible for reducing the songbird population. Stealing eggs I did abhor! They may not be as smart as the well-studied, bashful ravens, but I saw them as pugnaciously determined survivors, much like us, of our tough urban environment.

Recently, I was sitting on my balcony, amused by the clumsy walks of both crows and people. A crow on the roof peak began to caw. He or she— there was no differentiating plumage to distinguish the sexes—seemed equally interested in the wrappings from a Twinkie and some road kill. Suddenly, transported back to the Sonoran Desert, I stifled my self-consciousness, and cawed. The bird cocked its head, as though surprised, hesitated, then cawed again. For a few insanely wonderful minutes, we had exchange after exchange. Our conversation had begun.

"A Perfect Place for Kids"

*Children have never been very good at listening to their
elders, but they have never failed to imitate them.*
—James Baldwin

Children have more need of models than of critics.
—Joseph Joubert

Judith, Timothy, Shelley, Niki, Lydia, Nate, Anna, Justin, Kara, Jina. All born
since those first planning meetings. Would 2001 be the first year Cambridge
Cohousing failed to spawn a child in our six years of being together?

Every year since 1995, the adult cohousing community had become the
collective godparent to one or more infants. A child-favored, child-intense,
infant-adoring culture this was; we took seriously the African wisdom that "it
takes a village to raise a child." We gleefully responded to middle-of-the-night
labor pains and honored the birthing and adoption stories of new parents.
Adults competed for the privilege of walking a colicky baby in the dining room
so that the exhausted mother could have a relaxed dinner. Announcements of
a pregnancy, most likely at a general meeting, were received with hugs, toasts,
and promised loans of stroller, crib, clothes.

But what was happening now? Did community supplant libido? Had
ours reached its procreative best? Maybe the middle-age cohort was tipping
the balance. Along with other grandmothers, I slyly reviewed the house-to-
house roster for signs of a replacement generation: were there to be no more
children?

True, our carefully budgeted square footage didn't encourage much
population growth. As it was, of the ninety-seven residents at the millennial
head count, just about one-third were children under sixteen. This figure
included the several part-time children who regularly visited a parent. The
number escalated abruptly, however, with the inclusion of grandchildren;

these can be a little dazed by this place at first, then take their visiting rights seriously—but what reasonably sociable child wouldn't?

Then, just as the seemingly infertile year was drawing to a close, Ken and Lynn returned from their Fulbright year in Indonesia, the infant Justin of our memory now a determined toddler. His parents were laden with gifts and photos, and bursting with news: Justin was to have a sibling, our first twenty-first century baby.

During those early planning sessions, it seemed to Ed and me that inordinate time was spent searching for strategies to entice young families into our den. If cohousing was such a great way to live, I mused, then why weren't families clamoring to join? The first family to back their commitment to the project with money, Nathan and Dori with four-year-old Barbara and Judith *in utero*, were hailed as the gurus of the modern family. With stinging frankness, they shared their opinions: we weren't child-friendly enough, we weren't low-priced enough, we didn't understand the current demands on young families. In short, we were rich, middle-aged, and white.

"If you really want to attract kids," Dori insisted, "you could signal your seriousness by paying for childcare during meetings, allowing *both* parents to participate without interruptions."

Wow! The proposal smacked of creeping socialism. Yes, I was committed to an age mix, but it would never occur to me to expect others to pay my babysitting expenses. More surprised than opinionated, I thought the idea fell somewhere between bribery and brilliance. (I am surprised to be saying this now; I must be more of a product of group-think than I realized.)

Our eventual decision to allocate specific funds for the collective good was a giant step in community-building. Now that childcare dollars are an accepted budget item—right along with water and sewer fees—it's difficult to recall just how polarizing and emotional the idea once was. Our first serious conflict, as a matter of fact, with a stormy road to consensus.

As I recall, Dori's comment sent up shock waves in the group. For some of us, the very thought had never entered our minds. Share the costs of *other* children's care? A brazen, appalling idea. Even some parents of young children had trouble with this proposal.

But after eloquent words were spoken about the meaning of community, and after a long, heated discussion, we agreed to try it for a year. Now, more than ten years later, never is child care payment mentioned. This is one of many, many ways a group of separate individuals evolves into a community.

Our painfully won "tithing" also accomplished the hoped-for effect: young couples did appear at our early meetings—married, unmarried, same-sex, with children, without children, but all full of hopes. (The latter, knowing that children were a high priority, felt obligated to reveal their family planning programs.) They would check us out, sometimes return, often not. I wondered whether I, in their shoes, would have stayed. The appeal was unmistakably there, but such a life-defining decision it must be. To blend personal family values along with the stresses of parenting into a still-evolving culture would be pretty daunting.

Forty years ago, with three school children between five and ten, Ed and I were having our own differences as parents, daily struggling with issues of authority, discipline, and sibling rivalry. Could I have exposed my feelings of inadequacy then to such an intimate group? Everyone would know what a terrible mother I was. How could I give up the privacy of our own dining room? I wouldn't know how to be sure that the community would believe in and support the values I wanted to convey to my children. The decision must have been a wracking dilemma, one that calls on a degree of courage and trust I'm not sure Ed and I could have mustered.

Thirteen families, fortunately, have found the vision and the dollars to take the plunge along with their born and unborn children. And they all seem more sure of themselves than I ever felt. Thanks to their confidence, they have helped to create a tapestry of Brueghelesque richness. Daily, we benefit from the resulting lively, interactive brew that may be less than family, but more than most kin.

The mix defies categorizing, but a few vignettes about "our" children may help. To me, from my safe distance, they are fortunate children: the better for having parents who tapped the support and resources of the community to undertake the difficult task of parenting. These children are now growing up in an expanded circle of belonging.

We often hear the question, "Are cohousing children different from other kids?" It's the one subject about which I would have liked, from our beginnings, to have planned solid research. Seen from the sidelines, Cambridge Cohousing is not paradise, but there are opportunities for kids at various stages of growth to take advantage of—new friendships, adult models, and activities such as cooking, babysitting, and music. But children still fight; shy ones still withdraw. Some fuss when called in at night and some go through very public tantrums. They also tend to be watchful of one another, to dote on the babies, to join together in imaginative play. And even with gates ajar, I've never seen a child of any age go outside them or into the street. A parent or cohouser always seems handy to referee a skirmish, retrieve a ball from the street, soothe hurt feelings, or return a child to its parent. The children attend almost as many schools as there are kids; one family home-schools its three. Do all these spontaneous social interactions make for better, happier people, as they learn the fundamentals of tolerance and fairness in childhood?

The Pretty Good Lawn

I looked up from my apple crisp to see one, two, now three little girls solemnly emerging from the playroom, each pushing a carefully dressed doll in a miniature baby carriage. In tight single file, the little caravan moved through the crowded dining room, barely skirting the buffet table. Diners parted to let them pass, seemingly agog as the three-year-olds, cooing reassuringly to their babies, marched to their biologic destinies.

A lot of action takes place in the dining room, where thirty-five to forty of us choose to eat dinner together three nights a week. On one particular day, as I entered, I saw four-year-old Ronnie circling the center table, touching each corner as he went round and round at a good clip. Uttering some jargon or other, he appeared obsessed. As I neared, I heard, "Cal, ca, ca … a!" and as he made another circle, "li… f … C-a-l-i-f-o …" and on and on until he figured out how to spell the state. With each labored phoneme, his watchful mother, standing inconspicuously in a corner, proudly and a little nervously, followed her son's agonizing road to mastery. As I approached her, she quietly told me with what excitement he was learning how to decode the language. We marvelled together over the magic of the developing mind.

If we needed a metaphor for the thorny process of group formation throughout a construction project, the Window might be it. Initially uneasy with the idea of their young children being in a room without them, and adamant that toddlers must have visual reassurance that a caretaker was nearby, parents requested an unobstructed two-way view between the dining room and adjoining playroom.

The Window became a test of our child-friendly intents. The architect balked; the builder balked; the Design Committee balked. The wall in question was a firewall, and the building code forbade a window in a firewall. Parents didn't budge.

The reluctant architect returned with institutional solutions such as thick wire-embedded glass. Absolutely not! The Children's Committee bridled at the mere thought of seeing their children through chicken wire and vice versa. What emotional mark would *institutional* glass leave on our children? exclaimed the prickly parents. And on our beautiful dining room? meekly complained the Design Committee. The architect returned with a final suggestion: a German product, a very thick, expensive glass that could withstand extreme high temperatures. With a building variance, it might just do the job. Delivery time: unknown. Cost: twenty-three thousand dollars. Damn the cost, said the elated Children's Committee.

Such intense feelings required resolution, but the embryonic cohousing group was hurtling into other, more ominous concerns. Our manufactured homes were behind schedule, and the discount the company offered had expired, meaning costs would rise—and many future owners were on fixed incomes and modest salaries. Such construction delays, cost overruns, and internal politics can unite homebuilders anywhere, so it was little wonder that, pitted against the bigger question of the project's survival, the Window issue faded.

The Window, fast becoming a symbol of opacity rather than clarity, ushered in other unresolved issues. Periodically we got side-lined, veering down the byways of child development, cost, trust, safety, aesthetics, and the always-hovering fairness. Each age cohort was inclined to feel that another was being favored in these issues.

Now, a decade later, I no longer hear mention of the Window. In this particular case, neither strategy, negotiation, nor consensus resolved the conflict. Time alone took care of the human stalemate: familiarity and growth on the children's part reduced anxiety on the parents'. At common meals, toddlers eat a required bite or two of pasta, always an alternative on the menu, climb down from their high chairs with nary a backward glance at the parent, and head straight for the playroom. A distressed toddler knows just where to find his parent.

Every now and then, screams or a crash prompt a flashing stream of ever-alert parents who head for the playroom to tend to the bedlam. A just-like-home crisis but, in this setting, shared by many. Ears have taken over for eyes. Separation anxiety is real, but chances are it would have never been ameliorated by a window.

Alex at nine, an ardent Red Sox fan, dreams of playing baseball, but he steers away from the loose, raucous game on the lawn, hilariously enjoyed by all ages, not to mention a couple of dogs.

He's quite explicit about the reason. "My leg muscles don't work so well. Soon research will fix this Muscular Dystrophy."

Seemingly indifferent to the gleeful screams from the close-to-football-field-size lawn, he once wanted not one but both of his grandparents to join him in the dining room for the "Game of Life." The cook team was in the kitchen; Marsha was trying to do her part, but four-year-old Victor needed attention. Could he join us? she asked. Of course. Alex explained the board game to him. "Unlike Monopoly," he said, "a player accrues life events rather than real estate; like Monopoly, you might make a lot of money." Victor chose a career path, but when he picked a "Fired" card, he did not want to go the college route. (Later I learned from his mother that going to college to him meant leaving home, a concept for which he was not yet ready.) In the middle of his next turn, in an ordinary voice, he turned to Ed and asked, "How come you got to be so old?" Without missing a beat, Ed responded, "Guess I just want to stay here a long time." They both earned an extra hundred thousand for candor.

In the failed blizzard of 2001, the undisguisedly gleeful weathermen, in their joy at predicting a doozie of a snowstorm, called it wrong. So convincing were they that "No School" announcements started to appear twenty-four hours before the first flake fell. The result: three snow days! Winter vacation barely over, this was a double blow to parents—an emergency made for cohousing. Whereas most mothers' stomachs gird for the stretch, here I noted a momentary flinching, maybe, but then heard such conversational fragments throughout the day as, "T. can come to our house," "C. wants to play dress-up, and there's a whole chest of costumes in the children's playroom," and "Let's play games in front of the fireplace … I've got a lot of cheese but no bread."

By morning, almost twenty children from four to sixteen, with a preponderance between five and eight, had commandeered the common house, with living room cushions piled into a fort. In the foyer, L.'s "train," a pink cotton blanket, dragged behind her as she swished through. Through an open apartment door, I glimpsed four-year-olds in a noisy game of War, one player just now stomping out, on the edge of tears. East End and West End parents were in the kitchen pooling supplies for a lunch of grilled cheese sandwiches. A storm-stranded visiting adult was overseeing a pool game in the Rec Room. No one seemed to be coming unglued … another of the miracles of cohousing.

Midmorning, with a library project in mind, I sauntered to the common area in search of muscle power and set my eyes on a little huddle of thirteen- to fifteen-year-old girls. Dare I break into their world?

I explained: "Books for the library—several shelves of biographies—need to be moved from the fourth to the first floor, labeled, alphabetized, and reshelved. Will you help me?"

Silence. Did I detect fleeting glances of contempt? They dutifully, wordlessly, trudged behind me as we made our way upstairs.

Surrounded by four unresponsive teenagers, facing twenty running feet of books, I reviewed the task with them: stamp each book with "Cambridge Cohousing Library," weed out any duplicates (which means reading the titles), transfer via grocery cart to new shelving on the first floor, and, most challenging of all, alphabetize by subject. I worked alongside them, commenting occasionally—to myself apparently—about a book that I loved, and one I didn't. Suddenly, afraid to look, I sensed they were moving with purpose, that the sulking has ceased. Lenore had set aside a book to borrow, one that I'd referred as good; they were squabbling over a system for stacking. They argued over how to alphabetize; Alice thought she had a better system and defended it loudly. Then Kathy addressed me directly for the first time in our three years of living here.

"Jean," she asked in a pleasant, conversational voice. "Does *Gift from the Sea* go under *G,* or under *L* for Lindbergh?"

Oops! An urban toad!

"Let's Have an Art Show!"

*You can never plan the
future by the past.*
—Edmund Burke

Rising above the din of the dining room, someone's voice proposes, "Let's have an art show!"

Anne responded first. "That's a wonderful idea. How about February?"

Others chimed in.

The idea was quickly echoed by Theda who added, "We can combine it with our cohousing dedication!"

I weakly agreed, seeing Ed's enthusiasm, but, in truth, a shudder ran through me, the artist's wife. That mention of an art show hits the spouse of an artist much like a fourth daughter's engagement announcement strikes her mother: Yes, there's to be a joyful occasion, but after several daughters or several dozen shows, one thing is certain: much work lies ahead.

Ed's photographs, magically enhanced by a powerful computer, were wonderful. They filled #410 with beauty, and spilled over into proud displays in every available niche here. His major concern about the move had been the loss of work space, which had covered the entire third floor of our former house. He's happiest creating entirely unique images from the high-tech palette of the vast cyber realm, using his endless inventiveness. From some deep bond between him and his computer, he could, by scanning a snapshot, or even a tiny section of one, rework it through many iterations of double-clicking and screen-gazing to produce a miracle of color, design, distortion, wit, composition, tension, and balance, rarely with much resemblance to its birth mother.

His work was much admired. Among those who love it, an exhibit came as good news. Outsiders cannot, however, understand the angst that accompanies the mounting of a show. In the first place, there are all those questions hovering in the shadows: Am I ready to exhibit? Will the show have a theme? Will it be juried? What image or style for the invitation will send just the right message? What is the right message? There are the discarded canvases, the failures, the rejected submissions of past shows. So the first phase is about decision-making, a period during which the artist's self-esteem is more fragile than usual.

Then, much like for a wedding, the spate of planning begins: the gallery, the date (expect a blizzard or an overlooked holiday), the invitations to be negotiated with a California printer, the schlepping, the intricacies of hanging, and, last but foremost, the food. That creative finger food looms large for planners. And don't forget the matter of publicity and attracting critics. More weddings are blessed by spiritual advisors than art showings by kindly reviewers—or any reviewers at all.

In coho-lese, all of this experience was BC (before cohousing). Thus, my knee-jerk response to "Let's have an art show!" turned out to be one of those many vestiges of my past that lagged behind our new reality. The planning period, in fact, went something like this.

Anne, as head of IDA (the Interior Decoration and Art Committee), was fairly bursting with agendas: "Why, this will be a wonderful incentive to put the picture molding up that we took out of the construction budget due to cost overruns. I'll ask Miriam and Howard if they will do it. Miriam is very skillful at carpentry. She helps build houses in Roxbury with Habitat for Humanity. The walls of our common spaces beg for art, and the light is quite lovely."

Theda cheerfully offered, "I'll design the invitation. Maybe you'd have time to have it reproduced in Harvard Square, Ed."

Ed and Theda, our two professional artists in the early years, have captured the lion's share of the wall space. All who have ever dabbled in paint, ink, photography are encouraged to show their work. An astonishing variety and level of quality awaits hanging as other residents courageously overcome shyness and submit their works. The exhibit date is put on hold pending Theda's completion of a number of ceramic works in progress, a new direction for her. This is in addition to her full-time job at a local publisher. Other delays arise. I slump in my chair; this doesn't bode well. Is this a way to run a show? IDA neglected to clear the event through the committees that coordinated the calendar and common area use. After all, any of the nearly one hundred people within our forty-one units may have designs on the fifty-five hundred square feet of common space that we jointly own. We're still learning how to share this huge home of ours. In the end, several months elapse before the date is finalized.

To Ed, I groused, "What's an art show without invitations?"

The reception nears but copy for the announcement has yet to be seen. Unbidden, a couple of days later a draft for the invitations appears in our box. Ed rushes off to the all-night copy service to get a proof. I should have caught on then that I could stop worrying. Why, this is going to be a collaboration. No one, but no one, is agonizing over this except me.

But no show is without its glitches. The printer undercolored, overcharged, and misplaced the master. Despite my "I told you so" announced to no one in particular, by the week of the show, stacks of cards promising "tasty snacks" simply appear in the mailroom. A sign encourages us all to "invite your friends." While a bit haphazard, I was forced to admit to myself that this procedure beats the master mailing list Ed and I used to sweat over. But would anyone come?

Meanwhile, back at #410 I rail to Ed: "Exactly who is going to prepare these tasty snacks?" That same day, Theda, in passing, sweetly asks me, "Can you and I fill in food items that other artists don't bring?"

I mumble something, probably "Of course," then grumble to myself and to Ed.

Reception minus two days. On the notice board in the lobby, quietly posted during the night (I should remember that Theda is a night person), a sign-up list appears—cheese, crackers, fruit, dip, paper cups, wine, whatever you want to bring. Halleluiah! It used to take me days making lists, revising menus, shopping, and nursing my aching back.

On the day, early Saturday morning, Howard and Miriam appeared with a ladder and a few assorted tools, ready to inaugurate their newly installed moldings. Without fuss, artists stacked their productions against the wall. The elevator carried Ed's handsomely framed photos to the living room; crating, delivering, packing and unpacking the car are all eliminated. He is spared the usual fretting about scratched glass and bumps in the road. A half hour before the opening, carrying my food contribution, I go downstairs to help set up, dreading that I will find a foodless, guestless space.

As suddenly as the show was conceived, the space has been converted into a quite beautiful art gallery. Platters of food have been dropped off, flowers grace the buffet table. Someone has added a colorful cloth, some silver trays. In a few moments of amiable bustling, arrangements are completed. Sam begins to pour wine as the first guests arrive on schedule. Insiders and outsiders alike come together to admire the work of our twenty-two in-house artists. Three or four trained, professional artists and the rest—including a couple of children—closet painters, water colorists, print makers, etchers and sketchers with surprising abilities, all overcome their shyness to exhibit their—our—works. I submitted a point-and-shoot photo that came out very well although I do not include myself in the talent category. A good party, a good show, even without sales and, alas, without reviews!

A humbling and liberating experience for me. Although I have used the word "interdependence" in explaining cohousing, I am only now beginning to fathom its true meaning. I find I prefer to share rather than shoulder responsibility. Several proverbs, worn but true, spring to mind: many hands make light work, all for one and one for all, no one is an island unto himself. In past years, I often felt alone on that island. But now, the tides of cohousing are filling in a peninsula where once stood lone isles.

Common House art exhibit

Sign Up for Dinner

*We want to share and interact with each other
through social activities, celebrations, and practical
tasks, such as cooking, dining ...*
—Cambridge Cohousing Vision Statement

*... the ritual of communal
dining is the most abominable of Society's abominations.*
—W. G. Sebald, *The Rings of Saturn*

"The pizza man is here!" shrieked several children, spying the delivery man with his insulated carrier at the front gate. "Don't bring me broccoli!"

It was 6:00 PM, Monday; families were arriving promptly with baskets, holding dinnerware and drinks, ready to claim their preferred seats in the common house dining room. Betty and Mike, the meal's coordinators, had arranged the tables; Mike paid for the ten pizzas for which he would be reimbursed in due time. He and Betty had ordered just the right assortment after consulting the computer printout in the pantry: veggie for the vegetarians, cheese-only for the kids, no tomatoes for Curt, no peppers for Anne, pepperoni with everything for the other adults. They arranged the pizza boxes buffet-style and warmed up leftovers from the weekend meal. Those adults long-tired of pizza brought potluck dishes. Their meal would cost less.

Monday dinner can be lush or lean, depending on the potluck contributions, but high spirits are not limited. Neither is noise. Even hearing-impaired residents tend to stay away or else seek out the farthest corner to complain about the acoustics and concoct schemes for reducing the decibel level. In good weather, the kids finish in minutes and rush outside to play.

Monday is also the occasion to honor those with birthdays during the upcoming week. When Shirley or Jaimie or Betty comes through the kitchen door carrying a huge, decorated, icing-rich cake with glowing candles, kids pour back into the dining room from lawn and playroom, eyes wide, lips puckered, poised to blow. No matter whose birthday, they never tire of this ritual.

Pizza Night, another of those building-blocks of cohousing, revived and fueled the ardor of many a wilting task force, committee, and work team throughout the organizing years. Now, ten years into residency, Pizza Take-Out, once the staple of a kitchenless Common House, became institutionalized as the anchor of the weekly meal routine.

Approximately the first year of cohousing, it residents were without a kitchen. Construction-budget overruns took a toll on completion of the common kitchen. Dishwashing equipment was postponed. This intrepid crowd, however, eager to share the good fellowship that only food can galvanize, once again ingeniously adapted to our shifting circumstances. At first, that meant potluck dishes, concocted in our individual kitchens. Men, women, and even children invented contributions: soup was popular, vegetables prepared in delicious variety, beans, beans, beans in every possible form, and treatments of tofu found in no cook book. Satisfying? Mostly, yes, but pressure mounted for a stove of our own. The hat was passed. Then one Saturday, Ned and Marion ventured out, returning with a monstrously heavy, used gas stove, enabling cooking teams and shopping teams and, of course, cleanup teams to be organized.

Today, a meals-finance team periodically creates yards of printouts rivaling the Excel spreadsheets of major corporations. This data is spread out in the mailroom, so residents can check their charges, dinner costs, payments and reimbursements to shoppers, as well as personal food preferences and allergies. (Children under twelve ring in at half the price for a meal that typically costs between three and four dollars.) Then every six weeks, the easel with sign-up sheet appears in the lobby. You fulfill your voluntary meal obligation by signing up to cook or clean three times in this period.

We can now witness the culinary feats that our neighbors have been itching to show off, often dishes of near-restaurant standards. We can choose to dine in style—buffet or family—with wonderful offerings, three nights a week, with on average forty of our neighbors and their guests, who are always welcome, as long as you sign them up by the deadline. Every meal is an event.

Food, glorious food, is for me an enduring passion. To say "glorious," however, ignores the first quarter of my life when, of my many nemeses, food was up there near the top, hardly a source of nurture or comfort. Thrice-daily battles were the norm in my family.

Is it possible not to be able to recall a single standout meal, a comfort food, a holiday favorite? First, you have to understand, my household was ruled by fiat, not choice. One word—"must"—ran our lives. What was put before me and my two siblings was never removed until finished—even long after *rigor mortis* had seemed to claim the messy mounds on our plates. Surreptitiously attempting to dispose of morsels brought consequences, and my father instigated a strict monitoring system to thwart such "flagrant defiance." He was a man who carried control to an extreme, even beyond that prescribed by Dr. John Watkins, the authoritarian psychologist whose pronouncements made many children's lives miserable. Did my parents read that stuff? I'm not sure, but my father would have invented the harsh child-raising regimen of the 1920s and '30s if Watkins hadn't staked out the territory for him.

Two memories emerge from the monotony of childhood meals—a blur of browns and bilious greens, and the gray "mush" of breakfasts. One was my mother's spice cake, made with thick coffee frosting, reserved for birthdays—one of the few items that she did not assign to the maid. Another was the Thursday hamburger feast, the maid's night out, and also Father's, as he went to eat dinner those nights with his austere, humorless German family—his mother, spinster aunt, and bachelor uncle.

This elsewhere gathering of Methuselahs was a high-point of the week for my mother—and for me and my siblings. When we got home from school, the ground beef waited in a bowl, ready to be enhanced. We chopped onions and added ketchup, egg, and the essential Worcestershire sauce. We then salted the mixture heavily and shaped it into patties. I secretly but liberally ate what menus, years later, featured as *steak tartare*.

No force-feeding was required on Thursday nights; my siblings and I even abandoned our fighting. Afterward, with dishes cleared, we readied the dining room table for the weekly games of Old Maid, Authors, and Flinch. Our timing was always excellent: we finished and scored the games and proclaimed the winners precisely as Father's car turned into the driveway.

Fortunately, when Ed and I were married, I left my childhood eating problem behind in St. Louis. Unburdened from a legacy of family recipes, I became a culinary *tabula rasa,* with only the following in my quiver: a copy of *The Joy of Cooking* (its renowned author, Irma Rombauer, was an acquaintance of my mother), a bride's wish to please her new husband, and my newly discovered appetite. The constraints of wartime food-rationing were also a force in the tiny kitchenette alcove in our New Haven studio apartment that was my training ground. A bare-bones cooperative grocery store within walking distance—no coupons, no ads, no leaders—was my sole supplier. It was just the basics for a first-time, part-time cook. And my first menu for guests, for some unretrievable reason, was creamed sweetbreads on toast!

Although my romance with food began with marriage, there was little time to practice the art of cooking. When we did eat, most often, Ed and I met for dinner in the cafeteria of the hospital where he was an intern. Sometimes, I ate alone when Ed's pediatric patients needed him more than I did.

Chemistry of one kind or another preoccupied the rest of our time. In those low-tech days of 1944, Ed dreaded the possibility of hurting tiny babies with needles in order to do the required bloodwork himself in the hospital lab. Similarly, my premed lab courses were not inspiring; I often hurried through the experiments to return to the hands-on chemistry I practiced in my kitchen lab—the the birthplace of my obsession with food.

"You must have *appizza* in New Haven; it was invented here," I was told several times by new acquaintances. Nothing in my Midwestern food experience had prepared me for such a novel, proactive approach to food— food as pleasure, as something to be sought out. Food, as distinct from basic provender? Here was an entirely original way to look at a once-hated chunk of life. So in hindsight, although a series of unfortunate things happened to us in that year in New Haven, I took away a burning interest in anything to do with food.

Finally, I searched New Haven for its *appizza*; I knew only that it was Italian. The road to the built-in brick oven proved to be short, and I gleefully brought the large box to the hospital to share with Ed on his break. Unfortunately, he was delayed by a new admission, so, oh so cleverly, I upended the box, placing it between wall and radiator to keep its contents warm. Several hours later, my precious *appizza*, still warm and redolent with olive oil, had slithered through the flimsy box and onto the floor.

Pizza delivery has improved since 1945 but, even now, at our cohousing Pizza Night, the shrieking children can bring memories of cheese oozing out from under the radiator.

Is my personal food history relevant to my interest in a living arrangement that features common meals? I think it is, just as a lifelong interest in golf will draw aficionados to buy homes ringing a course or artists to populate artists' lofts. Likewise, our cohousing meals have come to represent, I am convinced, an amalgam of resident food histories as well as rationales for joining.

Tamara, a displaced Russian, periodically brings unfamiliar dishes and eagerly awaits to be questioned about their ingredients and origins. Keith, the household head of six hearty eaters (I last counted three grills in his postage-stamp back yard), confidently, efficiently, proceeds with an ethnic dish, maybe an Indian curry. He prefers to work alone, often into the night. He and Jackson are consummate chefs, both sparing nothing in the quality of their ingredients. Dennis's concerns about pollutants include off-gassing from plastic and china plates, so he eats his carefully selected items from glass only. Rose, from a Midwestern farming community, brings the passion and extravagance, generosity and drama of the coloratura soprano she is to her leadership of a cook team. She and I share the memory of a German specialty, fried brain sandwiches. With pleasure, Leo recalls years of cooking in a summer camp. Greg and Dalenna, as faculty and house parents, appreciated the ease and sociability of boarding-school meals, when their children were growing up. Nathan and Dori, from kibbutz to cohousing in a crooked path, have raised the standards of vegetarian food for us and somehow quietly steer their three young children away from tempting meat selections. Paul and Ann Marie work together to reproduce the recipes of several generations.

Two still-warm brownies, a loaf of cranberry bread, or a fabulous dessert simply appear in the #410 kitchen at any hour. (Easy access to each other's units encourages exchanges.) They are from another Anne, the one who keeps Ed supplied with sweets, and the one who expresses a life force by sustaining people through difficult times. It was she who mobilized all those who rallied to feed Ed and me when I returned home after a hip replacement—a touching demonstration of care that is vivid proof of the miracle of this place. Anne, a self-described military brat, always seems to be the first to know when someone is in trouble; she's there to do what she can.

But I surprise myself. In contrast to an earlier self, who daydreamed of opening a soup restaurant, less and less do I see myself as a leader of a cook team. For one thing, there is the heft factor: the amount of energy and muscle calculated to order, shop, lift, carry, wash, peel, and stir for over forty diners is physically daunting. And my visions of no-splurge, no-waste, satisfying soup, bread, and cheese suppers compare feebly with the elaborate spreads that can appear. It may be my fate to remain a perpetual helper, a clipper of interesting recipes, and a small-scale necromancer in my #410 laboratory.

The foundations of cohousing are many—lofty ideals, innovative design in support of social commitments, intergenerational living, some drudgery, a haven for the like-minded. But of all foundations, dare I suggest that the bonds forged around providing provender are among the strongest? Somehow these bonds tap the generosity, the hospitality, the reaching out, the problem solving, the information exchanging, the loaf-by-loaf building of community. A work activity is barely underway before someone brings newly baked cookies or freshly picked apples or a modest bag of chips to the laborers. An "I hate to eat" person is hard to find here.

Does everyone pitch in evenhandedly? Make no mistake, we have not discovered the formula for utopia here. Cohousing is prochoice: you can share in common meals or you can retreat to your own kitchen. In fact, a not-so-covert subtheme of our community might well be dubbed "The Shadow Residents." Resentment can occasionally flare up toward those whose lives rarely intersect with the rest of ours. The mailroom, designed to guarantee that paths cross regularly, is centrally located. Packages for a handful of no-shows pile up for days, then disappear in the quiet hours of the night. Shadows do not paint, compost, or manage the guest rooms. Shadows neither help with meals nor share in the bounty, and they attend meetings rarely. They seem untouched by the muse of common dining. The chopping board and the soup pot are not, for them, the route to community. Their absences are wordlessly noted—by some with annoyance, by others with sadness.

What compelled them to join an intentional community? The cohousing model is flexible—it can wrap inclusively around the many needs and pleasures people have around food, and it can accommodate the minority for whom communal dining is an abomination.

Holiday Dialectic

Dialectic: The contradiction between two conflicting forces …
—The American Heritage Dictionary, 3rd ed.

Caged by tall buildings on both sides, the wind built force as it whistled through the streets. No traffic, no other humans, just the raw cold gusts to break the silence. Ed and I, each with a cane in our right hand, inched along wide sidewalks, wary of the ice slicks that could spell doom. Bent from battling the small gale as well as the bone-ravaging shrinkage of age, we sense the lights of the hotel marquee slowly fading behind us. Leery of offering support to the other, we unconsciously exercise the felt wisdom of survival: if one falls, we all fall. Shouldn't there always be one upright who can aid the other?

Having gauged and put in perspective the environmental hazards, we were now free to recall the evening and the 6:00 holiday sitting. After leaving the scorching warmth of the hotel lobby with its fireplace and maneuvering the several steps to the street, Ed apologetically admitted to disappointment with the dinner. I, agreeing, tried to find a context, one that would not diminish our indulgent but treasured tradition.

"Well, we've done the hotel dining rooms now. I think the mistake is ours for expecting that Christmas dinner would represent their best. Next year it should be Asian."

A long tradition, maybe a couple of decades by now—ever since our last local child loyally started juggling two family festivities—reserving Christmas Eve for family, Ed and I began carving out our own Christmas Day, just as we had in those other BC years—those Before Children. We felt we had hit upon a win-win situation. Our distaste for this *faux* religious holiday had grown over the years, along with my wish to simplify the seasonal swirl: a surfeit of belongings, the shopping-induced backache, the frantic gift-wrapping (although Ed enjoyed that part), and most of all for me, the pervasive "have-

have not" dichotomy forced into a sharp and painful pinnacle by the season's opulence.

Nonbelievers must fashion their own rituals. A leisurely Christmas brunch with empty-nest friends, maybe modest exchanges of books and homemade consumables. The day, then, was ours, to follow our wont: no contest, it was always the same—an afternoon movie! If pressed, I can probably recall half the titles over the past twenty years as well as the encounters with friends, predictably Jewish, in the ticket line seeking their own escape from emptiness. The 1981 movie *Reds* stands out, seen with several visiting children. The quintessential religious-political contradiction: Warren Beatty and Diane Keaton clinging to Christmas in the radical context of the Russian Revolution.

By now, our holiday tradition is well-established, but in the midst of tracking down the perfect movie, we still often ask ourselves if our move to cohousing called for rethinking that old philosophical quandary: was it to be the individual or the group? Was this one of those occasions when our commitment to our new "family" should outweigh personal indulgence? After some soul-searching, the "them-us" scale tipped toward preserving a treasured tradition.

So, forgoing any cohousing festivities and releasing our in-town children to spend guilt-free time with their in-laws, we continued our custom which, along the way, has gained a final feature, a finial to top the constructed day: a fine dinner, just the two of us, with a relaxed review of the holiday season and a wine to match the mood.

We acknowledge, however, to being very slow learners, with memories that fail to serve us from one year to the next. Said another way, shouldn't we have figured out by now that fine restraurants close down tightly on this most sacred of holidays? Are not hotel dining rooms, required as they are by law to remain open to accommodate the public, a poor second anyway? And are not reservations, while requested, seldom honored? (One year, turned away, we went home for the perfect omelet.) This particular year, the small so-called European-style hotel, the seemingly perfect choice, offered three sittings, a glossy menu with three *prix fixe* dinners, and no substitutes.

"Did you have in mind a light supper, dear?" Ed asked puckishly, as course after rich course was plunked down before us.

A long digression to explain why, after a late Christmas dinner, we were being shoved along deserted sidewalks by strong winds toward what, on any other night, would be a coveted on-street parking spot. But wait, what was that ahead on the sidewalk? Could tomorrow be a trash collection day, I pondered? (Ed later told me that, for a moment, the sight apparently gave him similar pause, making him fear that he had neglected to organize the trash detail back at cohousing.) Blue and white mounds, neatly composed on an oversize grate, rested near the curb.

Together, we wrestled the wind, slowed to a halt, and with a single gasp, in the habit of long-married couples, knew without words what lay at our feet. Something moved, and the worn toe of a boot appeared from under a bedsheet, scraping the sidewalk. Three interlocking mounds, each carefully wrapped, one white sheet, two pale blue, slightly rising and falling, each front-to-rear, heads-to-center, forming a curving, warming circle, fitting together as neatly as an Escher drawing, under the streetlight.

"Better Safe than Sorry"

When you are forty, half of you belongs to the past ...
And when you are seventy, nearly all of you.
—Jean Anouilh

My finger pauses, midair, over the "9." Did I really want to set in motion an irreversible force? Why, this could be one of those decisions—maybe my last—still within my control.

"A decision unmade is a life unchanged," "A toss of the dice from which there is no retreat" and other homemade aphorisms of choice, of dilemma, of delay and death, kept spilling out of my mind, unbidden. Hastily, I returned the phone to its cradle. On a scale of one to ten—ah, yes, that pain scale, almost as important to the healthcare industry as my Medicare number—this pain was maybe a mere four, hardly of a strength to unleash the city's rescue operations. On the other hand, the on-call doctor's words nagged at me. By his words and coldly final tone, he had signalled the end of our conversation.

"We're not going to resolve this on the phone," he'd said. "Better be safe than sorry. Just call 911." In the coming hours, this was a refrain I would hear from a choir of healthcare workers. But was he being—he didn't know me—perhaps just a tiny bit too cavalier? Still, his words, like the pain, echoed through me.

My distraught husband and wonderful friend from the apartment below—how reassuring it was to have Anne here—hovered around the bed, brows furrowed.

"Should I?" I looked at them. "Do you think I should call? This really seems ridiculous."

They asked me once more to describe the first chest pains, now half an hour old. Their worried expressions triggered my scoffing and a spate of lame jokes. This really couldn't be serious! I couldn't disrupt my neighbors yet again, unsettling them on their way to bed, calling attention to myself for a false alarm. I recalled those excruciating hip dislocations, no question then, but

135

that's what people would assume and remember. How many alarms—there must be a lifetime emergency quota—can a person send out before attention is no longer paid, before you're relegated to the dustbin? I refused to be perceived as an invalid.

The safe-rather-than-sorry blandishment finally won out. 9-1-1. So easy to dial, so impossible to retract. On the other end, a male voice of mellow baritone authority, less directive than the doctor but firm nonetheless, asked, "Where are you calling from? And your age, Jean?"

"What's the difference?" I jauntily shot back. "Chest pains are chest pains!"

I recognized the calm information-gathering technique and was immediately regretful, visualizing the checklist in front of him. High blood pressure? Family cardiac history? Age? I could see his risk assessment rising with my response to each question; I was falling squarely into the "silent heart attack" profile for women over seventy. At least I wasn't sweating and he couldn't tick off diabetes on his list.

I reassured him in my strongest voice, "I'm sure this isn't a heart attack. Please tell the ambulance not to put on its sirens." And then, did I really hear myself say, "It's out of character for me to have a heart attack"? It dawned on me that he politely cared not a fig for my self-diagnosis, my wit, my reasonableness. Why, he was likely translating my sassiness as fear.

"No, no," he said. "Don't hang up, just talk to me a little." In the midst of this conversation, three very large men, suited up in their fire gear, stiff-legged in their padded clothes, waddled around the bed. The leader—Could he truly be?—was a red-faced, chubby youth who, with grim urgency, fired more questions at me. Was there sweating? Arm pains? A previous heart attack? My chuckles increased with the pace of his staccato questions. I couldn't help enjoying the high drama, but, really, those giggles—were they coming from me?

"I'm really all right, but let's just go and check it out at the ER."

They had a different plan, it seemed. More uniformed moonwalkers arrived, filling the apartment. A party! A team of two came forward, a man and a woman. She knelt by the bed, introducing herself as Gigi. All seemed to listen to Gigi who, with a sympathetic smile, heard her patient's protests while deftly inserting an IV in her arm, quietly placing tubes for oxygen in her nose. Gigi's EMT partner displayed for all to see "the new nitro-spray—it looks like a bottle of nail polish." Then Gigi, the soul of competence, the picture of compassion, took a history, sent the patient's husband to the bathroom for a list of medications, started the saline drip, explained the three-tiered rapid-response system, and, with a wave, dismissed the firemen.

She had wrapped me up; I was now resigned and cooperative. She transferred me to a chair for removal to the ambulance, and not for a moment did she lose her dimpled smile.

Wheeled out of #410 into the lobby, I see Anne talking with somber residents, scared by the trappings of crisis as their imprisoned neighbor is carried to the elevator. Unlike the other emergencies, this time, I was grinning, attempting a good-bye wave with a free foot. I saw my floormates' faces as caricatures of tragedy and was determined to make this departure a distinct improvement over those others when I was strapped to a stretcher, writhing in pain on a scale of … way off the chart.

"What kind of housing is that where you live?" Gigi asked in the ambulance, en route to the hospital, then continued quietly to minister to her patient. "Do you smoke? On any drugs? Alcohol?"

Just like two women anywhere in an animated conversation over lunch, we jointly pursued parallel themes in the two-mile run to the hospital, medical facts intermingling with the subject of cohousing.

"We take care of each other," I told her, explaining how we were a little community of friends and neighbors with much diversity—in age, ethnicity, economics.

"And gays and lesbians?" she chimed in, as though she knew the answer.

"Oh, yes—and parents of gays and lesbians, all sharing some meals, some activities."

"I live in Sudbury with my partner and our dogs!" she responded. A shared laugh, a jostling over winter's potholes, and delivery to the hospital's emergency entrance followed. Ed joined us from his seat next to the driver.

Later, when I told him where Gigi got her adorable pixie cut, he lamented, "How do you learn so much? The driver and I didn't exchange ten words."

The ER, strangely empty, provided a background of soothing chatter, occasionally punctuated by outbursts of staff laughter. No urgency here, just a relaxed efficiency that matched "the pain will get better" mood. Blood drawing, EKG, chest x-ray, leads, cords and monitors all continued as the staff proceeds to rule a heart attack either in or out.

Ed and I had both spoken by phone to our intown daughter, who already had been alerted by Anne's call. "Go back to sleep. There's nothing to do now."

"Good, you've finished your testing for now," I finally said to the medical resident, and gathered my things to go home, where I belonged.

"Your husband can safely leave, but we'll be keeping you overnight," he replied. "All the results aren't in yet. There's no bed on the cardiac floor for a few hours; they will have to transfer a patient." I was a captive to caution. But yes, I knew, safe was better.

I glanced at my chart, which had been casually left open on the gurney. It read, "?Myocardial Infarction." That meant heart attack! I focused my full attention on the question mark.

Beeps, whistles, even a code call, provided a shield for solitary reflection. Stunned by the coldly clinical diagnosis in vivid black letters, I uttered the words to myself but only faintly comprehended. Alone, anchored to the gurney by taut lines, I viewed the ceiling, pockmarked with high-tech blemishes. My life was suddenly as unstable as the current Dow Jones Average. Mostly mimicking the Dow's upward trend of recent years, it has registered a few blips, of course, but now, with little warning, both plotted lines were dropping off. And into what? Illness, disability, dependency, recession?

Was this to be my future, I wondered, writ large on this ceiling? Was this that single moment when the sum of all life's parts, furiously juggled until now, crashed into permanence? Did hope freeze with this actuarial finality? How would Ed manage a night alone or a life alone? I simply could not die if he were to be left alone in that big house! Once more, I congratulated myself on moving us to cohousing in time ... oh, tomorrow's schedule! Who will pick up Alex at school? Am I to be deprived forever of one of the week's pleasures? Why, oh, why didn't I destroy those old journals? They were meant for no one's eyes ... certainly not the children's! What was I doing to my children! Their lives were so full, so encumbered these days, they really couldn't fit in a mother-crisis besides.

I smiled to myself, realizing how silly I was being. Then overcome by a sudden lassitude, I rolled over. Somehow, everyone would manage. Tomorrow, my return to Richdale Avenue would blot out the suspense from all those solemn faces.

Celebrating Diversity: Three Disputes

The worst sin towards our fellow
creatures is not to hate them, but to
be indifferent to them; that's the
essence of inhumanity.
—G. B. Shaw

From my fourth-floor bedroom window, the one that looks out to the west, I have a good view of the back of the tennis backboard. It parallels the railroad tracks across from cohousing. My windowsill, which holds an indoor/outdoor thermometer, a humidistat, and a pair of binoculars, serves as weather station and bird observatory. The American flag in the park across the tracks—flapping, straight out, or limp—is our crude but adequate measure of wind velocity. From a comfortable chair I can follow the yearly cycle of the community garden plots, watch the dog walkers, and observe every contorted tennis form the human body is capable of assuming.

The backboard, painted a milk-chocolate brown, a hundred and fifty feet down the tracks, is part of my early morning scanning ritual, as soon as the light hits it. This particular morning, awakened earlier than usual by the *thwomp* of tennis die-hards at play, I took my stand at the window. Immediately I noticed the yellows, whites, and greens of newly minted graffiti. With my morning revelation, I shouted to Ed, "The graffiti artists were here last night!"

Before the day was over, when the light was just right, after having earlier alerted Leah, Ed took his camera to her second-floor window and photographed the latest in his growing graffiti series. Leah, Ed, Ellen, Riva, I, and a few others passed around the word, as though we'd had spring bird sightings.

And just as magically as it appeared in a morning, could it rapidly disappear within hours, certainly within a few days. A city crew would appear, unload cans that looked suspiciously like paint from its orange truck, and, in minutes, ready the canvas for more surreal doodling.

For a couple of years, the mystery persisted, the familiar cycle of creation and obliteration continuing. The graffiti artists were never spotted—by day or night—although Ed and I looked carefully when our aging bladders got us up at all hours. I was certain, however, that the values shared by our group supported these rough attempts either to beautify the environment or to harmlessly thumb noses at authority. My eventual lesson: you must never imagine you are privy to the values and beliefs of others.

Assumptions can take us down questionable roads. I learned that while Ed and I were giving the indulgent nod to urban art forms, planners and developers were heralding graffiti as a sign and forerunner of neighborhood deterioration, and that citizens were passionately polarized on the subject. Did that explain the city's uncharacteristically rapid response? Was the public works department keeping close track of the backboard's desecrated surface? Or, if not, since when had Cambridge become so efficient, so focused?

Then one day I overheard a chance remark: George had asked the Design Committee for permission to put up fencing on his first-floor back porch.

This is when I learned that not everyone was in sympathy with the drawings or would agree that they should be recognized either as art or urban phenomenon. It seemed that other watchful but less-tolerant eyes had also been tracking the backboard's images.

"Does the noise of the train bother him?" I ask, naively. "A fence won't help much. What does he need to screen out?"

"He doesn't like to look at the graffiti" was the reply. "He considers it a blotch on the landscape and a sign of urban decay."

Graffiti across RR tracks

A few fresh-air mavericks of our community—in league with my grandmother's generation, I do believe—had, from the very beginning, held one wish—to have clotheslines! In advocating for these natural clothes dryers, they promised fellow residents that nothing smelled better than sheets dried in the wind and sun. Most members smiled patiently and moved on to other topics as soon as politely possible. But the "taste police," as the Design Committee was sometimes dubbed, reacted with horror.

"No, no!" we exclaim in unison. "This is not a crash pad, a slum. Why, we'd look like a tenement!"

Being a no-frills launderer myself, who celebrated the advent of the clothes dryer, I thought the feminist movement had buried this labor-intensive housekeeping practice for good. Nevertheless, an environmentalist corps of women with strong backs was asking to be heard. In the midst of larger decisions, the clothesline lobbyists withdrew, biding their time, only to rise again each season to search the glade, the roof, wherever a clothesline might be hung. No resolution to this dispute was in sight.

Around year seven or eight, however, new and more vociferous owners joined the community and, supported by renewed threats of global warming, became clothesline advocates. Jokes, giggles, and even a few tears emerged over the issue, but only partially diverted the force of the campaign. Finally, at a general meeting, we agreed on a trial period. The major objection was an esthetic one; any suggestion for a site was someone's view of a little piece of nature, not to be obscured by flapping sheets or drying underwear. But once the first collapsible umbrella line (and collapse it did) was in the ground, it was only a matter of time before it was replaced by a more substantial model, and, not surprisingly, supplemented by a second, even a third clothesline, before the snows came.

The profoundly emotional nature of "The Clothesline Episode" is not fully represented by this account. Only its transition from near tragedy to comedy by a recent skit in the annual No-Talent Show by one of its most ardent fans legitimizes the dispute and places it in the growing collection of family stories.

"You don't strike me as someone who hates trees, Jean. What do you have against them?"

I sighed. To me, a conservationist, a serious tree-lover, and a homeowner who kept a dying pear tree alive and bearing juicy urban Bartletts for fifty years after an arborist pronounced it dead of old age, this stung. I really didn't deserve such a reputation. But how to shake it?

Every time the word "tree" was mentioned now, my mind automatically returned to a decade-old memory. A friend's attempts to entice her elderly, failing mother to enter a retirement community—a very beautiful and peaceful one in the country—were received only with a sarcastic remark: "Now why on earth would I want to sit and stare at trees until I die? I know what they look like. I want to look at people."

As an advocate for trees, I can suggest many spots that need them, but not, please, outside my window or in front of my balcony. I didn't go through this rigorous process only to be *unable* to watch, in my old-old age, our active community frolicking on the lawn and our always entertaining street scene. Decades ago, a housewife named Jane Jacobs figured out that cities depended on observers and pedestrians for security and safety, a service that should be recognized and encouraged. I agreed! But with the proposed tree right outside my window, my views would be obscured by leaves half the year.

One woman, attempting to reassure me during one of our meeting debates on the matter, said, "Oh, but trees grow slowly. By the time they would get to the fourth floor, Jean, you'd be dead!"

Grounds Committee members would plant something, anything, anywhere in their relentless march to accomplish the greening of this land. And they had done a phenomenal job—until now. Grounds has decided the concrete patio could be used more in the summer heat if it were shaded by trees. Probably true. But the "ten stack" (#210, #310, and #410), in fierce unanimity, presented a unified front and would fight to preserve its sightlines.

The Jane Jacobs Club of Richdale Avenue, the community's watchdogs, should not be rendered impotent.

I had never played my red card and hoped trees would not trigger a first-time veto. The feuding was proceeding to the red-card stage, however, when George (the graffiti eliminator, I'm convinced) announced a sizable contribution of money from the sale of his former home and designated the funds to be used "to build and plant a pergola for the patio." A serious donation was, without doubt, a painless way to resolve a conflict, but this was not to be the end of the Battle of the Trees. The punishing economy swept in, obliterating the contribution.

We celebrate diversity here, and as such, we are learning to live in shaky, capricious, ephemeral harmony. Inevitably, along the way, we find some of our differences close to irreconcilable. Could anyone, however, have predicted trees, graffiti, and clotheslines to be among the more contentious?

Common House Laundry Room: no consensus

Ambivalence Resolved

A man builds a fine house; and now
he has a master, and a task for life; he
is to furnish, watch, show it, and keep it
in repair the rest of his life.
—Ralph Waldo Emerson

One doesn't discover new lands without consenting
to lose sight of the shore for a very long time.
—Andre Gide

I fumbled around in the dark car for the garage-door opener. Why wouldn't it stay on the visor?

"Just another of those things that doesn't work around here," I grumbled.

I was returning late from an Equal Exchange board meeting, tired, but why so unexplainably annoyed? The meeting had been tough and long, but ultimately successful. And, like at cohousing, we talked an issue through until there was agreement—but, really, this garage was a disgrace! People's overflow junk—mine, too—was randomly stacked in front of cars. Insulation, blown in during the harsh winter as a bandaid measure to deal with freezing pipes, was bulging like yellowed brains between ceiling joists. I stepped over ridges of salt, dirt, and sand formed by little eddies of water from last week's flood.

How long would these reminders of unrepaired leaks and inadequate heat be a semiconscious burr under the skin? Why did some people's cars stick out more than others'? There was little enough wiggle room in this garage—some day I might just ram an offender! A parking test should be a prerequisite for a condo deed!

With a composure I did not feel, my key on-the-ready, I walked purposefully toward the door, thankful that my assigned parking space was near the building entrance. Until safely in the building, I remained in the grip of that obsessional thought I had never uttered to anyone: what if someone was lurking in the shadows? I planned my every move, even allowing for an escape route. As soon as the lock responded to my key and I heard the comforting click of the self-closing door behind me, my entry ritual dropped away.

Regretting my outburst of disloyalty in the garage, I put my anxiety behind me, recalling how genuinely safe I felt here, so surrounded by caring, thoughtful people. As though to reassure myself and anyone listening, I exclaimed to the walls while waiting for the elevator, "It's all worth it! I love being here. And to have a covered garage is the height of luxury." Never in my half-century in New England had I or my car been so indulged.

No one was in sight, although the basement was lavishly flooded in wasted light. As I entered the elevator, a spill on the floor caught my eye. Now, in a flash, I suspected where my kvetching was coming from. It had been a challenge to tolerate some of the construction, and now, the housekeeping oversights, but I had. I had been able to suspend criticism during the moving-in period—my own chaos times forty-one households, I calculated. In this glow of camaraderie, it seemed best not to notice that some folks bore all the signs of the chronically messy. And ignoring the accumulation of dirt and clutter during the feathering-your-own-nest phase had not been too hard; as long as I could reach some semblance of order by the end of each day in my own flat, I was all right. People lived by different standards, I kept telling myself. But I couldn't fully dismiss caring how the common space looked, and my visual acuity increased whenever friends visited.

"Your house is always so clean and uncluttered," friends used to tell me. I hated the expression "clean and uncluttered." I seemed to hear it not as a compliment but rather as a flaw in my character, perhaps, an affinity for honoring order over unhampered enjoyment of life. I secretly suspected they associated clutter with a free spirit.

But by now I had learned to live with my neatness gene and could enter another's chaos without flinching or judging. At cohousing, I had become pretty adept at dodging the toys underfoot; I could handle magic marker on a wall and mold overtaking the common house refrigerator. My own flat offered refuge, but it was the common spaces, that middle ground between public and private, where the extremes of compulsive order and disarray met and would have to be negotiated and reconciled by us all. Those who found the latter conditions upsetting tended to take responsibility to alter them by bringing them up at meetings. Anne had been one of those, who in describing the kind of place she wanted to bring her friends to, had successfully pursued setting standards for the common areas.

Did I really want everything polished, perfect? I considered my friend's condo on the "right" side of Cambridge, which was always in ship-shape condition; fresh, very fresh flowers in a studied arrangement in the lobby, and no chance of figures crouching in shadows on her gleaming marble floors. Sarah's every request was responded to with alacrity by the twenty-four-hour concierge staff. (I could have, I reminded myself, chosen that life, too.) The landscaping was gorgeous, and it was all accomplished without committees or task forces on a tight budget. But absent was the pleasure of gardening together. The lobby gave off an ever-so-slight protective, watched-over atmosphere. To boot, Sarah, a wonderful cook, could not claim the satisfaction of cooking with others. And although she felt cared for and secure, an important difference for me was the employer-employee power imbalance that existed in that world. The concierge system, aside from its cost, would never have been welcomed in this setting—some residents would rise in rebellion at the mere thought of hiring people to do what we were able to. Here, there were dozens of concierges.

Surely this lack of control over my environment was what triggered my irritability. When I pull into the garage, there is no one to be angry at. In a spit-and-polish place, complaints went straight to management. Fire away, they're employees, they're accountable. But where could I aim my darts in cohousing? Even if I knew whose car was leaking oil, whose child dripped a popsicle in a long sticky trail in and out of the elevator, there was no "somebody" to respond to my complaints. Here, I could confront a perpetrator on the spot if I were tougher. I could send a carefully worded letter to the Managing Board. But a reply could just as well appear as an embarrassing agenda item at the next general meeting: "Okay, Jean, why don't you head up the item titled 'Cleaning Police?'"

Someone would surely suggest surveying residents to determine, on a scale of one to five, incremental standards of cleanliness: did we want our common spaces always to look as if professional cleaners had just left? Did we ourselves clean up crumbs and spills religiously, only a little, or not at all? Who threw away wilted flowers or recycled unclaimed newspapers? Where was that balance between the meticulous and the sloppy, the rigidly sterile and the distressingly casual? Because quantifying cleanliness was impossible, the discussion would then veer away from rules and guidelines and in the direction of "personal responsibility."

We gave this subject short shrift in the planning years. Most cohousing projects, in principle and for economy, do not hire any outside services; instead residents performed the chores. Still, I always felt that the matter was a potent one. In my many discussions with women who were living alone but exploring the idea of shared living, I learned that their reservations about pursuing shared living centered on the knowledge that people had differing housekeeping standards—and they expected those differences to be a major obstacle to harmony.

Yet, continuing my monologue, I still found myself glad to announce—to no one in particular—"This is my home!"

On that note, however, I had noticed, with surprise on occasion, that others, even strangers, felt quite free to make it theirs, too. I was sure that the U.S. Postal Service and UPS plotted their routes to make timely use of cohousing's conveniently placed lavatory near the mailroom. And though visitors felt welcome, as was hoped, families of visiting children felt welcome, too, and quite comfortable about invading the living room and Rec Room. It felt decidedly odd to find strangers ensconced in "my" library. Even odder was that, for a fleeting moment, I became the intruder, the owner unable to confront the unfamiliar face. How to create a hospitable atmosphere and also set limits on intrusion—that was still to be learned. Was it possible that the residents' haziness about this new form of living left a newcomer with an equally unclear sense of the rules of behavior?

My mind ran to the distant past, to my parents' home. An unfamiliar person would never have been allowed through the entrance of that gated community. Dinky, the genial nightwatchman who always gave my dates the once-over, discouraged prowlers and diplomatically steered any reeling teenagers in the direction of home. Dinky knew all the players, from bank presidents to maids and gardeners. Strangers were carefully vetted, no trash littered the wide curving roads of the posh development. Had I forgotten my dreams of a more friendly, more egalitarian, less suspicious and less fearful world?

Once, during a meeting, when the group of coho residents was bravely tackling the prickly subject of finding a comfortable way to live together, Howard offered this metaphor: "Many different people dance on the stage of our community. We learn to dance with all of them."

Sitting there, listening to Howard, the warm cozy high of that sense of *belonging* rushed through my body: this was a privilege, an extraordinary opportunity to find oneself in. To be able to talk frankly about differences, to hear oneself and others moderate a view or confront a bias or rankling opinion, is a rare occurrence. Oh, I hold no brief for changing the world a village at a time, but to me, it is ceaselessly amazing that the workings of community have a berth anywhere at all—not in a faith-based setting or a political caucus but in a secular, intentional home—it gives me shivers again just writing about it.

Although not frequent, dancing is an activity favored here. One dance that stands out was that of a mother-daughter sixtieth-thirtieth birthday party. The hostesses issued the same invitations to all of cohousing as they did to friends from other parts of their lives.

The dining room was cleared of furniture, opulent food came in the familiar platters and bowls, strobes and candles were added as lights were dimmed, a well-briefed DJ arrived. Families with kids came first, the littlest children scuttling in like puppies amongst the mass of feet. Adults, arriving in good time, did not as quickly make the transition from proper buttoned-up behavior to elemental physicality as the children. This is why we have dress-up clothes and anticipation—they are aids in the transition from dailiness to specialness. The rituals of sampling others' food, laughing with coresidents about a recent glitch in the trash procedure, taking on an auxiliary host role to welcome a solitary stranger, and, of course, having a drink, also all help adults to strike a party mood. Kids, on the other hand, toss over their barely acquired socialization, reacting to the stimuli of food, fire, darkness, and floor-shaking rhythm. And thus the party begins.

I am not a dancer. Ed and Anne subscribe to Boston's small but discriminating modern dance audience. On those nights when they are gone, I stay home and write. At the birthday party, Ed and I dared to try a timid fox trot when we heard "our" '30s and '40s music, but then returned to the sidelines to observe the generation gap play out. Our generation *talked*—we rarely danced—and we preferred Beethoven to The Beatles.

Regardless, I loved to watch my neighbors turn into different people, divorced from their mailroom and lobby personalities. I regretted that chasm that made me unable to kick, squat, shake, wiggle, bend, thrust, twist, hop, glide, and slide, but sadly accepted the fact that I would never dance like they did. I still had confidence that an Alvin Ailey, a Mark Morris, or some master choreographer in the sky had a bigger scheme in mind that included both dancers and observers together.

Departures and Arrivals:
The Second Cohousing Generation

Always an uneasy balance:
the group or the individual
—Unknown

By June of 2000, we reached a kind of stability in our relationship to the wider neighborhood. You might say each party, on its own side of the street, had drawn the neighborhood's measure and concluded, unconsciously perhaps, that the potential for significant interaction was limited. Except for occasional visits and conversations, beyond polite nods of greeting, we had few exchanges—as in many neighborhoods. For the most part, we cohousing residents had retreated to the increasing richness of our community life with its growing variety of activities, and some—the writers, the artists, the entrepreneuers—even returned to our own individual pursuits.

We certainly weren't at the block-party stage yet. (After all, Ed and I had lived on our old street thirty-five years before a friend and I arranged the first block party. And though at our new address, after about eight years, cohousing did organize a very successful one, subsidized by the police department, we weren't there yet.)

One event, however, did persuade me that these boundaries are loosely drawn and that hope is still very much alive. A cohousing resident received a call from the police, who had her bike in their custody. Its theft from behind our gate, they reported, had been spotted by a woman in an apartment across the street from us. Not only that, but the woman recognized the thief—a neighbor kid—and was prepared to identify him.

I wondered whether, earlier in our time here, her loyalty would have allowed her to come forward, whether, by now, she had just found enough redeeming features in her new neighbors to be willing to help us.

Following muffled reports of discontent, Roger and Clea, along with their daughters Jina, age five, and Lydia, age two—both cohousing babies—announced their plans to depart for new work and the novelty of a single-family house across the state. They were admired contributors to the formation of this place. Roger headed our first Managing Board. Clea helped create the Children's Committee and arranged for the childcare that freed parents to attend Sunday cohousing meetings. Both brought strong opinions, expressed with humor and gusto, to our meetings. We all followed Clea's pregnancies, provided impromptu audiences for Jina's developing dramatic talents, and celebrated the launching of Roger's second book.

So their news was met by gasps, followed by the silence of disbelief. On everyone's mind was: Can our embryonic group survive this departure? Not only were the adults involved in the community, but their children had a place, too. And then the inevitable question: Is a job change the only explantion, the real reason, for their departure? As mentioned, there had been some rumblings: overwork, stress over community responsibility, burnout, personal grievances, all mixed with yearnings for a quieter, rural life.

Watching children grow from birth places a claim on hearts, however. The bonds to Roger and Clea's children were strong for a host of surrogate grandparents, who often vyed to hold the baby at dinner while Clea enjoyed her meal. But we bowed to the inevitable, and the farewell ritual began—intimate, official gatherings, as there had been for the Wongs a year earlier. (They, our first "defectors," had heeded a career call across the country. Several families here stay in touch with them; the latest report is that Bill, a medical officer, just received orders to leave for Iraq with an advance hospital unit. I wonder if Cai Yi and Erin ever think nostalgically about cohousing as a place to wait out their personal upheaval.)

We are not a transient community. Moving vans do not come and go without note. Because the American culture is often so indifferent to such comings and goings, however, the contrast of these departures is the greater for us in cohousing. If community means a place where individuals are accorded respect and attention, and will be missed after they're gone, then we have succeeded in creating one. Themes of loss, however, must precede those of renewal. Pillars of the community leaving! Could the fledglings survive without the parents?

Goodbyes and Hellos

The departures raised questions still unresolved in our then brief history. Our self-selected community was built on commitment to values rarely found in the marketplace. Look how hard it was for us to find one another.

Some, even then anticipating the inevitable turnover, spent many hours concerned about the preservation of those values. For example, in the earliest days, people got pretty tired of my advocacy for organizing ourselves as a cooperative rather than as a condominium association. The way I understood it, was that a cooperative could offer certain advantages to a group like ours. One is that its board would decide on new residents—rather than the market value or purhase price. "We would," I argued, "have a crack at maintaining our hard-won diversity by reducing our vulnerability in the (already in 1998) rising real estate market and maintaining some control over the resident composition." From our waiting list of largely single, older women, we could have rapidly filled any vacancies, but why, when so far we had worked so hard to resist the pressure to build a retirement community! A quick scan of our decision-making process at that time, however, clearly indicated there was no hope of arriving at the consensus necessary to create a cooperative entity. In fairness, there were other formidable obstacles to creating a coop structure. So we would go the conventional condominium route.

To give some support to our strong value of attracting like-minded families as residents, we wrote into our bylaws that Cambridge Cohousing had a thirty-day right of first refusal. During this period the condo association or an individual member could choose to purchase the unit and hold it until an interested family from our own network came along. *Could* is the key word here; could, but it has never happened. Instead, our efforts went toward building a revenue stream for an affordability fund. Brent recommended what he called a "transfer fee" to discourage windfall profit-taking, on the one hand, and to return money to the community, on the other hand. A fee would amount to a diminishing percentage of the sale price of a unit, a figure based on length of residency. I was disappointed that our members rejected even such a token attempt to approach equity-fairness and affordability. If there were to be financial profits, young families, buffeted by uncertain career futures and potentially costly housing locations, were not willing to sacrifice *any* gains.

As it turned out, this edge property that we occupied, one that had been so disdained only a short time ago, had begun to soar in value even before we moved in. I concluded that while we may have talked and behaved like a cooperative, it seemed we only did so until the time came to cash out.

For Ed and me, however, and for others who intended to live here permanently, the intangible values and the developing traditions and beliefs of cohousing held priority over property values. The issue boiled down to how to preserve the hard-wrought values—both financial and social—of a still neophyte community when key people left. Even now, these values are fragile, easily wiped out by departures; preserving them is a hotly debated challenge for all intentional communities and, to my knowledge, solved by none.

The result: if our little village was to continue long enough to validate its vision, it appeared we would have to depend upon the open market for new members. How, I wondered, would a prospective off-the-street buyer view our open design, our toy-strewn central entrance, and our lobby with homemade covers on floppy cushions? Would our message boards noting "Water turnoff next Tuesday," "Tomatoes ripe for picking," and "Please, *please* sign up for lawn watering" push them off into flight? How did our five thousand square feet of common space fit a buyer's fantasies of a vintage Victorian house on a quiet street? Could a buyer accustomed to a monthly utility bill visualize a single electric meter for forty-one households?

Imagine a family fresh from a bewildering tour of stunning, expensive condos, each privately oriented to obscure the neighbor's view, with fireplaces and European kitchen applicances. Would they grasp a design—explained by a sales-driven realtor—meant to encourage group interactions, not to reduce them? Would they grasp the basement garage, a longish walk from the available unit and not adjoining it? Would they grasp the downstairs laundry room, shared by seventeen households?

"Whatever happened to the American dream?" exclaimed one potential head of household to the real estate broker, as an errant child on a Razor scooter came a shade too close to him for comfort. "In-house washer-dryers aren't sacred anymore?"

The energetic people, the scattered toys, the improvisational landscaping. The cheery voices and cooking odors emanating from the common kitchen. What would buyers make of it all?

"Maybe it's an ashram," they'd think. "An urban cult."

Any buyer would have to be drawn to an atmosphere of controlled chaos and have a chemical make-up that included a few wacky genes not to turn tail and run for the nearest building with a nice, impersonal concierge. But, I was glad to say, based on our early history of several sales, that my concerns were baseless.

After the Wongs left, Francis and Martha, spilling over with enthusiasm, childless but hopeful, found us through a cohousing lead and attended several meetings, asking questions and eventually seeking—imagine!—our *approval* to purchase the unit at a huge mark-up. They knew about the flaws in the heating system, about our funky wiring, about the list of other projects that had to be postponed for lack of funds.

Once they joined, they volunteered for everything, introduced Ukranian food in great quantities to common dinners, and initiated a poetry-reading series.

Next, Leah and Al, also through word-of-mouth, with four children, *chose us.*

Everyone knows that the dynamics of a group change in unpredictable ways when members enter or leave. Still mourning Clea and Roger and Jina and Lydia, seeing little of Al and Leah and their kids in those first few days was a positive and a great relief.

"Hey, they seem nice, but let's let them get settled before we overwhelm them," some would say. Or, "Four children, for a net gain of two," the counters would point out. "That's a lot of adjusting."

But the astute balcony watchers were in for a surprise. Before the new family had fully unpacked, it had mobilized the cohousing children, and some in the neighborhood, in cooperative play.

We nodded approvingly from our several perches. "Wonderful!" I heard someone say later. "It takes kids to break the ice."

Long before Al and Leah came here, I had been watching "that boy" across the street, whose name I later learned to be Richie. Maybe nine or ten, he had spent August bored and restless, hanging over and walking on the railings of his front porch. Between arguments with an older girl, probaby his sister, his attention was always glued on our lively kid-filled cohousing scene. Now, clearly itching to join Al's children, I imagined that Richie was plotting his strategy from his stoop. He soon ventured as far as our picket fence, watching pleadingly as Al tossed multiple frisbees to his kids, Dolf and Emma. When the hoped-for invitation did come, he leaped over the fence to join the game until dark.

The next day, Richie bravely entered our gate and politely knocked at Al's door, asking to play. Thereafter, his growing success was not tempered by restraint. Quite the opposite, in his eagerness to belong, he mismanaged his next entry. The temptation to share his celebrity with others in the neighborhood, whom he likely barely knew, overcame him. Soon, urged on by their new Pied Piper, unfamiliar kids, prisoners of summer and hungry for new playmates, piled out of entryways.

"Come on, bring your sister, too," Richie said, no longer waiting for the gatekeepers, Dolf and Emma. Yearning to explore our "attractive nuisance," strange kids swarmed over the place. They invaded the lobby; they discovered our Rec Room. Al came home in the evening to crowds of children hoping for a frisbee free-for-all. The balcony folks could now be heard to utter a strangely familiar theme, "Whose house is this, anyway?"

It was a genuinely thrilling moment to watch our newest resident, Al, armed with several frisbees, channel the energies of more than a dozen kids from the ages of two years to late teens. Not so thrilling to witness that, as darkness descended, cohousing children were called indoors, but no parents crossed the street to claim our visitors.

The next day, they were back in force; but without Al to orchestrate the performance, things got a little ragged. In a tone of both amusement and concern, Anne asked George to add the "invasion" to the agenda for the next general meeting.

How else was a sympathetic community to respond? Hooked by our own utopian language about goals of diversity, we had wordsmithed our way into this dilemma.

Well-intentioned adults can learn, however. The discussion that followed at the general meeting was reasoned and compassionate; no longer did we have to wrestle *ad nauseum* with fifty social consciences before deciding on a course of action. The group's willingness to talk it out, to hear one another's fears and anxieties, resulted in greater cohesiveness, and we rapidly arrived at an agreement that reflected the group's level of comfort that was recorded into the minutes.

The protocol at cohousing is similar to that of any household; one does not enter without an invitation. Invited guests are welcome; they are the responsibility of their hosts. Children should discuss with their parents before inviting guests. Parents are expected to monitor both guests and hosts.

Al was smilingly sheepish when he apologized for what he called "my naive, open-handed embrace of the kids. They began to overrun our house, too."

Then one day, not long after that meeting, I was startled to realize I hadn't seen Richie—not even across the street from my balcony.

"Oh, he moved away," I learned in response to my inquiries. "New tenants have moved in." How could I have missed that?

Wherever Richie is now, whatever fence he is plotting to scale for social gain, he deserves credit for having left us with the raw material for dealing with these nettlesome boundary issues.

Double Creme, Triple Trouble

Cheese—milk's leap toward immortality
—Clifton Fadiman

"You and Ed don't come to Pizza Night anymore, do you?" Velma queried me in the elevator.

"Not often," I agreed. "We're trying to eat less—this place is putting the pounds on us and we're weak-willed. Neither of us can resist pizza." A simple enough exchange, but it set in motion an internal monologue as unstoppable as my recent avoidance relationship with food.

I knew very few people who shared my particular preoccupation; in fact, only one. Douglas, an old friend, and I discovered that we each woke up in the morning with the day's food options piercing the fuzziness of sleep. Before putting a foot on the floor, we planned dinner—not from cookbooks but from our memory of the refrigerator's leftovers. Doug's special absorption was shopping; mine, cheese.

Cheese, glorious cheese. Soul food, link to the past, curds of infancy. From peasant formula once *affinaged* (another of the new words I've learned lately—it means ripened) in bacteria-filled barns to a savory for kings. Once baby's first finger food, now still finger food—a hostess's status symbol. I can still call up many of the benchmarks of my romance with cheese. For every phase of my life lurks a cheese memory.

I recall sometime around age seven pleading for permission to take to the streets on my new two-wheeler to pick up cheese at Wydown Market. You see, at 7:30 every morning, including Saturday, my mother telephoned her day's grocery order into Wydown, to be delivered before lunch. That day, they had neglected to bring my most coveted item. As I pedaled home from the market, feeling very grownup, visions of the long cobwebby strands of melted "rat" cheese, in all its velvety orange allure, whet my appetite in anticipation of the prize: the perfect grilled cheese sandwich.

Ordinarily a picky eater, I was also very penurious with my twenty-five-cent weekly allowance. Maybe I was around ten when I circled the local dime store, deciding whether I could really afford to lay out twenty cents for a variation on the theme: a sublime cream cheese and olive sandwich at the soda fountain at Kresge's five-and-dime.

As I grew older, my repertoire expanded to include stronger cheeses. Still vivid is my midnight craving when pregnant for an intolerably fragrant Roquefort. Poor Ed. He always wished for a normal wife with whom he could share ice cream or peanut butter.

My father loomed large in my search to understand this passion bordering on addiction. Alas, he fueled much turmoil in our household with dramatic tales of his exalted role in the business world and his far, far to the right political lectures, which he reserved for the dinner table. In his nightly histrionics, he produced at least one off-color Depression-era joke about Eleanor Roosevelt.

But in the arena of food, my father set high standards, which I happily internalized: a preference for strong, sinus-clearing odors, stomach-churning tastes, plenty of salt. Pickles, herring, and dark, dense breads and cheeses. Liederkranz! Limburger! The rottener the better. It was a nostalgic German's delight.

On a recent tour of a Vermont cheese factory, the connection between cheese and salt became abundantly clear. After the curdling stage and before fermentation, when the whey had been drained off, salt, in shocking volume, was literally shoveled into the vats, and then mixed and stirred with a huge wooden rake. Recalling now my father's salt dependency, I wondered whether it had any place in my fondness for cheese.

My nine-year-old grandson had refined his salt habit to an exquisite extreme: he now simply dispensed with the cheese he always loved and rapturously consumed coarse, gray, hand-harvested French sea salt directly from his hand. His salt craving comes from both sides of the family—a sure-to-please gift for his father is yet another shaker of exotic salt.

Of further interest to me is that my father, I, my son and son-in-law, and their sons, all know the agony of the migraine headache. Lately, medical inroads have diluted many of life's simple pleasures; once a highly recommended food, cheese has taken an especially hard beating. Increasingly, however, studies name high salt intake a culprit in fat acquisition, high cholesterol, high blood pressure, and very possibly, migraines.

The deliciously creamy Saint André now carried for me, double its butterfat weight in emotional conflict, a burden that lingered far beyond its heavenly taste on my tongue. As such, I'd rather spurn the research findings and imagine that cheese is a socially acceptable vehicle for what the body needs. Like the menthol that makers of Kool cigarettes long ago introduced to hide their deadly drug, the smells and tastes and textures of cheese tend to mask the great quantities of salt. And like a chronic smoker who is convinced to quit after seeing nicotine-blackened lungs in a science exhibit, I watched with growing horror as the grainy white salt cascaded into the curds. The message became clear: my father's legacy, in addition to an aging metalworking factory in the iron belt, was a dietary minefield.

How comforting and convenient it would be to explain my addiction as an inherited genetic disease! But genetic weakness or not, the problem lay with me. I had no self-control, not even a shred of restraint, when it came to cheese. No matter how many mind-tricks I played, a cheese board at a party tugged until I could not resist.

"Just one morsel more," I'd think.

Even the cheap stuff—over salted, globby, streaked with orange dye, and surrounded by a waxy rind (or, mounded in small cubes to stretch the quantity)—was irresistible. This sounded like the language of addiction, but I was *not an addict!* Well…

I kicked a sleeping-pill habit without aid; could I lick this myself? Or did I need to go the detox route? On the other hand, I mused, a twelve-step program may be in order. Total deprivation would never work; the first failure would only lead to a breakdown of confidence on the way to the nearest cheese shop.

Sublimation, I thought, may be my salvation. And with the aid of cohousing as my "weight watcher," my forum, and my stage, I could go about transmuting my unmanageable dependency into socially, psychologically, and gustatorily rewarding activities. This was accomplished, the self-help folks said, by taking *ownership*. In this case, by understanding the history, the husbandry, the manufacturing, and the culture of cheese-making. By flushing out my personal preferences, I could rise above gluttony.

But first, I had to persuade myself that the supply would not vanish; there was no need to stockpile. Unlike fickle love, the supply must remain steady, if small; I needed not to consume it all at once. "Linger and savor" would be my motto. Whatever cheese represented—love, acceptance, belonging—could be satisfied in small daily doses, delectable portions of Camembert, Raclette, Morbier, Stilton, or Tallegio.

In these two ways—by replacing quantity with quality and immersing myself in the cheese culture, I would reverse the path of the too-frequent guest at wine tastings, a path that always ended with gallon jugs of rotgut.

Ed helped, while Anne and Dick looked on, amused. They unearthed a map of Vermont, noting local cheese farms. Surrounded as we were at cohousing by supporters of local agriculture, CSAs (Community Sustainable Agriculture), and organic products, it was an easy step to narrow our search to makers of regional sheep and goat cheeses. I went to nearby cheese shops, talked to the proprietors, enrolled in a class, and bought a book. Then, together, Ed and Anne and Dick and I pinpointed some destinations before setting off for western Massachusetts and Vermont. I felt like Shackleton tackling the Antarctic.

After only a few hours on the road, a new world opened up to us. Stop at any natural food shop, and you'd find inveterate proselytizers of local artisanal cheeses; it seemed an invisible chain linked them all. They were generous with information and surprisingly happy to impart it to novices. The password—*chevre,* if you want to appear knowledgeable—would almost certainly bring out samples along with directions to "Susie's farm, where a herd of twenty-seven goats accounts for eighty to a hundred and twenty quarts of milk per day through the summer." At the farm, we learned that it was illegal to milk ewes for sixty days after their lambs were born, and that for a certain number of days more, their milk produced a seasonal delicacy in France, in the region of Savoie, called *Persillé de Tignes.* Such a cheese, we understood, was now made in New York State.

Then setting out on this rare vacation, feeling far from home, we discovered rural Vermont. Following local directions down dirt roads, we actually located Hardscrabble Road, at the end of which was a sun-splashed green valley, complete with grazing sheep. Spotted among them were several dark objects, which the farmer told us were llamas—monitors, you might say, to protect the sheep from marauding coyotes and foxes. His wife, the *affineure,* he informed us, was in her sealed, sanitized barn "setting" milk that would eventually journey to specialty shops in the Northeast—one a few blocks from Cambridge Cohousing.

Feeling like explorers who had indeed discovered gold, we returned to Cambridge, ready to share our new products and knowledge. Within an hour, we opened the wine and assembled our treasures on a large tray with labels and flavors heretofore unknown to our hastily summoned guests. The impromptu cheese tasting catapulted me into an overnight expert at our cohousing gatherings; now my advice, on occasion, is even sought. My refrigerator always contains a small goat or sheep selection, lately even a fine French or Spanish sample.

I have a new fondness for goats and sheep the world over, my morning awakenings are the richer for exposure to the cheese trade, and my personal detox program has proven to me that the connoisseur can overcome the glutton: I have shed a few pounds. Learning, however, carries with it the risk of unearthing unwelcome truths. I find I still cannot resist the second, even the third, slice of pizza. But far worse, on good authority I am told that Midwestern cheese fans, unlike their coastal cousins, tend to spurn cheddars in their natural pale yellow color. It turns out that, along with the salt, an orange dye, annato, is added to the mix. So after all, my cherished memory of orange rat cheese is a sham

Metered Energy: A Metaphor

I was in the basement of a Somerville apartment building, visiting my friend Vicky, a gym pal of fifteen years and a jewelry maker whose studio was in this renovated basement. Sporting my new earrings, I walked out with her, when I stopped dead in my tracks, my attention riveted by a bank of electric meters. Five rows of eight meters each, sparkling, readable, lined up like an Andy Warhol pop-art display on a freshly painted wall. I was staring, stark still.

"Are you all right?" Vicky asked.

"Oh, sorry, I'm fine, really … are there really forty apartments in this building?"

Vicky had always viewed me as a model for the aging woman—older than her mother and easily twenty-five years her senior. I worked out with her generation and thus far had escaped the "old lady" stereotype, but now I sensed she thought I was displaying sudden onset dementia, in front of forty electric meters.

"C'mon," she said, gently taking my arm. "Let's go upstairs to my apartment and have a cup of tea. How is Ed? Is he still making fabulous photographs? You two are so amazing; you seem so—" This is the way Vicky always talked but this time she cannot quite finish her sentence.

"It's okay," I said, reassuring her. "I'm really all right. I was just startled for a minute. Cohousing has forty units … actually forty-one … but only a single meter. Can you imagine that? One meter for the entire complex!"

The image of those meters, neatly lined up for easy monthly reading and billing to individual residents, packed a visceral wallop. It was the "individual" part that leapt out for me. When posed with the choice between separate or together, alone or cooperating, independent person or group entity, our cohousing planners presumed, in all instances, the latter—engaged as we

161

were in collective thinking for the collective good. Then we simply took off, always in too much haste to explore the ramifications of departing from the traditional ways of doing things. We were so committed to carrying out this ambitious vision that perhaps we unwittingly risked discarding some perfectly useful practices. For instance, would stick-built housing have served us as well or better than manufactured housing? Were we fully aware of the level of construction quality we would sacrifice for the goal of affordability? In our determination to underscore our egalitarian ethos, had we neglected to head off the fairness issue now looming? Would we have heard Lao Tse if he'd been among us?

As I stood immobilized before the meters, a whole series of scenes passed in spurts before my eyes, like a video on rewind. Moments of DOC debates about energy savings, how we could best implement our mission of sustainability? A speeded-up Katherine, head wagging at a ridiculous rate, urging a twenty-first-century take on the environment. A hasty debate about the economic good sense of setting ourselves up so as to qualify for nighttime commercial electric rates not available to individual residences. The video slowed down here, and I took a closer look.

We did touch on, for some moments, the question of equity—would there be resentment toward larger users? A brief response that our common commitment to energy savings would discourage abuse and that our condo fees (based on percentage of ownership) would reflect higher fees for larger users. We teetered back and forth on single or separate individual meters, until Don's "Oh, no!" came through with guttural disapproval and heavy irony.

"It's a little late to redesign the whole electrical system …" he'd stated.

And thereupon began the parade of consultants at DOC meetings; one persuaded us against a single power source; another located forty-four small discontinued meters, available to us at a discounted price, which, the salesman promised, would fit neatly into our unit electric panels.

Fast Forward a few weeks. New information brought a reverse in direction once again. The mini-meters *did not* fit and could be tailored to do so only at considerable expense. Ours now, they were relegated to the East End electrical room, useless, unsellable, where they still reside, one of the castoffs in the wake of a fast-track social experiment.

Ten years later, with utility bills through the roof, we continued to search for the individual metering solution.

The meters are but symbols, or motifs, of very core matters of any intentional community: fairness and money. And now, they had both returned to haunt us. Our kinda-sorta policy, a feel-good abstraction initially based on good intentions, was being tested. Complaints about unfairness had emerged in other areas, as well, such as gardening, meal preparation, and decorating common spaces, but those over electric meters become the most vivid, as reduced utility bills turn out to be a myth.

Starting with the energy crisis in California, energy rates everywhere rose significantly. In response to that rise, our community morphed rapidly into a state of hyper-alertness.

Peter points to the owner of a hot tub. "That must cost an arm and a leg to heat during the cold months."

Other examples of "flagrant wastefulness" hit the gossip circuit. "So-and-so's lights are on day and night: I shouldn't have to pay for that." Or, "What about those people with Jacuzzis—they use extraordinary amounts of power and water!"

Greg grumbled that we had too many light fixtures in corridors and the dining room. "What hedonist designed all this lighting?"

Monitoring and looking over one's shoulder do not bode well in a cooperative living community, however. Affordability and income diversity were easier to spell out in a vision statement, it seemed, than to live with on a daily basis.

Seated in our living room, Doris, grim-faced and pale, sighed. "I have come to a decision that I want you two—and a few others—to know about before I make a public announcement. I am putting my unit on the market. It's been an agonizing time for me but I've decided I simply can't stay here— for several reasons."

Ed and I look at each other, quite shocked and sad. Doris was a vital part of us. We knew about her dissatisfaction with the poor progress on the long-overdue repairs, but why couldn't she, like others, ride this out? Would her decision escalate into an exodus, a turning point for the community? Were others dissatisfied enough to leave?

"I just can't watch this process anymore," she continued. "I have lost any confidence that cohousing can pull this together." And then, of course, because money is always a big factor, she told us that she would not be able to afford the special assessment that was clearly in the future.

"But, Doris," we argued, "your unit has much more value now, even if you haven't got the cash. A loan wouldn't be hard to get."

"No, I've climbed out of debt before—I'll never go back there again!" Then, as might be expected, she had other complaints; clearly, they had been building. "It just doesn't seem fair that a few must carry the load. And the Managing Board does not seem willing to take on that beast."

Here it was then: money and fairness, that potentially damning pair of pollutants, toxic to healthy group life. Certainly, Doris's "comfort level," a phrase she used several times that night, was lowered by covering trash duty recently for absentees. She had reached her threshold for frustration. I wondered whether a money matter—or a fairness matter *alone*—might be resolved, but as a double-header, we were over Doris's limit.

I may have wished that everyone was aboard with cohousing's philosophy for fairness but then, since money concerns did not top my list, my preference would have been to pay for the services—not yet an option, it seemed, in a mixed-income, participatory community. It was also troubling to many that the sweat equity poured into this place had added immeasurably to the value of our real estate. Wasn't there some moral obligation on the part of those who sold at a considerable profit, to give back in some fashion, to return a fraction of their largess to the community?

Fairness is hard to quantify. And based as its assessment is on raw emotion, is it ever truly achievable? A friend who works with community housing groups similar to Cambridge Cohousing once estimated that he would feel more than satisfied with our degree of participation. His own experience was that 10 to 20 percent of residents in these types of communities became involved, and he was amazed at my guess that only 10 to 15 percent of our households kept to themselves. We both agreed that fairness was not a measurable entity; there are levels of fairness and different ways to be "in it" together.

Could we have designed better ways of managing ownership and turnover? My experience now convinces me that all long-term groups, if they are to survive, must address two critical issues very early: getting in and getting out. In hindsight, had we been able to find consensus on entry and exit policies, we might have simplified the living in between.

The power odyssey continued. In a burst of initiative, Miriam lit the way, carrying it to new levels.

Throughout the dissension about utility costs and equitable payments, Miriam, an early-retiring organizational consultant, listened quietly from the sidelines. (Although, I thought I heard her mumble once to Howard at a meeting, that user fees were regressive, and that we needed to use *less* energy overall, not tattle on one another for using more.) Like all of us, she was concerned about rising costs, especially for fixed-income budgets.

Her concerns about dwindling natural resources were already well-known. But rather than join the complainers, she moved to the research and development arena, where she discovered what she called a "near-revolution" looming on the horizon: dramatic improvements in residential lighting technology.

People were wary. More than one person at the meeting on energy exclaimed, "We've known nothing but the incandescent bulb all our lives. I can't just throw away my stock of spares!"

What she learned, upon cultivating the local electric company, was that it wanted to be our ally, to collaborate with us using new products. The power company shared our concern about efficiency and productivity.

Who can say why some people, quite aside from personal gain, alone take on a project that would overwhelm, or that would lie beyond the capability or imagination of, most? No one would have predicted that Miriam would become our lightbulb czarina. But in the midst of a personal crisis, she surveyed the entire community's lighting supply, systematically visited each unit, and worked with owners to assess their needs. At our flat, Miriam talked wattage, kilowatt hours, baffles, and CFLs (compact fluorescent lamps), to which we were shifting a significant amount of our lighting at very little cost.

"And from industry experiments, we know," she added, "that pleasanter, less-glaring light could actually lower the decibel level of our acoustically challenged dining room."

This phase was not without its detractors; the debate got testy. In fact, "debate" is a polite word for what Miriam experienced. There was questioning, yes, but also resentment, competitiveness, jealousy, challenges to her credentials. It seemed personal initiative, in our multi-leader community, was admired, applauded—and suspected. It could be affirming and confidence-building when it ended in success; it could also cause the faint of heart to make for the exit. Perseverance in the face of opposition and criticism was a trait essential to the ongoing rejuvenation of an intentional community.

Single-handedly, Miriam acquired for Cambridge Cohousing large quantities of fixtures; long-lasting bulbs of various shapes, sizes, and voltages; uncounted *pro bono* consulting hours; and three two-man workdays, all at bargain-basement costs. More significantly, she negotiated a state-of-the-art closure to our persistent but unfocused sustainability argument. She was only one of many who, when the future of this social experiment periodically clouded over, rose phoenixlike to reset our compass.

Preserving a Lifestyle

Dear Friends in Cohousing,
We want you to know about a hard decision we
have just made. Within the next three months our family
will return to Ithaca where we used to live. After
weighing the benefits of our life here in Cambridge
Cohousing which have been great indeed and the
opportunity to forward our careers in a familiar setting
it seems that a move at this time, before the school year
begins, is the right thing for our family …

There it was, prominently posted in the lobby, again shattering the illusion of permanency. I hated these announcements! It felt like a precious fabric being ripped. I now know that the fabric can be repaired, but, still, the mending job is never invisible, and in the repair process, special threads are inevitably lost.

All departures from cohousing have been of families, and they always take with them our collective investment in them and their children. In this case, Petra had been an infant when we'd begun planning; Niki, then three, was a shy cohousing baby—we must have come across as a wall of people. Her two mothers, Ellen and Riva, had put as much thought into joining us then as I'm sure they did into making this move. Were they unhappy here? "They are very private people" was the only response I heard to that question. But did we fail? At some level, these leavings were like rejections, and like rejections, they were hard to face. Were we sensitive enough to the lesbian experience? Some departures we can comfortably file under "Career Move" or "Remarriage." This one was murkier.

Several years ago I predicted to myself that Petra could some day become the community's documentarian; behind those large, watchful, bright eyes there had to be a video recorder. Nothing escaped Petra's lens. My most vivid memory is of that beautiful little face shyly peering out from behind her mother's leg, but she followed every step of my recovery from hip surgery, questioning walker, crutch, and cane. It was during that time when, right under our balcony, we witnessed her metamorphosis from wary to outgoing and confident.

Her thoughtful, serious parents brought special skills to our community life. Both became able group facilitators, and each at different times propelled the Children's Committee, organizing playroom and outdoor equipment. They took on their share of meals and work projects. Incredibly attentive parents; a self-sufficient family. If there was a profile of the model cohousing resident, the Smith-Jones family was it.

The first reactions to the news were dismay and disappointment. But as the initial impact took its place in the bigger picture, we knew what we needed to do. This had happened before—three times now. High on the list of frequently asked questions about such situations: What have you done to ensure that community values will survive the departure of its founders?

Regrettable as the loss of each household was, such events were unavoidable. There was hope: in the three previous sales, the subsequent buyers, by word-of-mouth, had found *us*. It appeared we may not drift into becoming a retirement coummunity after all. And as a result we're gaining some confidence that this community housing model will probably survive the social challenges; it's the financial ones now that seem intractable. The first sale in 1999 stunned us into recognizing the reality of the marketplace. According to independent appraisals, our project was keeping pace with the phenomenal rise of Cambridge housing prices in the 1990s. We just continued to hope that informed purchasers would be willing and able to pay a premium for what one of us then dubbed "the social factor."

A very simple procedure exists for entering cohousing. No brokers, no advertising. Just sign up with The Friends of Cambridge Cohousing for a nominal fee, attend some events and meetings, and join us for a meal or two. When a unit becomes available, you will be quickly alerted. "Quickly" is the operative word; cohousing has thirty days to find a suitable buyer to recommend to the owner/seller. After that, the negotiation is between the owner and the potential buyer.

So as soon as Ellen and Riva's announcement appeared, we referred to the Friends of Cohousing waiting list—what we jokingly referred to as the RRRTF (Rapid Response Resale Task Force. A couple of days later, George, a single father of two teenagers who visited him regularly, stopped me in the mailroom. Veritably bubbling with a new idea, he said, "Let me run it by you."

Upon hearing his idea, I was less than enthusiastic, but suggested he put his plan in writing for all to consider. Wanting more space, he proposed to buy Ellen and Riva's unit, adjacent to his, open up the common wall, and make the two units into one for himself.

"I have always felt cramped ... I have a lot of stuff ... I came here from a large house ... I need to feel free to play my drums whenever I like." Our bylaws specified that a resident had the opportunity, before an outsider, to make an offer. The letter created shock waves from East End to West End. A large townhouse—and maybe two—and no family!

"Oh," added George later, "my other idea is to rent part of it to a young family who would fit in here." With this, the community erupted.

Could George possibly not know that he was tangling with two revered cohousing dictums—"the more kids, the better" and "no renters"? On the matter of rentals, the bylaw committee was prescient. It was early convinced that renters could not be expected to have the same commitment to our complex physical and social organization as owners. The Managing Board, therefore, would consider only short-term sublets.

The Smith-Joneses were, of course, free to sell to anyone they chose. George was poised to make them a formal offer. Had the condo association been financially able, in this instance, it might well have bought the unit, holding it for a family.

Ellen and Riva's sensitivity to the community's needs must have made this an uneasy period for them. They supported cohousing's wish for a family with children yet they'd also have liked to accommodate their neighbor and themselves with a rapid sale.

Several families came to look, their children swarming over the play structure and instantly bonding with our kids, but none made an offer. Meantime, voices were simmering in opposition to the possible loss of a voting unit and a family, to the consolidation of valued space, to the structural luxuries George planned for his new townhouse (hot tub, built-ins)—items he saw as essential and others viewed as excessive because they would raise the bar for future purchases.

Strong-minded people lived here; some began expressing their opinions to George in formal letters—a communication mode of last resort. Customarily, messages were posted in several places, e-mails flew, notes were dashed off on napkins. But a real, old-fashioned letter? Almost unheard of. A palpable tension replaced our usual easy-going social exchanges. The RRRTF cited reasons why George's plan was doomed to failure. The mounting concerns were inescapable. Various individuals tried to intercede. (One letter writer, however, alarmed at the community's interference, supported George's right to do what he wanted). Then, suddenly, George himself suggested a meeting of the entire community.

Realtors would shudder. What kind of a real estate transaction was this? Was it going to be done the old American way or would the voice of peers issue the final word? I find the term "proactive" distasteful, but it does describe what happened next, an extraordinary departure from any property sale I have ever known. Our cohousing culture clearly presumed that we shared a tangible interest in the entire project. Together we bought it, developed it, designed its space, oversaw its construction. Each member, therefore, had a stake in the whole. While a court may not have supported this view, the court of peers was a powerful one.

As George said, "I do not want to live in a place that doesn't like what I do."

The meeting began at 8:00 on Thursday night in the living room. As chairs filled, others were brought in from the dining room. The conflict brought out, like a fire alarm, some usually not seen.

Howard, who had volunteered to act as facilitator for the discussion, had carefully prepared for the meeting by talking beforehand with George and agreeing on some ground rules. In his introduction, he emphasized the importance of being respectful to one another as well as to George. George then asked to speak first. He wanted the group to understand his physical and psychological needs for more space, his continuing dissatisfaction with the unit in spite of his elaborate renovations.

"I'm just not happy there." Pausing for a long moment, he then added, "I've been terribly hurt by the responses I've had, those letters under the door—why don't people just talk to me? The way I feel now is that I'm not sure I want to live here. And I think I'm a little fearful that this discussion will get out of control."

Howard assured him that he would rigidly enforce boundaries in order to make this a safe place to speak out. In fact, he did admonish an early speaker for an accusatory tone of voice.

Dalenna then eloquently reminded us of her expectation upon coming here—that life would be simpler, that together we would commit to working toward environmentally sensitive living. This expectation had been a major factor in her and Greg's decision to join us.

"We would not be able to buy here at the current cost of housing," she added, and then went further to say that she found it distressing that a few members focus so much on energy-wasteful amenities and materialism.

Ken B., in his customary, rational manner, produced a detailed technical analysis, from the construction perspective, of the inadvisability of combining two units.

Ken T. talked about his wish for a strong, constantly replenished foundation of children to counteract the retirement rate and aging of the current population. "We need the strong and willing bodies of their parents, too. Doesn't there seem to be an abnormally high percentage of bad backs, bum shoulders, and tennis elbows, thus reducing the number of physically able adults?" he concluded.

One crusty contrarian insisted that the community should let the market rule. "George can take over the entire place if he can pay for it!"

The facilitator took a poll of what individuals hoped would happen to the unit. Two preferences outranked the others. The highest of the two was for a sale to a family. The other was for a compatible buyer who understood and shared our goals.

George stirred in his chair and asked for permission to speak. "I've been listening carefully, and I have just decided that I want to withdraw my proposal to combine the two units. I will sell mine to a family, buy Ellen and Riva's next door, and renovate it to my liking—and move my drums to the music room in the basement!"

One of cohousing's finest hours, I thought, limp with fatigue, on my way back to #410. Two hours had been consumed! But if eighty people-hours could confront and resolve a serious conflict among its members, the time was well-spent. We were no longer a neighborhood at war over the expansion plans of one of our own. No one shouted, harangued, or threatened legal action. Whatever you call it—community-building, mediation, consensus, kangaroo court—while not completely satisfactory for anyone, it had circumvented corrosive and lingering resentments.

I was proud of George. Could I have done as well? Would I have caved, cried, or cavilled under pressure? Had he been intimidated? Somewhat, certainly, but he would have been more so if he had proceeded unchecked with his plan. Was the community smug with victory? I saw none of that, only a sigh of relief that our mini-crisis had been resolved and that the community fabric was already undergoing repair.

Urban winter on The Pretty Good Lawn

"Just How *Do* You Get Along?"

*Democracy is a small hard core of
common agreement, surrounded by a
rich variety of individual differences.*
—James Bryant Conant

If there's one most-asked question about this experiment in living, it's this: "How do you get along?" It ranks above "Do you all eat together?" and "How can you stand all those meetings?" Getting along implies achieving a reasonable harmony with people who bring a wide spectrum of attitudes, beliefs, and behaviors. For me, and others too, the challenge of it is with us dawn to dusk, a Greek chorus hovering off-stage.

Springing to open the foyer door from the inside so Joy doesn't have to put down her packages and dig for her key is but a tiny gesture. As is following toddler Kara for a crucial few minutes while her mother tends to the scrapes of three-year-old Justin who has fallen off his tricycle onto the concrete patio. And being sure Ruth, on crutches, can respond to a fire alarm. And collecting Velma's mail during her vacation. These are everyday, ordinary things, you might well say, that people do for others everywhere. Here, however, while spontaneous in the execution, they are the result of deliberately designed building blocks for a civil and respectful community. Favor following favor, the accumulation creates a bank of good will, and slowly, solidly, we benefit from the atmosphere of interdependency that we had all once just envisioned.

Of course, neighborliness is not unique to cohousing. Cohousing cannot claim ownership of civility and respect. These concepts, even practices, are not foreign to people living in apartments, villages, and enclaves the world over. But cohousing can play a large role in engendering these qualities in a community.

As a bride in a strange city, with a frequently absent intern/husband, I found none of these civilities. I came to know only one person in our low-rent apartment building, another stranded and lonesome medical wife. My yearning for connection must have been what others were referring to when they sang the praises of their neighborhood, proclaiming, "I will never leave here. I'd never find such good neighbors again." Cohousing: the balm for loneliness. The idea of cohousing, the very word itself, has come to tap deep hopes and expectations for social connections, even though sometimes bordering on delusion. To my knowledge, the purchase of a house does not (excluding those restrictive, negative covenants) come with a social contract. In contrast, however, our cohousing agreement, as spelled out in our vision statement, is specific, comprehensive, idealistic, and hopeful. In short, it is a paraphrase of the Golden Rule and, with the addition of some environmental guidelines, is the refrain of that Greek chorus many of us hear in our heads. The document is based on trust, and carries with it few rules and fewer penalties. It bears no signatures. Its failures, to me, are minor in proportion to the enormity of its achievements.

What makes the difference between a fortuitously genial neighborhood and one that deliberately plans its own path? For me, it's a matter of two words: "intent" and "opportunity."

In my old neighborhood, the chance meeting played a large role. Acts of God brought us streaming from our houses. Standing in the street together experiencing the eerie temperature drop, wind, and yellow haze of the Worcester Tornado of 1953 sealed a friendship that for me still continues. But otherwise, and especially during the winter months, I rarely communicated with my immediate neighbors except to wave as we backed out of our driveways. Twice, Ed and I responded frantically to ninety-five-year-old Eliot's Lifeline emergency calls, only to face false alarms. Was that what I thought I would miss? Here, opportunity abounds. Winter is the coziest season; we're like cows collecting under trees as a storm approaches. It's the time to chat, to check out the common living room, to sit around the fireplace, to catch up with the messages in the lobby, to shelve a few books in the library. An encounter is not dependent on fire or flood. It is not left up to chance.

At Richdale Avenue, if I haven't seen a particular friend for several days, it's "Have you been away, Dalenna?" or "It must be tax time, Doris (an accountant). We never see you." If the frequency of physical encounters is a significant factor in building a community, a simple mathematical computation can be applied for doing it, and probably was by our architects. But opportunity alone, without stated intent, is not enough to create a cooperative group. (We know about those luxury condominiums with public meeting rooms that are sadly underutilized.) The cohousing template carries a lot of simple wisdom. Housing units face each other, the placement of the common house expands opportunities for encounters, small private households encourage the use of common spaces. But none of these features would carry the same weight had they not come packaged with an intentional community. And in a responsive and committed intentional community, opportunity and intent reinforce each other.

When you think about it—and to me it's absolutely astounding—I and many others here are loosely plugged into the lives of probably three-quarters of our fellow residents. Without any systematic tracking, I have a fair sense of the comings and goings of maybe seventy-five people at any given time. I call it Jean's Seepage Axiom: A large part of the group culture is the result of seepage of a barely acknowledged but steady flow of social, behavioral, and sensory interactions that take place within it.

Going beyond the spontaneous concierge-like courtesies, we step up to another level of kindnesses and exchanges. These require some thought and planning and even inconvenience on the giver's part; mainly, they presume an alertness to and some empathy for the events and feelings in the lives of those around us. While our society tends to attribute these characteristics as being natural to women—and that's true here, as well—a number of men are also very proficient in such behaviors. "Oh, you're off to Toronto on Wednesday. I'll take you as far as the Blue Line if you can leave by 2:00 PM," Dennis offered to Janet once at the dinner table.

The critically timed offer of a car, bringing food from a shopping trip to an ill neighbor, peddling an unused theater ticket, and helping out with children for a limited period—these are but a few examples of so many acts of kindness. And while not everyone lives within this culture of courtesies, I believe most residents have access to some cadre that exchanges favor.

Another category of social interactions is what I call personalized acts, which occur in the choreography of deepening friendships. There are many examples—the loan of a vacation house, hosting a friend's family, accompanying a neighbor to a critical medical appointment, traveling together. How many neighbors will follow your ambulance to the hospital in the middle of the night? Anne and Dick did that for Ed and me and others countless times, and then arranged for community-delivered meals to the convalescent.

In addition to intent, what sets cohousing apart from the traditional living arrangement is opportunity. An invaluable informal network of resources is here for the asking—resources for medical help, entertainment, travel, education, technology, art, music, politics. We are, in fact, our own Web site—both literally and figuratively. Opportunities to access these real and virtual networks abound—conversations, bulletin boards, the dinner table; an admired book passed along, a successful recipe copied and distributed; a fairly traded-coffee-buying club, or word-of-mouth recommendations for a dentist, plumber, flute teacher, summer camp, psychologist.

There is a steady flow of informational calls, messages taped to doors, in-house mail, and thank-you notes. Several years into living together, we have a rich fund of information and contacts, enabling us to respond to an array of requests from borrowing a suitcase to making a midnight run to CVS.

Once, within a few minutes of our struggle to hang a picture, Dennis appeared at our door with an electronic stud-finder in hand. How did he know? But more important, his trove of electronic gadgetry served a dual purpose: in addition to helping us, it offered a social opportunity for a lone bachelor.

Humans are social animals who yearn for connections. The base of our interdependency pyramid grows increasingly solid over time.

Visitors commend us for being a benevolent community. And we are. Touring architects and friends of friends of friends alike have given us raves for being a considerate and responsive place to live. People who have lived here or stayed here with friends continue to return, their enthusiastic praise inferring that such a community is indeed rare. The vignettes they might see, and the sounds and smells on any given day are rather ordinary: several children cooperating to hoist baskets of wood chips by rope to the top level of the play structure; enticing odors wafting from the kitchen where a cook team prepares dinner; a couple of gardeners on their knees planting perennials along the fence; the sounds of a piano lesson coming from the living room.

Yet that balance between privacy and togetherness continues unabated. Everyone's need is different, I'm sure. When we've had enough noise, food, or people, for example, Ed and I will not sign up for dinner. Some residents may also feel a bit smothered by the displays of togetherness, feeling pressure from the socially active atmosphere. These people desire more privacy; they could do with less "inter-" and more "in-dependence." Still others prefer to substitute a brief "Hi," wave, or smile when passing in the hall for the obligatory conversation they fear is expected.

On the other hand, most adults who live here are quite good at protecting their psychological boundaries by clearly defining their emotional and physical limits, often with humor. I recall Velma saying once, "You don't want me to work on your project. I'm all thumbs. I'd ruin the whole thing." Dori never makes eye contact as she hurries out to work early in the morning. Another man settles for a winning smile as he takes his children to preschool.

Greg and I share a year of birth and, along with two or three others, living with artificial hips and something we discovered just recently—a profoundly mortifying childhood stutter. Last year, a few weeks into a siege of pneumonia, Greg placed the following Xeroxed note, in his inimical style, in everyone's boxes:

COHO CONVALESCENCE

FIRST, a great big "Thank you" to Jina, Nikita, and elders who sent cards, offered help, visited, brought food (wonderful), one plant (just right—I have a brown thumb).

NEXT, status report: If you've not had pneumonia but have experienced mono, that's the present sensation—feel okay if inert, crave little stimulation or company. Prognosis: maybe two more weeks of same. b-o-r-i-n-g.

LAST, what I learned: From watching & experiencing, help is commensurate with need. I was stroked sufficiently, not too much. Let's not work into a "have to show I care" mode, putting a burden on carer & caree. This is excellent as is.

I admired his way of acknowledging support yet discouraging a cascade of well-wishers. He clearly set his personal boundaries for being ministered to by stating, essentially: Sickness is no fun, but it's his bad luck. It's his job to get well and not to burden the community. It's ours not to nurture unreasonably. I crumpled the note and tossed it in the wastebasket. A day later, still remembering it, I retrieved it from the trash.

There's another, much smaller, category of residents. They've been referred to in a number of ways—nonverbally, with raised eyebrows, or in such terms as "the missing" and the "no-see-ums." No account of how we get along can be complete without noting that a predictable minority (as few as 10 percent, I've read in some social-science research) of every group does not comply with its norms of behavior, loyalty, or participation. It should be no surprise that the majority—the rest of us—can find this aggravating. I'm reminded of the saying, "The absent are always wrong." There is that danger of sliding into an "us-them" culture.

Although in cohousing, I find that a remarkable tolerance still exists; the absent are not rejected. The Quakers among us are ever hopeful and—if I read it right—tend to lead the charge for inclusion. We once designed a graduated set of strategies—from friendly reminders, personalized invitations, even hints of fees *in lieu of* participation—to re-engage the reluctant joiners. When all outreach failed, there was disappointed withdrawal. But make no mistake, the message was clear: the door is always open. And then the unexpected happened. Joseph once made a rare and unannounced appearance at dinner, receiving an all-is-forgiven, spontaneous round of applause.

Here, the Greek chorus might choose to take a break from considering the *opportunity* for social encounters and speculate again about *intent*. I'm probably not the only one who would've loved to know what Gerald, Dorothy, Nell, and Joseph were thinking during those long, demanding planning meetings on Sunday afternoons. Were they sizing up their neighbors, with the hopes of finding a real estate bargain, a home, and a few soul mates? Were they biding their time and calculating their profits, banking on our obscure edge-property to appreciate in value? Somehow, I found it hard to attribute malevolence to their disengagement.

Were there any signs in those early days predictive of future remoteness? Yes, probably a few, but inclusion and self-selection were mantras, whereas delving into personal motive was always anathema to this group's beliefs. Were they socially uncomfortable? Naive about or blind to the obligations that would accompany the hoped-for benefits of such a venture? Did they just recently find the cooperative effort abhorrent? A midstream change of mind? Or was it a distracting personal matter, a new relationship? We may never know; all that's certain is that there must be stories.

The real question, however, is whether it really matters. They are, after all, our very own ten percent.

Although I find myself increasingly detached and mellow toward the subject of nonparticipation (aging is responsible, I am convinced), some residents, chronically and intermittently, are incensed. A few decades ago, I might well have joined the ranks of those who felt duped, ranting alongside them about fairness, using the common lines: "They had to know what they were buying into," or, "I don't really care if they choose not to come to dinner, but they're not sharing the responsibilities." I'm not so complacent, however, as to wonder if they haven't forfeited their right to red-card (veto) a proposal. At moments of high tension, others go farther, advocating fees, fines, even expulsion. But at heart and by choice, we are a determinedly *laissez-faire* bunch of people.

In fact, if truth be known, I find myself more curious than angry. It takes talent to avoid people around here—how do the no-see-ums manage it? How late at night does one have to pick up mail to remain invisible? Have they lost interest in food since our original meetings, and aren't they just a little curious about the common dinners?

There I go lumping "them" together as though "they" were actuarial numbers. I've decided that it's draining to expend energy in attempts to shepherd the "delinquent" into the fold. In the end, it's the deceit, less than the absenteeism, that galls. I'm reminded of our infamous "tie" during the lottery's critical unit selections, resulting in one of those extra-hour sessions when Dorothy persuaded us to favor her with a two-bedroom apartment over a nice couple who subsequently dropped out for lack of a unit. She presented a strong argument: cohousing was the ideal place to bring up the foreign child she was about to adopt. She'd have a built-in community of godparents! We welcomed the child with open arms, but very soon, a veil of silence descended. What went wrong? Dorothy picked up her mail and occasionally occupied her apartment and a parking place, but her sentient life took place elsewhere—until she disappeared for good.

Initial impressions are hard to shake. Ed and I were "old" when we came, and we remain the oldest couple. We'll always be seen as old, especially to the children. As elders, we were exempt from certain strenuous efforts, but at the same time we were aware that this role could become a stereotype that distances us from others. When we moved in, I was limping quite noticeably. Within a few months, I had hip-replacement surgery and some subsequent ER runs, from which I returned wearing a variety of splints and braces. Yet although free of these for years, for many, my *persona* is frozen as someone who is impaired or handicapped.

Another example of how roles stick is that Anne, Dick, Ed, and I moved in from the same address as a friendly foursome, by chance to apartments under/over each other in the common house, thus reinforcing an image of inseparability. They did help us through some rocky times; they buffered our entry in so many ways. Did it take us longer to assume our rightful roles for being cocooned?

Entering a new group is a time to define oneself. For the widowed and divorced, that poses a special enigma—a portion of their stories is missing at the outset; they must choose how much to bring with them as their contribution to the group identity. Single women anywhere will tell you that couples are slow to include them in their social activities; I've heard such mutterings here and feel awkward about couples-only social occasions. Other single residents, since moving in, have found or brought out of the closet relationships new to cohousing. Some of these partners now make cohousing their home and are valued members; others are shadowy figures

Group characteristics show up well in dining-room behavior and seating patterns. To me, it's always interesting to observe who eats with whom. There are six tables that seat eight to ten diners, with a serving table in the center of the large dining room. Our *zeitgeist*, in the three common meals a week, each enjoyed by twenty-five to forty-five residents who have signed up a day or two in advance, is casual. There is no dress code, unless it's jeans. Compared to dining rooms with assigned seating, we are "patternless"; that is, there is freedom to sit wherever one chooses. The atmosphere is very informal. To spice things up every now and then, we put on some smashing dinners to which we bring our best manners.

The surge around the buffet table resembles cheerful, low-level pandemonium. I find it interesting that, given all the problems we have ingeniously tackled and resolved, we have barely touched the issue of crowding around the food table. My guess is that the eager hilarity at the serving table simply negates the presence of a problem. We're hungry, we're curious, we're reasonably polite, we enjoy seeing friends, and we do not place the highest value on order. Should an announcement or an introduction be necessary, hands are raised for silence. One nice custom has evolved: the lead chef describes the menu, lists its major—and possibly allergenic—ingredients, points out the vegetarian alternative, announces the children's selections, and then introduces the Cook and Cleanup Teams. Hosts may then introduce their guests.

Often people will reserve seats for a small group, perhaps including a guest, bring a bottle of wine for the table. With the permission of the lead chef, someone who neglected to sign up is allowed to attend if there is enough food. A latecomer can comfortably take any empty seat, in fact, is roundly welcomed.

Accounts of Danish cohousing suggest that dinner is the time for families to be together; I see little of this. Families with small children may sit together initially, usually close to the playroom and where the highchairs are. As soon as children are old enough to drift away from parents, however, they seek out other children. At times, a parent will join a child, or all family members will split up.

If there is any dining pattern, it is the endless—and fruitless—quest for the least noisy table in an "acoustically challenged" room. A perpetual task force is looking into that.

In the nearly fourteen years since the core group first assembled, there have been no scandals, marital separations, or divorces. A couple of long-term relationships have not survived, resulting in the non-owner partner moving away.

Several families await medical miracles and clinical breakthroughs for combating devastating diseases. We're one of them, always acutely keyed to research bulletins about muscular dystrophy; two other families focus on multiple sclerosis. Some serious wishing is done with every birthday cake that comes through the kitchen door.

Among the over-sixty-five cohort there are serious and chronic health issues, periodic crises. People are solicitous and concerned, ready to help when appropriate, but take care to avoid fawning and crocodile tears. After all, this is a healthy, vigorous community.

The intergenerational model is a wonderful one for children to grow up with—my own children, deprived of role models, knew only slightly two long-distance grandmothers. Here, the announcement of a pregnancy, the birth of a baby, is a time of great joy. Wonderful parties celebrate both the parents and the newcomer in a whirl of hope and promise.

With others, we sweat through the agonies and uncertainties of *in vitro* fertilization, kindergarteners' first days of school in a big urban system, dreaded colonoscopies, losses of relatives and friends. And we're all acutely alert to that critical call to our resident awaiting a kidney transplant. The epilogue contains an update.

Some may say this account is too much about demographics and too little about personalities. My friend Sheila once said to me upon reading a draft of my manuscript, "You're not telling us the bad stuff." I recall reddening a little; she was both right and wrong. I wasn't revealing the litany of tensions during the construction period that threatened to upend us all. This is "family" after all. Neither she nor anyone else needed to know that I had a run-in with X, a temporary falling out with M, and a every now and then a bout of hurt feelings.

I refuse to expose any details about our not-quite-perfect honor system except to say that food is occasionally missing from the common refrigerator; messy trash can appear in an unlikely spot; not every dog owner, all the time, scoops the poop. The same is true of rumors. You will not find them here, either serious or silly. They appear; they heat up, they cool down. As one of man's earliest news networks, the best method for reducing them is a reasonably transparent environment.

This utopia has not, however, defeated internal gossip. It would be an unnatural group that has and I'm becoming radicalized on the subject. Viewing it as inextinguishable in an organization, I see it as having a salutary as well as a destructive function (and, of course, wonderful grist for the Greek chorus). Held to a reasonable level, gossip can be a safety valve against a buildup of hostility. It keeps people informed, edgy, and involved, and can correct outlandish imaginings; it can bring out new initiatives, even uncover new leadership. Several researchers were quoted in a *New York Times* article in Science Times of August 6, 2005, in an article entitled "Have You Heard? Gossip Serves a Purpose." One writer, David Sloan Wilson, (*Darwin's Cathedral: Evolution, Religion, and the Nature of Society*, University of Chicago Press,

2003) says that "gossip appears to be a very sophisticated, multifunctional interaction which is important in policing behaviors in a group and defining group membership." In other words, it's not all bad. Others have claimed that it provides comic relief and can help us better define ourselves. Within the dynamics of an ever-changing community, gossip has to be recognized as an important and potentially healthy and useful mode of communication and community building.

While public behavior is never synonymous with private behavior, my guess is that the discrepancy is less marked here than in lots of organizations. Our lives intertwine like thick shrubs; there is little room for secrets. Just a small example: there's little point in whispering behind my back about, say, "my stubbornness" in regard to having trees planted outside my window, when, in fact, it's public knowledge. Occasional jibes come my way; for the sake of protecting my sight lines, I can take the remarks and prefer that they are out in the open. This relative transparency, I believe, encourages an atmosphere in which the inevitable antagonisms have a chance of being flushed out and diminished.

Is it worth it? Why do we do all this, go to all this trouble? Now I am circling around a long-held premise of mine, something we do not talk about a lot. Our stated reasons for being here are many, but there's one that we all hold in common, regardless of *how* or *whether* it is expressed. This is the most basic reason: humans need connection.

In some measure, the intimate details of life are integral to satisfying this need. Those for whom social connection is a conscious need and those who can hear the insistent refrain about "getting along" learn to balance the angst, the emotional exposure, and the "bad stuff" with the warmth, the generosity, and the hopefulness of living alongside each other in this disorderly, sprawling not-quite-a-family, imperfect democracy.

...by talking together at meetings

...by participating in decision-making

...through a network of committees

The Kaleidoscope of Community:
An Epilogue

Civilization is a movement—not
a condition; a voyage—not a harbor.
—Arnold Toynbee

Like sun worshippers everywhere, we gave high priority to the siting of buildings. All of our units are oriented toward the south—allowing, for most, some views of the street with its pedestrian parade and the juggling of vehicles by drivers who, surprisingly often, politely take turns as they make their way through the single lane left by parked cars. Schoolboy motorcyclists noisily claim the entire street. I look at these constantly variegated pictures as though through a kaleidoscope—the optical instrument intriguing to all ages.

From windows and balcony, my mirrored kaleidoscopic lens takes in the Pretty Good Lawn, with its phalanx of children and its collection of many sizes of colorful balls (once I counted thirteen from my balcony). Contrails festoon the huge sky; and for a while after 9/11, the chilling sound of military fighter planes commandeered the empty, grieving universe.

Beyond the railroad tracks, the view from our rear bedroom windows is charming and intimate, like a detailed painting of the Boston Garden. A row of attached townhouses with their handkerchief-sized gardens, separated from the tracks by a retaining wall and a collage of fences. The patchwork of the city's community gardens with their seasonal changes, tennis courts, play lot and picnic tables, often the daytime rendezvous of inhabitants from a nearby halfway house, who while away untold, cigarette-filled hours. Periodically, the police drop by to check, and on rare occasions, take someone away with them. And, of course, there are the infamous graffiti exhibits. The train completes the picture. My lens picks up, then jumbles, the elements of a 1950s-era iconic America at its best—leisure, home ownership, diversity, dogs, community responsibility, travel, food production, happy children—

and arranges them into constantly changing patterns, shapes and colors. And while I watch the incredible agility of skateboarders leaping over a picnic bench, I cannot miss the American flag that waves over all.

Until, with a jiggle of the kaleidoscope, a haunting event disturbs its usually pleasing arrangements, reminding me that from childhood to my octogenarian years, trains are destined to be both a nostalgic and a tragic presence. One night, around 11:00, as we were about to go to bed, bright, flashing lights from the park drew Ed and me to the window. An engine and its six cars were stopped perhaps fifty yards down the tracks. Then just below our window, a sight unfolds that is forever seared in my brain. Four floors down, the body of a young woman lies splayed on the tracks. A single pink shoe a few feet away rests on blackened cinders. In the distance, but nearing, we hear sirens scream, see more lights flash. Ed and I, in one voice, gasp, "Suicide!"

Lying between the rails, her body appears unscathed; her head and face, except for a crown of red hair, damaged beyond recognition. As my benumbed brain begins to function, and as suicide, to Ed and me, becomes a given, I keep asking myself, "Why *here,* why *this* particular spot? What brought her *right here* to end her life?"

There she lies, alone in death, surrounded by dutiful male strangers. I very much wanted to go and sit beside her, another woman to help bridge her transition from here to eternity. At such a moment, the little village and the larger world melded into one.

It is eleven years now since we moved here. A respectable length of time to store thousands of images, although none as grievous as that of the train's force that night. The ever-present kaleidoscope has striven to spot patterns, but the rate of change has been daunting. No wonder social-science research is so difficult. How can you possibly *control* for infinite variables?

Cambridge Cohousing is neither a sterile laboratory nor a mathematical given; it's a dynamic, flowing, constantly altering one-and-a-half urban acres, with a full complement of people. This must have been true as well for the early nineteenth century intentional communities—the Oneidas, the New Harmonys, the Amanas—although from our long look backward, they appear static, a paragraph in a history book noting their dates of birth and demise, along with a few dreary, obsolete facts. I recall a story about my research of New Harmony; I had one of those epiphanies that, correct or not, I will nevertheless always cherish.

It goes back to my "beginnings" in the chapter by that name. My mother kept stories of her past carefully veiled, the result, I suppose, of an unhappy childhood. In response to her children's interest in that part of her life, such as "Take us to see where you lived?" Or, "Where did your father come from?" she had precious little to say.

"Oh, you children wouldn't be interested in *that* old place," or, "I really don't know—maybe Illinois … or was it Indiana?"

So I am almost as uninformed about my mother's family history as are friends whose families perished in the Holocaust. What she did tell us was that, somehow, George Rapp Medell appeared, suddenly, in St. Louis.

"This handsome man (Mother did say this much about her father) met your widowed grandmother. They married and lived over their grocery store in North St. Louis."

My grandfather died when I was a few months old, taking all knowledge of his mysterious origins with him.

Decades later I read about New Harmony, Indiana, and its charismatic founder and leader—George Rapp! Spellbound, I began to weave my own story together with his. I envisioned my grandfather as the wayward grandson who, unable to tolerate the allegedly tyrannical authority figure, left the community, drifted for a time, then turned up in St. Louis to start a new and settled life. The geography is possible, the dates roughly fit—but the characters? I believe I'll fall back on creative license rather than attempt to track down the facts. I like believing in the utopian version, that I have an historical, even genetic, legacy to explain my absorption with community-building.

Through the indefatigable efforts of Kathryn McCamant and Charles Durrett, cohousing is no longer a gleam in the eyes of a few, but a living reality for many. From those first years of endless talk, when ideas fell on more deaf than hearing ears, its progress has been remarkable, especially considering the long lead time required for such a project to reach fruition. From the mere handful of such communities that existed when Cambridge Cohousing was born, now more than a hundred—containing from as few as nine to as many as forty-four households—have been completed or are in development. Sprinkled throughout the East and West Coasts, they have also penetrated parts of the Midwest, and about half a dozen more are in various stages of development in Massachusetts.

The pioneering of early groups such as ours—and their generosity in sharing information—fostered a warm-spirited culture and a slightly faster learning curve for subsequent project initiators.

Nevertheless, the time required for planning, designing, funding, and permitting should never be underestimated; established neighborhoods can take a dim view of this intruder known as cohousing. And although some aspects of the development process have been streamlined, the democratic participation of future residents is what distinguishes cohousing from almost all other housing types. The process cannot, therefore, arbitrarily be cut short or speeded up.

At the time of our formation, so great was the initial enthusiasm among novitiates that strangers from opposite coasts who shared this passion spent countless hours communicating, trading advice, and answering questions. This insatiable curiosity among believers was aided by the rapid growth of e-mail; that and word of mouth have always been cohousing's best advertising tools. From the first homey newsletters with a tiny, local readership, to a national journal, and now, to an online magazine, which was reported to receive around a hundred thousand hits a week when it first appeared in 2004. (www.cohousing.org/magazine)

During the recruitment phase it was soon clear to cohousers that one of Cambridge's basic precepts, that of ethnic and racial diversity, was not to be fully achieved here. Surprising to many, it turns out that cohousing offers little interest for most minority groups except Asians; it is largely the choice of white, middle-class, moderate-income Americans.

Other precepts have been carried out more successfully. The guiding tenets of the Danish founders have largely been respected and integrated into local architectural styles, both at Cambridge and at other cohousing developments in different parts of the country. The philosophy of participatory democracy, even with its inescapable inequities, is well reflected in our governance; though every cohousing project evolves in its own way, all endorse community participation.

Multigenerational living is undisputed, although three external factors have posed bumps in the road for Cambridge. First, young families have been hard to lure, in large part due to the cost of urban housing. From our nearly thirty children at the onset, as property values have appreciated and children have grown, we now count about half that. Second, the once-midlife folks are now well into the elderly category, and this age-skewed population has very little turnover.

And finally, we got to a point where we could fill the unit with waiting-in-the wings elderly single women. But the inevitable march of reality told us that dependency was just ahead, and, again, we did not profess to be a retirement home. Recognizing this nationwide demographic trend, Charles Durrett, co-author of *COHOUSING*, has been developing senior cohousing—not all seniors choose children as housemates.

There was a time when Ed and I woke up to the sudden realization that *some* of us were showing signs of age. I observed that each end of the age continuum seemed to sport more rapid changes than those in the middle.

Overnight, the babies were in school, the mid-lifers limping, losing hair and height. And judging by the number of ambulance calls, breaks, bends, scrapes, and joint replacements, the latter were the ones who are straining the healthcare system.

At common events now, the walkers and wheelchairs collide with the tricycles, and work committees muse over the challenges posed by a dwindling labor force.

But Cambridge cohousers are still a resilient bunch. Two directions exist for us and they're not mutually exclusive: to adapt cohousing to the needs of normal aging and to intensify the recruitment of young families. I personally hope to replenish the children.

Our community structure has undergone much streamlining, as has our consensus and facilitation processes. The nine-member Managing Board of the condominium association is now responsible for all the tasks that come under condo bylaws—governance, finance, and maintenance. The physical plant is its bailiwick. It makes decisions by majority vote, whereas the condo association operates by consensus. Its members are elected for two-year terms; all members are encouraged to take a turn.

The nonstatutory Community Life Committee (CLC) is the social-concerns arm of the organization. Committees and task forces are coordinated by the CLC. Income from the guest rooms provides most of the funding for Children's, Meals, Design, Grounds, Library, and Events Committees, and others. In conventional condominium associations, these functions either do not exist or are subsumed under the Managing Board. We, however, have always been in the ambiguous position of behaving and thinking like a cooperative, while legally organized as a condominium.

Sometime, someone will write the definitive story of the evolving organization of Cambridge Cohousing, complete with interviews, flow charts, graphs, and budgets. Still, it will not be the story of a homeowner's honeymoon. The budget shows annual increases, including the most recent assessment, an agreement to raise condo fees in order to build a more adequate reserve fund.

Although fixed costs leave little room for negotiation, there are informal ways to reduce expenses that simultaneously tighten the web of community. Negotiating swaps of and barters for services such as child and pet sitting, sharing cars, buying in bulk, pooling equipment, (e.g., small machines, tools, DVDs, books, magazines), exchanging toys, games, and clothing. All can save considerable amounts of money. In addition, our lead cooks are enormously ingenious about creating meals for dozens of diners that are delicious, nutritious, inexpensive, and continually less dependent on meat.

In condo lingo the word "assessment" can raise blood pressure and set off diatribes of blame and accusation among condominium owners everywhere. An assessment is a one-time-only, designated sum of money that a unit owner must pay over and above the regular condo fee; it is often labeled a "special assessment fee." Its purpose is to fund nonrecurring items not included in the operating budget. To some, it is a euphemism for unaffordable amenities. "Did we really *need* this new landscaping?" or "Not all of us can afford a swimming pool."

Few at Cambridge, however, would argue that luxuries are the issue; rather, it is safe balconies, rotting wood, leaks, insulation, and our state-of-the-art heating-and-cooling system. In its short life, the Managing Board, in a systematic repair of construction flaws, has been forced to declare three special assessments, even though the values of our units have appreciated dramatically. That does not produce cash in hand for the dreaded assessment in income-tight households.

One of the original hopes, which has become fantasy, was that cohousing would prove to be an economical lifestyle, sharing, pooling, and bartering as we do The rising costs of utilities, labor, and supplies on top of a backlog of repair and maintenance projects have been disappointing for all, but especially for those on limited incomes. For anyone in this financial position considering cohousing, it is worthwhile to understand the demands of both new and old buildings over time.

In the enthusiasm of planning a cohousing project, it is very tempting to convince one another that the ability to regularly pay the mortgage and the taxes is the extent of one's financial obligation. Who knew that signs of aging tend to appear in buildings after about ten years? And in our case, we continue to repair old flaws as we discover new maintenance surprises. Also, does everyone remember that condo fees know only one direction—and that is *up*?

Some conflicts appear to be indigenous to cohousing, requiring decisions that can be made based on only very personal preferences. The *Cohousing Magazine*, Vol.17, No.1 (www.cohousing.org/process) points out that many of these reappearing conflicts begin with the letter *P* and are common to all cohousing communities. Cambridge is no exception: we have spent inordinate amounts of time thrashing out problems relating to Pets, Parenting, Painting, Parking, Participation, and Process. We in Cambridge, however, can also add a few *C*s, such as Clotheslines and Color, and elaborate on them in spades. Anyone living here has stories of the highly emotional nature of these topics. To balance any such episodes, however, there are incredible reserves of humor that are essential for negotiating our way through the landmines. Fortunately, some people's talents lie in rescuing a potentially drop-dead issue and whisking it away into rejuvenating moments of laughter and redirection. Humor has been the surest tension-reducing balm.

To me, the survival of this community after weathering its first ten years—with its strong personalities, forty-one units, multipronged mission, play space, vegetable garden, and below-ground parking all tucked into a once grubby city industrial lot—is nothing short of miraculous.

Reinventing our lives is what many of us feel we have been doing, not only to adapt to our new space but to recover from the many small sword-crossing moments when the question, "How are we going to live here together?" echoes through the buildings.

Then, in between those moments of challenge and growth, often from the midst of a palpably stalled meeting, a voice emerges, uttering the word "party ... we need a party." And like a flame moving along a fuse, the mood alters from heavy to buoyant, and someone else adds, "Let's celebrate the Solstice on Saturday; we could stand some brightening around here."

At Cambridge Cohousing, countless events have touched not only the lives of residents, but those of our relatives and friends as well. The requisites for a good time are few and simple—a feeling of camaraderie, a suitable space, and food and drink. Incidentally, our little village has all the ingredients, lending itself to the imaginations of its residents as they set out to mark life's special occasions.

When I try to recall the many varied occasions we have celebrated here, my mind goes back to an early party. We all have our favorites. Others might recall the dedication, a bat mitzvah, a child's birthday party, a wedding. Or, perhaps a talent show, a poetry reading, or a recital. But my favorite is that of Ed's eightieth birthday and its convergence with our first months here.

How often does one suspend disbelief, make a huge leap of faith, leave a much-loved home after fifty years? How many seventy-nine-year-olds forfeit the warmth and hearth of a dependably heated house for the fluctuating temperatures of a still-uncompleted cohousing flat? Or opt for bone-wearying meetings of consensus building over the serenity and predictability of a well-earned retirement? Although now settled in a wonderful, spacious, sunny apartment, originally Ed had no more guarantee of success than his wife's prophesies of ... well ... enough said.

Thus, my self-imposed challenge while recovering from a hip replacement was to find a way to mark these significant events for Ed. Anne and I independently had the same idea and thrashed out every detail together. She organized the food contributions and volunteers, filled the rooms with flowers, and made appetizers, cookies, and a fabulous birthday cake. I prepared dozens upon dozens of Chinese eggs, sent invitations, and wrote countless lists.

My vision was both intimate and large-scale—bringing under one roof rarely seen friends and family from our outside life together with new friends, and blending them all into a bang-up party. After having filled our friends with this strange concept called cohousing over the past several years, we had watched as their eyes glazed over with doubt, bewilderment, boredom. We needed to demonstrate the virtues of urban cohousing—one of the last mini-movements of the twentieth century—in order to erase what they surely viewed as our creeping senility. It was clearly time to join these strands of our life, to make us whole. In short, we needed a party! We needed a time to forget our HVAC woes. We needed a time to supplant Punch List items with invitations, to celebrate the wisdom of age and the courage of experiment, to place the old, enduring friendships alongside the new, still-fragile ones. We *needed* Ed's eightieth—and a housewarming.

At first the idea was logistically overwhelming, as bringing such a vision to fruition required staff and caterer. But no! "Cohousing" was the operative word here; friends rallied to celebrate the patriarch and to show off our unique community. In doing so, we achieved an unintended bonus—the sprucing up of our Common House, then occupied for less than a year. It looked beautiful and wonderfully welcoming.

But while our generous common areas would certainly hold the almost two hundred guests, the challenge was to keep them circulating. Tapping the talents of a few neighbors, we created a self-guided tour, using a numbered-program card indicating food stations in the library, living room, mailroom, and playroom, and then finally, in #410. In search of food, guests could be counted on to move around.

It worked, except for a traffic jam that occurred in the common kitchen where two sushi chefs skillfully demonstrated their art, barely keeping up with the demand. Without the help of our Korean neighbors, I'm not sure I alone could have negotiated such kitchen theater.

Childcare was provided in the playroom while parents partied. Resident experts explained our complex heating/cooling/hot water system to interested guests. A parking amnesty was pre-arranged with the Cambridge Police Department.

Then the ringing of a bell by our Seattle grandson summoned guests from various parts of the building to the dining room, where I introduced our family to all and turned the spotlight on Ed. Poems were read, sentiments expressed. Not everyone could see, and those standing in the back did not hear well, but the mood was festive. Cohousers presented Ed with a check to be used to purchase a weathervane to grace the future roof gazebo; the choice would be his—a grasshopper, a bull, or perhaps a train. Only one condition accompanied the gift: he *must not search for consensus*. The evening ended with a medley of 1930s and '40s show tunes played and sung by our resident soprano/pianist with words supplied for all those under seventy.

The celebration was to become a kind of marker.

Anyone here can recall subsequent occasions observing our other significant passages. Most recently, on January 20, 2009, we used our affinity for galas to honor our new president with a whopping Inaugural Ball, a formal dress affair complete with dancing. Many here had worked hard to elect President Obama.

One celebration we will not have is for Ed's ninetieth birthday. After a long series of illnesses, he spent his final two weeks in the hospital, his last days in palliative care. From the nursing staff's gossip network, I learned they assumed he was "a famous man," because he had so many visitors. Famous, who's to say, but he was a much-loved man to whom many came to bid their farewells. The memory of seven-year-old Danny from cohousing, walking confidently up to Ed's bed and patting his hand is one I shall always treasure. Unable to speak or move, Ed responded with the only sign of recognition he was capable of: a slight raise of his bushy left eyebrow.

Before the eyes of all, his life, his pleasure in living here, was diminished. His ready smile, however, remained until Christmas Day of 2007, when his hospital room quietly filled with family and friends. A stroke had deprived him of speech, and his mobility was reduced to that one bushy eyebrow, his final gift to each entering visitor. After our sixty-four years together, he left me alone but not abandoned; a few nights after his death, members of the community gathered in the common living room, and, one after another, spoke about the meaning his loss held for them, each in a beautiful and moving manner.

His was the first expected death. Both Joseph and Phyllis had died suddenly, Joseph in a fall and Phyllis peacefully in her sleep. Each was honored in a similar way. Phyllis had recently celebrated her eightieth birthday with a summer family reunion on the patio, when she introduced those of her large family who could attend. Even she was not always sure of the current count of grands and great-grandchildren, who arrived from all over the country and Canada. She was a vital part of Lynn and Ken's family; a pioneer in our cohousing venture, having given up her home in California to remake it with us; a grandmother figure to many children; and a model of courage and independence.

"*Namo amitabhaya hri … namo amitabhaya …* " chanted the mourners seated cross-legged on green floor cushions in the lovely Buddhist center in

Brookline. We were transfixed as the flames licked away at the photograph of Joseph resting in a small urn. For most of us from cohousing, this was our first Buddhist ceremony.

A few weeks earlier, Joseph had been found dead on his kitchen floor, presumably having fallen, surrounded by the icons of his days and nights—empty beer bottles. This serene service, with alternating periods of reflection, meditation, and memories, was the first opportunity to think quietly about Joseph's life over the past eight years. His sisters recalled a younger, sprightly wit, a fun-loving albeit unfocused man, a light and jocular manner, a curious mind. But to us whose span of knowledge was relatively brief, Joseph was our inscrutable guide through a dizzying learning curve—steep at times, sluggish and meandering at others.

Each of us separately came to the realization that, except for momentary flashes, his dormant talents would not express themselves at CCH. Oh, we heard an occasional reference to Shakespeare, to his favorite e.e. cummings, or to his pleasurable moments chopping wood through a long Maine winter. But here, Joseph did not lift as much as a stick. Although he stated a wish to learn to play the music of his idol, Scott Joplin, and Rose offered to give him free piano lessons, he was unable to muster the resolve even to walk down the hall to her unit.

Joseph was a presence from our first meetings. His quiet demeanor was not unfriendly; the faded Red Sox cap all but obscured the friendly, twinkling eyes. Despite the scraggly beard and overlarge, overused sagging pants, topped by a faded plaid shirt, he carried himself with dignity. With a stealthy, evenly slow pace, he seemed to glide across the noisy meeting room. He claimed a front-row seat and, statue-like, surveyed the assembling group. He responded to overtures, even made few himself. But on those Sundays when he failed to appear, his absence was noted. A frail but intense presence was missing and missed.

Had he called? Was he ill? Did he need a ride? (Heavens, no! He often came on his ancient-model motorcycle.) Should someone check? In time, someone always volunteered to seek him out, to gently restore him to the fold.

Early on Joseph assumed a role, an identity as well defined as that of an acknowledged leader: that role of Dependent, the one whose silent cues elicited the well-meaning advice, support, and succor of his fellow cohousers. He was to give a new dimension to the meaning of diversity. Joseph had found a safe harbor, and we unquestioningly took on the responsibility of fulfilling his dream. Why then, didn't this collusion work?

None of this was said then, of course. But when the incidents of his self-destructiveness and disruption of others' lives increased, each in his or her own time came to see the folly of attempting to take responsibility for someone else. It's been called "enabling" and is doomed to disappointment and failure.

Joseph is now part of our collective history: we've learned that caring communities both attract and are anathema to substance abusers. We shared a similar belief system of hopefulness and the power of the group to influence and change behavior. While we're all familiar with rare exceptions, we had to learn that the reversibility of the power of alcohol on a vulnerable temperament is unlikely. We had to discover that a community is inevitably negatively impacted by a member who drinks to excess.

Another dreaded concern in this situation was the fear of fire. For a long time, people showed remarkable tolerance to the behavior that Joseph displayed; it was when individual and group safety were threatened, that people wrestled seriously with their consciences, asking themselves the ultimate question, "In the event of Joseph's death or that of another, will I have done all I could have?" It was then that cohousing decided to help find a more protected environment for Joseph before his accidental death. We wrestled with our mission in regard to the long-term care of poorly functioning residents and reminded ourselves, not for the first time, that while we cared *about* our members, we were unable to care *for* them.

Joseph's expectations for living here, it turned out, were quite specific, if flawed. He was aware that he required a constantly engaged audience. When asked, he frankly expressed that he'd thought there would always be someone in the living room, in the kitchen around a coffee pot (or a Pepsi jug, in his case), in a place where he could talk with them. He needed "noise" to fill his own emptiness.

Had he been able to mobilize his energies, ratchet up his participation just a little, he could have found a niche here, and for doing so, he would have found appreciation, kudos, and rewarding social interactions. But he was unable to make use of us.

To this day, his grandfather clock remains in the lobby to remind us that Joseph was honest in his despair, funny in his breadth and scope, and clear in his immutable non-response.

The eldest of our steady stream of children can now vote, a significant benchmark for a politically savvy bunch of people. They are out in the world; they travel, they live in foreign countries; they seem so independent and capable, but remain close to family.

I would love to hear how they describe their childhoods to their peers. Were they happy, intimidated, content, mystified? Did they feel they belonged to this experiment? Or were they outsiders? Had they found good adult role models or just too many? For me, one of the most satisfying things about this place has been the opportunity to be part of the growth of these children and to watch from the sidelines.

Of the original nearly thirty children who were here during the inauguration of cohousing, the two oldest are now college graduates. Fast on their heels are several more at or nearing college age and an additional small squadron in the early elementary years. This last cohort, with one exception who entered at age four, knows no other home than cohousing.

Beyond raw numbers and anecdotal accounts, it's impossible to profile this group of two to nine year olds. There's a lot of interest in the effect of cohousing on children's development. Some want to hear stories of an imagined *kibbutzim* life of special talents nourished in an atmosphere free of conflicts or tensions. Others would love to crow over tales of wanton abuse or *Lord of the Flies* abandon. Sorry, I assure you that these treasured kids are firmly rooted in their families, and their unique personalities are being etched more and more clearly as they grow older.

And I'd argue that much of their success was rooted in the opportunities they received in cohousing. Not all, all the time, but most entered wholeheartedly into various activities. And playing outdoors was the norm for them, where the play structure and the Pretty Good Lawn are Rorschachs for creative play.

A few, at adolescence, have socially retreated, avoiding meals and chance encounters. Others have expanded into the larger world without abrupt ruptures with cohousing peers and adults, then pick up again on holidays. Most have exhibited strong bonds resulting from their positive personal interactions in cohousing for over ten years.

I wish we had thought more about how to discover unique differences in the development of a child raised here as compared to one reared in the single-family house. When we had the opportunity to venture into such an undertaking, we were too absorbed with Process, Paint, and Parking.

Because watching children over the years has always been an interest of mine, I will tell you a few of my own random observations, often from my balcony, casually observing the kids in very informal settings—outdoors, in the Common House, and in my sporadic interactions with them. I am not theory-building but merely offering some comments as a part of any account of cohousing. My overall impression is that those who have participated in the cohousing experience, especially those born into it, are very fortunate children.

Pairs of special friendships form and fall apart, but in outdoor play the age spread is broader than often seen elsewhere. Acts of kindness and helpfulness by older children are common. Put another way: they all tend to play together.

In recent years, as they've become so accustomed to each other, there is remarkably little fighting, name-calling, or crying beyond the occasional tearful outburst or accidental injury. They are not angels, but they have learned a lot about how to settle their differences—with the help of nearby supportive adults and older children. And it's not too much to say that they respect, and appear to like, each other. It should be remembered that these children, except possibly in their own houses, are never free of adult presence, although they seem unaware of it. To what extent that unconsciously affects their behavior, I have no idea. Some kind of study comparing cohousing and noncohousing kids in school would be interesting.

In the early years, discipline was a sensitive issue for everyone. Parents wanted no interference since disciplinary and parenting styles varied greatly among residents. No one knew how to behave comfortably when children misbehaved in public; what was misbehavior anyway? Now that familiarity and trust have grown, these questions seem to have evaporated. In somewhat romanticized versions of cohousing, children appear to have a community full of parental substitutes. My reading is that. while parents are increasingly comfortable with the support, their children's upbringing, now as before, is their business.

Each stage of growth presents new challenges for everyone. For example, there's general agreement that teens should be able to use the Rec Room to entertain their friends in a supervised environment. A couple of times, however, there have been some infractions. The whole community then must become engaged in "refreshing the guidelines."

With an ardent environmental philosophy supported by recycling, composting, and use of nontoxic materials, Cambridge Cohousing is determined to play a role in the battle against global warming. Dalenna and Greg founded a committee dubbed the LLP (live lightly please). Periodically, they bring to our attention information about sustainable practices and often raise their voices, along with others, against waste and cohousing policies they view as damaging.

Once, Dalenna came to a General Meeting with a small plastic bag, the contents of which she dumped on the floor before our eyes; it represented the miniscule weekly trash collection of a two-person household. I'm not sure this demo reduced Ed's and my trash output, but it did raise our level of guilt and our hope that, going forward, no one would see us carrying our numerous bags to the trash bins. Others have since taken over the LLP and function as an educational resource for increasing awareness and potential action. A number of households have necessarily replaced old vehicles with hybrid models. Dalenna and I each own one of cohousing's "fleet" of Priuses, which now make up about 20 percent of our cars.

A frontal attack was finally made on the growing bicycle crisis. A survey confirmed what everyone knew: almost two hundred bikes were too many bikes! Many households, even many individuals, had multiple bikes. Even more than with cars, it seemed, people become very emotional about their obsolete, unused bicycles. Recognizing the high level of attachment, gentle encouragement on the part of the Bike Committee was required to enable them to channel some donations to Bikes Not Bombs, others to yard sales and trash. Without the nostalgia, we now have a more manageable bike storage room.

Every now and then a friend will ask me, "How are you getting along with your neighborhood? Is there more assimilation than when you first came?"

I have to tell them that we have arrived at a fairly comfortable stage—no memorable strides, no daunting setbacks, no ambitious projects.

Nods and hellos are exchanged on walks to the subway or inside the corner store. With spring always comes a gaggle of young African-American men, hanging out curbside around their cars, their man-talk blending with the surround of sound from their car radios.

And just this week, Martha, who runs the series of poetry readings held at cohousing for area poets, told me that she and Ma Yu, across the street, are thinking about starting a literary press. A nearby condominium association, without its own common space, holds its annual meetings in our dining room. Thread by thread, we weave the fabric of community.

Recently, with an increase in street robberies in the area, a neighborhood group asked to hold a meeting at cohousing. Attended by the police chief, the city councilor, representatives of community agencies, and many neighbors who had never been here before, the meeting taught us that fear of crime can accomplish what good intentions often could not. As our exposure broadened, our message, "Know your neighbors," was adopted by a nervous neighborhood.

Many dozens of pieces of exercise equipment—inoperable, in need of adjustment, of questionable safety, and duplicates—were unloaded here during the move-in period. For years, they idly sat in a corner of the basement. Until, that is, member initiative and exercise mania took charge.

Howard, bent on creating a small, well-equipped gym, procured financial help from the CLC, developed a design, and mobilized others to build a privacy wall and a lockable door (to make the room inaccessible to children). He then culled through the exercise machines, bikes, treadmills, weights, and manuals. He donated or disposed of the discards, sometimes needing to soothe regretful owners. Finally, he installed rubber flooring, a clock, a radio, and a TV, and opened our new facility—a most welcome amenity.

Throughout the process, he carefully informed the membership of the progress and invited their input. But, alas, shortly thereafter, following the purchase of a new, sturdier treadmill, he and Miriam announced that they were getting married and would leave Cambridge to retire to their New Hampshire home. He left a fine legacy.

It is spring—and another season without the crows. Other birds have returned, but the crows have completely vanished. No early morning squawking, no territorial fighting, no beady-eyed stares and, worst of all, no conversations. I miss them, though I hear no regrets from others—only sounds of relief. Some lay their absence at the feet of West Nile Virus, but although the bodies of a few afflicted birds have been found, why wouldn't we see more evidence? Will they recover from this avian genocide and return to Cambridge?

I'm often asked why families leave cohousing. There are a number of reasons; a few examples might help understand some of them. But you cannot think about those leaving apart from their replacements. Good-byes and hellos are likely to collide as we bid farewell to the old, extend welcomes to the new. Every departed household evokes its cluster of special memories and we're all conscious that the long-term health and viability of the community depends on people who choose to be here and to embrace our goals.

The Wongs were the first family to move in and lived here a few weeks alone—with the carpenters. They were also the first to leave, with Bill's return to the navy. Shortly after 9/11, he was assigned to the Iraq theater, leaving wife, Jitae, and Erin, then four, in San Diego. I often wondered then whether a family separated by war missed the benefits of cohousing. Martha and Francis, already in the cohousing network, purchased the Wongs' house; the transition went smoothly. They have become parents of the two youngest cohousing members now living here.

Roger and Clea send happily settled messages from Central Massachusetts and report enjoying a life of more control than the one they had in conjunction with forty other households—back when Roger was the first chair of the Managing Board. Their daughters, Jina and Lydia, can walk to school; they are excited about their large house and lawn. They've left fast friends here and periodically return to visit. And Al, Richie's erstwhile host, and his family of six, bought Roger and Clea's townhouse, after learning about cohousing through mutual friends.

Riva and Ellen now share a college teaching post in Western Mass, and on a visit to Cambridge Cohousing, announced that they intended to marry as soon as the Massachusetts ban against same-sex marriage was lifted. They reported loving their "simpler, more rural" life and were enlarging a small house. Their daughters, Petra and Niki, are also thriving and fall back immediately into lively play with their cohousing friends. George bought their slightly larger townhouse and moved next door; Lillian appeared from Washington to visit, and, already familiar with cohousing, bought George's place in the course of an hour.

When Rudy sold his small unit to Janet just before his marriage, he was reluctant to leave, but never expected to return. His marriage was short-lived, however, and he and his daughter Moira came back and bought Joseph's old flat. We welcomed them with open arms. Janet, after eight years, has just bought a townhouse across the tracks within sight of cohousing. This move triggered an ambitious three-unit shift, enabling Joy and Sam, who is now fighting cancer, to move from a third- to a first-floor apartment. None of these negotiations required a realtor.

From a single-family home to a smaller flat was the experience of many of us, but for Reba and her daughter Kira, the route was reversed. They came from an African American neighborhood to occupy a unit owned by the Cambridge Housing Authority. Reba used her time at cohousing to improve her financial position, acquiring an excellent job at a nearby university. At a general meeting, she proudly announced, to a round of applause, that she was to move on to be a homeowner and a landlord in a nearby city. Cohousing as a way station: a novel idea.

Doris outgrew her studio apartment, but another concern induced her to leave cohousing. As a member of the Managing Board, she learned about the scope of anticipated assessments and was fearful that she would not be able to afford them. She returns often to visit, still signs up with cook teams, and not so secretly harbors the idea of purchasing a larger flat here "if only the costs weren't so high."

The Soos left after his recovery from a kidney transplant to retire to the Cape, thus opening up an apartment for a local couple with coho inclinations. Paul immediately threw in his lot with the LLP, a special interest. Ursula joined the clothesline lobby as well as facilitating an in-house Yoga class. The Soos will be remembered for many things—bravely trying to make the transition from the rigid culture of their homeland to cohousing's faith in cooperative endeavors, extending their ready friendliness, sharing their wonderful meals, and making generous loans of their elegant, large rice cooker.

And then Shirley and Jackson, Jason and Laura! Who would have suspected? How can we possibly extol them sufficiently for their contributions to this community? We panicked momentarily with the familiar lament—How will we manage without them? Then we bucked up, remembering that this had happened before and that we knew how to circle the wagons to survive. Shirley and Jackson had a contract with a private school out of state, the one their college-bound son attended. They felt they gained much and owed much to this organization for turning their son's life around and affording their family countless other benefits. They rented out their townhouse each year that created an annual "constitutional crisis" for cohousing since it conflicted with our non-rental policy. Their intention was always to return but the cohousing philosophy, embodied in the bylaws, supports permanence and commitment by discouraging long-term rentals. The Managing Board, after consulting with the general meeting, allowed them waivers, four of them. This year they returned with a big welcome.

In the meantime, there was a hole, a large one. Who would step up with their bubbling humor, their dramatic talents, their graphic materials, their meals, the candor, the ready laughter, the kindness? Who else but Laura would give us the pleasure of watching the gymnast flourish from child to young woman? Their four-year absence did bring an infusion of interesting renters to enrich cohousing. Finally, relief from these heated discussions came. Return they did. And in this extended process, we all gained a new family in the last renters—Carmine, now the wife of Carol, the two mothers of seven-year-old Enrico.

The intricate details of our real estate history are not necessary to make the point that we are an unconventional property. Suffice it to say, we play a form of musical chairs that I see as another instance of our readiness to bend our hard-won policies in the service of a strong and vital community.

This place breeds books like mice. We have a couple of big-name authors, several poets, and then a few late starters like me. As a result, Cambridge Cohousing has hosted several signing parties through the years.

I like to believe that the clandestine writing group I organized was in good part responsible for our success in completing two books and a play. Three of us met faithfully every other week in #410, each conscientiously bringing fortnightly drafts to be critiqued during the two-hour sessions. My single condition was that *any mention* of my book beyond my apartment walls was strictly off limits. It worked!

"We" finished Janet's book, held a play reading at cohousing for Ted's opus, and all the while quietly read my many drafts. Cohousing friends celebrated the first two events with us but remained unaware of my work until my recent announcement.

The View from #410: When Home is Cohousing is my response to all those doubters, including myself, who feared that "all those meetings" would be anathema to privacy and productivity.

Acknowledgments

Every sentence, every chapter was read first by Ed; he was never too busy, too tired, or, even in his last months, too sick to read the latest version. While the subtleties of grammar were not his primary focus, as a visual artist, description and narrative were. He loved seeing my translation, *my view*, of our life at #410 blossom on the page. And for one who felt threatened by memory loss, he relished, relied on, and envied my still-intact ability to recall. He was my anchor and wellspring during this decade-long adventure.

After moving to cohousing, in an attempt to jumpstart a dormant wish to write, I joined a six-session class at the Cambridge Center for Adult Education. The class was offered by Judith Nies, a Cambridge writer and the author of *The Girl I Left Behind: A Personal History of the 1960s* (Harper Collins, 2008). Several talented writers were there for much the same reason as I; we were all mature adults who had, until now, set writing aside for more worldly pursuits. Jumpstart us, Judith did. At the conclusion of the class, several of us continued to meet at #410. For Ted Allen and me, the timing was right; the others reluctantly dropped away. However, Sarah James, a new cohousing resident, joined us. In our several years together, we hosted a reading of Ted's unpublished play, celebrated the publication of Sarah's *The Natural Step for Communities: How Cities and Towns can Change to Sustainable Practices* (New Society Publishers, 2004), and launched my first book, *Intimate Tyranny: Untangling Father's Legacy* (Centora Press, Cambridge, MA, 2008).

Now I have come out of the closet with cohousing friends and neighbors with the announcement that *The View from #410: When Home is Cohousing* will be published by iUniverse in conjunction with my own Centora Press. To Sarah and Ted, a large thank you. Dick Tonachel's editorial skills, Andrea Mason Nolin and Gwen Frankfeldt's cover design contributions, Brian Kane's computer support and Ed Mason's photographic contributions have been invaluable. Furthermore, through Judith Nies I met Emily Hiestand, (Cambridge author of *The Very Rich Hours, Angela The Upside Down Girl* among others, both published by Beacon Press, Boston, MA) who had faith in this book from the beginning and was extraordinarily generous with her suggestions. I am very grateful. Thank you, Judith, for your value-added class.

Jean K. Mason
Cambridge, 2010

Appendix

The Cambridge Cohousing VISION STATEMENT

** The purpose of the Cambridge Cohousing group is to create an urban residential community in which the architectural and social organization is designed to inspire and enhance the daily lives of its inhabitants. We are committed to Cambridge as a city—its vitality, history, convenience, and diverse populations. Our goal is to create a mixed-income community where children and adults of varying race, ethnicity, religion, sexual orientation, and ability can thrive. We hope that our cohousing life, and our individual and corporate participation in our surrounding community will be a healthy, healing force within our larger culture.

** We envision a community composed of a variety of sizes of private homes—probably including townhouses and apartments—and a common house where an assortment of shared functions are accommodated. All community spaces will be handicap accessible and private homes will be designed to accommodate a variety of physical and social needs. We are also resolved to create an environment that embodies principles of quality, simplicity, and beauty. We want our site to be large enough to include common gardens, outdoor children's play and general recreational spaces, as well as some private gardens that are part of the individual homes. We plan to locate our community within walking distance to public transportation. In design, construction, and development of our site we are committed to environmentally sustainable practices. We will emphasize conservation, recycling, non-polluting energy sources, and other environmentally sound practices.

** We share a commitment to the idea that cooperating in the endeavors of daily life brings the pleasures of sociability, greater economy of resources and effort in daily tasks, the warmth of an extended family, and the probability of a rich variety of friendships. In our interactions, we seek a balance between privacy in our own homes and our wish to be with others, living independently as well as interdependently. We want to share and interact with each other through social activities, celebrations, and practical tasks, such as cooking, dining, childcare, maintenance and through other shared work and problem solving. Honoring our varied experiences, we intend to follow a consensus-based process respectful of all points of view. We believe that through living together and especially working through our differences, we become stronger, more peaceful contributing members within the larger global community.